C R E A T I V E
HOMEOWNER®

GAZEBOS

& Other Outdoor Structures

CREATIVE HOMEOWNER®, Upper Saddle River, New Jersey

COPYRIGHT © 1995

CREATIVE
HOMEOWNER®
A Division of Federal Marketing Corp.
Upper Saddle River, NJ

This book may not be reproduced, either in its entirety, in any form, by any means, without written permission from the publisher, with the exception of brief excerpts for purposes of radio, television, or published review. All rights, including the right of translation, are reserved. *Note:* Be sure to familiarize yourself with manufacturer's instructions for tools, equipment, and materials before beginning a project. Although all possible measures have been taken to ensure the accuracy of the material presented, neither the author nor the publisher is liable in case of misinterpretation of directions, misapplication, or typographical error.

Manufactured in the United States of America

Editorial Director: David Schiff

Editor: Joseph F. Wajszczuk Jr.

Writers: Drew Corinchock
James Russell
David Schiff
Joseph F. Wajszczuk Jr.

Copy Editor: Candace B. Levy, Ph.D.

Art Director: Annie Jeon

Graphic Designer: Karen Ellis Phillips

Illustrators: James Randolph
Paul M. Schumm

Photo Research: Alexander I. Samuelson

Technical Reviewer: Douglas Goodale

Cover Design: Annie Jeon
Cover Photo: © Walter Chandoha

Current Printing (last digit)
10 9 8

Gazebos
LC: 94-071873
ISBN: 1-880029-04-9

CREATIVE HOMEOWNER®
A Division of Federal Marketing Corp.
24 Park Way
Upper Saddle River, NJ 07458
Web site: **www.creativehomeowner.com**

METRIC CONVERSION

Length

1 inch	2.54 cm
1 foot	30.48 cm
1 yard	91.44 cm
1 mile	1.61 km

Area

1 square inch	6.45 cm^2
1 square foot	929.03 cm^2
1 square yard	0.84 m^2
1 acre	4046.86 m^2
1 square mile	2.59 km^2

Volume

1 cubic inch	16.39 cm^3
1 cubic foot	0.03 m^3
1 cubic yard	0.77 m^3

Common Lumber Equivalents

Sizes: Metric cross sections are so close to their nearest U.S. sizes, as noted below, that for most purposes they may be considered equivalents.

Dimensional lumber	1 x 2	19 x 38 mm
	1 x 4	19 x 89 mm
	2 x 2	38 x 38 mm
	2 x 4	38 x 89 mm
	2 x 6	38 x 140 mm
	2 x 8	38 x 184 mm
	2 x 10	38 x 235 mm
	2 x 12	38 x 286 mm
Sheet sizes	4 x 8 ft.	1200 x 2400 mm
	4 x 10 ft.	1200 x 3000 mm
Sheet thicknesses	¼ in.	6 mm
	⅜ in.	9 mm
	½ in.	12 mm
	¾ in.	19 mm
Stud/joist spacing	16 in. o.c.	400 mm o.c.
	24 in. o.c.	600 mm o.c.

Capacity

1 fluid ounce	29.57 mL
1 pint	473.18 mL
1 quart	1.14 L
1 gallon	3.79 L

Temperature

(Celsius = Fahrenheit – 32 x 5/9)
(Fahrenheit = Celsius x 1.8 + 32)

Nail Size & Length

Penny Size	Nail Length
2d	1″
3d	1¼″
4d	1½″
5d	1¾″
6d	2″
7d	2¼″
8d	2½″
9d	2¾″
10d	3″
12d	3¼″
16d	3½″

Safety First

Though all the designs and methods in this book have been reviewed for safety, it is not possible to overstate the importance of using the safest construction methods possible. What follows are reminders; some do's and don'ts of basic carpentry. They are not substitutes for your own common sense.

■ *Always* use caution, care, and good judgment when following the procedures described in this book.

■ *Always* be sure that the electrical setup is safe; be sure that no circuit is overloaded and that all power tools and electrical outlets are properly grounded. Do not use power tools in wet locations.

■ *Always* read container labels on paints, solvents, and other products; provide ventilation, and observe all other warnings.

■ *Always* read the manufacturer's instructions for using a tool, especially the warnings.

■ *Always* use hold-downs and push sticks whenever possible when working on a table saw. Avoid working short pieces if you can.

■ *Always* remove the key from any drill chuck (portable or press) before starting the drill.

■ *Always* pay deliberate attention to how a tool works so that you can avoid being injured.

■ *Always* know the limitations of your tools. Do not try to force them to do what they were not designed to do.

■ *Always* make sure that any adjustment is locked before proceeding. For example, always check the rip fence on a table saw or the bevel adjustment on a portable saw before starting to work.

■ *Always* clamp small pieces firmly to a bench or other work surface when using a power tool on them.

■ *Always* wear the appropriate rubber or work gloves when handling chemicals, moving or stacking lumber, or doing heavy construction.

■ *Always* wear a disposable face mask when you create dust by sawing or sanding. Use a special filtering respirator when working with toxic substances and solvents.

■ *Always* wear eye protection, especially when using power tools or striking metal on metal or concrete; a chip can fly off, for example, when chiseling concrete.

■ *Always* be aware that there is seldom enough time for your body's reflexes to save you from injury from a power tool in a dangerous situation; everything happens too fast. Be *alert!*

■ *Always* keep your hands away from the business ends of blades, cutters, and bits.

■ *Always* hold a circular saw firmly, usually with both hands so that you know where they are.

■ *Always* use a drill with an auxiliary handle to control the torque when large-size bits are used.

■ *Always* check your local building codes when planning new construction. The codes are intended to protect public safety and should be observed to the letter.

■ *Never* work with power tools when you are tired or under the influence of alcohol or drugs.

■ *Never* cut tiny pieces of wood or pipe using a power saw. Cut small pieces off larger pieces.

■ *Never* change a saw blade or a drill or router bit unless the power cord is unplugged. Do not depend on the switch being off; you might accidentally hit it.

■ *Never* work in insufficient lighting.

■ *Never* work while wearing loose clothing, hanging hair, open cuffs, or jewelry.

■ *Never* work with dull tools. Have them sharpened, or learn how to sharpen them yourself.

■ *Never* use a power tool on a workpiece—large or small—that is not firmly supported.

■ *Never* saw a workpiece that spans a large distance between horses without close support on each side of the cut; the piece can bend, closing on and jamming the blade, causing saw kickback.

■ *Never* support a workpiece from underneath with your leg or other part of your body when sawing.

■ *Never* carry sharp or pointed tools, such as utility knives, awls, or chisels, in your pocket. If you want to carry such tools, use a special-purpose tool belt with leather pockets and holders.

Photo Credits

All photos in this book are for illustrative purposes only. Plans and specific building instructions are included only for the eight projects in Part Two.

Back Cover: (clockwise from top left) Dick Dietrich, Phoenix, AZ
Bill Rothschild, Monsey, NY
courtesy of California Redwood Association
H. Armstrong Roberts, Inc., New York, NY

p. 1:   Bob Braun Photography, Orlando, FL

p. 6:   Dick Dietrich, Phoenix, AZ

p. 8:   Bob Braun Photography, Orlando, FL

p. 9 and 10: courtesy of California Redwood Association

p. 11:   Dick Dietrich, Phoenix, AZ

p. 12:   (top) Dick Dietrich, Phoenix, AZ
(middle) Photo/Nats, Auburndale, MA
(bottom) Robert Valleau, Melabee M. Miller, Hillside, NJ

p.13:   (top left) The Terry Wild Studios, Williamsport, PA
(top right) Mark Gibson, Mount Shasta, CA
(bottom) H. Armstrong Roberts, Inc., New York, NY

p. 14:   Fox Landscape Architects, Melabee M. Miller, Hillside, NJ

p. 15:   (top & middle) George Mattei Photography, Hackensack, NJ
(bottom) Marilyn Stouffer, Rodale Stock Images

p. 16:   (top): Dick Dietrich, Phoenix, AZ
(bottom): courtesy of Vixen Hill Gazebos, Elverson, PA

p. 17:   Dick Dietrich, Phoenix, AZ

p. 18:   Classic Pool & Patio, Indianapolis, IN courtesy of
National Spa and Pool Institute, Alexandria, VA

p. 19:   T.L. Gettings, Rodale Stock Images

p. 20:   Bob Braun Photography, Orlando, FL

p. 35 and 37: courtesy of California Redwood Association

p. 66:   (top & bottom left) Photo/Nats, Auburndale, MA
(bottom right) Michael Schimpf Photography, Lansing, MI

p. 67:   (top) courtesy of Cedar Shake & Shingle Bureau
(bottom) Dick Dietrich, Phoenix, AZ

p. 68:   courtesy of Owens Corning

p. 69:   courtesy of California Redwood Association

p. 70:   Specialized PhotoGraphic Design, Convent Station, NJ

p. 79:   courtesy of Wolman KopCoat

p. 81:   (top): Photo/Nats, Auburndale, MA
(bottom): Susana Pashko, Envision, New York, NY

p. 82:   (left) The Terry Wild Studios, Williamsport, PA
(right) Michael Schimpf Photography, Lansing, MI

p. 84:   Marilyn Stouffer, Rodale Stock Images

p. 88:   Mitch Mandel, Rodale Stock Images

p. 89:   (left) Scott Star Photography, New York, NY
(right) J. Michael Kanouff, Rodale Stock Images

p. 90:   (top) J. Michael Kanouff, Rodale Stock Images
(bottom) Specialized PhotoGraphic Design, Convent Station, NJ

p. 91:   (clockwise from left) Mark Gibson, Mount Shasta, CA
Marilyn Stouffer, Rodale Stock Images
Scott Star Photography, New York, NY
Specialized PhotoGraphic Design, Convent Station, NJ

p. 94:   (top) John Schwartz Photography, New York, NY
(bottom left) Michael Schimpf Photography, Lansing, MI
(bottom right) Scott Star Photography, New York, NY

p. 96:   (top) Michael Schimpf Photography, Lansing, MI
(bottom) Specialized PhotoGraphic Design, Convent Station, NJ

p. 98:   (left) courtesy of Southern Forest Products Association
(right) Scott Star Photography, New York, NY

p. 101: courtesy of Wolman KopCoat

p. 105: Specialized PhotoGraphic Design, Convent Station, NJ

Table of Contents

Building Your Personal Retreat

You sit back, enjoying a gentle breeze wafting across your face. All is quiet except for the chirping of birds. You feel like you are a million miles from the hustle of daily life, but in reality you didn't have to travel at all to get there. You are enjoying a gazebo, pavilion, or arbor right in your own backyard. Your satisfaction with your outdoor retreat is enhanced because you crafted the structure with your own two hands.

This book is designed to help you create an outdoor structure that perfectly fits your family's needs and desires. The book is divided into two parts: Part One is filled with chapters that will show you how to customize your project into exactly the structure you want. Part Two contains step-by-step plans for several gazebos, pavilions, and arbors. If one of these plans matches your needs, then by all means, build it just as described. But if you have something different in mind, Part One will help you transform your vision into reality. In Part One, you'll learn how to lay out your project, build a foundation, construct the frame, install the deck, design the rafters, and build the roof. You'll learn the pros and cons of various outdoor finishes, and you'll even find a chapter that will help you choose a paint scheme. A chapter on maintenance will help you keep your project beautiful for many years to come.

Building a garden structure is one of the most enjoyable projects a do-it-yourselfer can undertake. Unlike most home projects, you won't make a disrupting mess inside your house. You'll be out in the sunshine, exercising your creative carpentry skills.

When you embark on your garden building project, you'll be joining a history spanning almost to the advent of gardening itself. Some of the first to appreciate the luxury of a small structure in the midst of their gardens were the ancient Egyptian pharaohs. In fact, the pharaohs ordered murals of their gardens painted on the walls of their tombs so that they might bring the beauty with them into the afterlife. In China, the Taoist religion revered natural beauty; garden structures were a natural and essential component of many compositions. The Chinese embraced these simple structures for their ability to provide a release from the pressures inherent in an advanced civilization (and that was in 4000 B.C.). Many centuries later, outdoor buildings caught on in the rest of Europe. By the start of the Renaissance, no proper garden could be complete without its own outdoor structure.

Gazebos and other outdoor buildings had their most profound impact on the Victorians. With the advent of the Industrial Age, more people were living closer together, and the new pressures associated with this new urban life necessitated more garden retreats. Gazebos were a natural complement to these garden getaways.

By the mid 20th century, these types of buildings had lost some popularity to front porches and open-air decks. But today, more and more people are rediscovering the pleasures of a special outdoor structure. Nothing can match their distinctive feel—how roses can be trained to envelop an arbor or the way that a summer shower can seem to isolate you from the rest of the world. It's not surprising that these structures are enjoying a new surge in popularity.

A bit of advice before you pick up your hammer: You'll save untold amounts of time, work, money, and frustration if you take the time to plan your project carefully before you begin building. Planning is essential for visualizing a project; it's also a way of thinking and working out problems before they become expensive or time-consuming mistakes. If you do not plan, you might just end up "managing crises" and will probably be disappointed in your final project.

Difficulty Scale

There is a difficulty scale rating presented for each project: one hammer if we consider the job an easy one to do, two hammers if it's moderately difficult, and three hammers if it's difficult.

Easy

Moderately Difficult

Admittedly, ratings are our opinion and are subjective. You may or may not agree with them. In any case, the instructions and illustrations will show and tell you in a clear and concise way how to tackle each project.

Difficult

Structure Is for You?

...gh to decide which outdoor structure ...ance the usefulness of your yard. ... the separate retreat offered by a gazebo, or would you prefer a vine-covered arbor or a simple pavilion over a patio? The size and style of your design depends on the number of people, activities, and equipment you intend to accommodate. The style and materials you choose should also harmonize with your house and landscape.

Gazebos

By definition, a gazebo is meant to be a "gazing room," an isolated structure intended to offer a panoramic view of the surrounding landscape or garden area. It is meant to serve as a haven, a quiet place to take a moment to catch one's breath as the busy world continues outside the garden.

During the late 1800s, gazebos became a focal point in proper Victorian and Edwardian English gardens. By the middle of the 20th century, their popularity began to wane, as more people opted instead for more modern-looking front porches and, later on, open air decks. Today, gazebos are being added to homes where front porches and decks already exist.

Gazebos are the most complex, but also the most adaptable, projects described in this book. Your gazebo can be very open or entirely screened in; giving you essentially a room separated from the rest of the house.

Pavilions

The pavilion originated alongside the gardens and pools of India. Along with the desire for water in their gardens, the people of India sought shade from the grueling sun and a place to sit, contemplate, and enjoy their surroundings.

The pavilion remains a great place to relax or to entertain during the summer months. Classically, it is a simple rectangular structure with either a slat or lattice roof. Often, it is set above a concrete or paved deck. The pavilion may be freestanding or attached to your house, sometimes acting as a transition between the home and pool.

The simplicity of this structure should encourage you to try your hand at a little custom design. Depending on your preference, you can roof your pavilion with lattice or you may decide to build a conventional rain-shedding roof like the one on the "Pavilion With Gable Roof" project on page 134. Similarly, the side walls may be completely open, or you could install lattice panels and plant some climbing vines to provide additional shade and/or privacy.

Gazebos and pavilions both offer welcome breaks from the summer sun. Gazebos can also be used as rainy-day retreats.

Arbors

Ancient Egyptian wall paintings depict vine-covered structures that resemble the arbors of today. But it was the Romans who took the idea of the arbor and ran with it, creating an abundance of designs most similar to the arbors we now know. During ancient times, these structures provided shade from the scorching sun. Arbors still do that, but today they often serve also as decorative entrances to many gardens.

Arbors are a perfect example of the beauty that can result when people work in harmony with nature. We build the arbor, plant vines at the base, and then let nature weave a fragrant flowering cover. Because the plants serve as roof and walls, the basic framework for an arbor is quite simple: Posts set directly into the ground act as vertical support members; cross beams and joists form the open framework of the roof. Grid facing constructed of wood slats or sturdy lattice also can be fastened to the framework to provide additional support for the climbing vines.

One way an arbor differs from its lighter cousin, the trellis, is that it is designed to support the heaviest of vines. Of course you can use your arbor to support the lighter varieties too. Check with your local nursery to see which vines will flourish in your area.

Gazebos are as popular today as they were a century ago. Whether it is boldly standing out amid a background of skyscrapers or quietly nestled within the trees, your project is certain to become the centerpiece of your property. A gazebo can restore an old-fashioned elegance to today's hectic pace by serving as a comfortable place to sit and talk. Climbing vines or flowers can be trained to make your project look like it grew out of its surroundings.

A well-designed outdoor structure will be as much a joy to look at from the inside as it is from the outside. Planning is the key to capturing a beautiful view. Just as important is the project itself; a well-crafted project will command its own audience. Careful attention to detail, such as a well-proportioned bench or artfully joined rafters, provides much more than simply a spot to sit out of the rain.

Gazebos take us back to a near-forgotten era. Once, the ornate decor impressed royalty; today, millions more admire their timeless beauty. Sawn balusters, gracefully curving brackets, and decorative frieze boards are a few of the options you can include in your project to make it uniquely your own.

Part 1

PLANNING AND DESIGN

THE CHOICE IS FUNCTION

Function, more than anything else, should determine the size and shape of your outdoor structure. For example, let's say that you know you want a gazebo with a hot tub . . . and you like to entertain. After thinking it over, you realize that you usually have about 10 guests. Now you have enough information to establish some basic design parameters. Begin with the hot tub. How many people do you want to accommodate at one time? If you wanted an additional seating area, the space would get larger. If you added a gas grill, the space would get larger still. As you add equipment and activities, you take on more people-circulation problems, requiring still more space. You might start out thinking that you want an 8-foot octagonal gazebo, but after analyzing what you want to do in the gazebo—its function—you may realize that the four-sided pavilion serves you better.

WINDOW SHOPPING FOR A PROJECT

Unless you are very comfortable working in two dimensions and envisioning how something will look in real life based on a set of plans, you are going to have a number of questions concerning general qualities of your project. It is impossible for this book to determine whether or not a specific project can accommodate this year's Memorial Day picnic, or if a roofline will look too steep next to the neighbor's shed, or if one project would look better than another if it was placed next to your rose garden.

The most effective preliminary research is simply to study existing outdoor structures. When you see a structure you really like, think

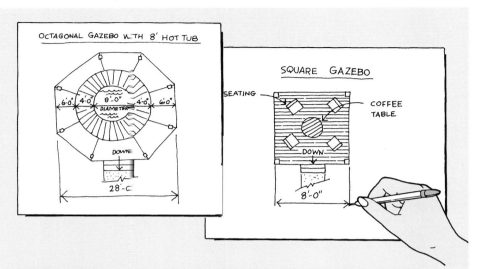

Take the time to sketch out your project before construction begins. Include in your drawing any furniture or accessories that you may want. Careful planning will help you choose the right project for your needs.

Study existing outdoor structures to analyze what you like and don't like.

Planning also includes the surrounding landscape. A brick path leads to this quiet retreat within the trees.

about what it is about the structure that excites you. You can learn just as much by a close look at structures you immediately dislike. Look for the design mistakes you want to be sure to avoid. Town parks, botanical gardens, and new housing developments can all offer invaluable research material. You might even try introducing yourself to those individuals who have a project in their yard, explain your interest, and ask if you might get a closer look at how it was constructed. There's a good chance that they will be flattered by your interest and will be happy to answer a few questions for you.

Look at all the different applications for these projects. Some may be used primarily for entertaining guests, others as quiet nooks to sit and enjoy the sun. Electric lights, barbecue grills, even hot tubs can be incorporated into the design to accommodate the desires of the owner.

Take time to inspect the details of how the structure was constructed. Was the project set in a concrete foundation or is it resting on concrete pilings? Notice how some techniques and materials influence the overall appearance of the design. For example, metal fasteners can help create a strong structure, but they may look mechanical compared

with hand-cut joinery. Pressure-treated wood creates a different effect from redwood or cedar. Seeing these woods in real life, perhaps after a few years of weathering, will help you decide which wood you like best. Some of the designs discussed in "Customizing Options" on page 88 are more time-consuming than others, but seeing just how much a little trim can enliven a project might inspire you to try cutting your own custom slat balusters.

This is also a great opportunity to compare different solutions to problems. For example, when trying to build in a little privacy, did they use lattice, plant shrubbery, or a more creative option? What problems have they discovered? What do you see as problems in their particular design?

Finally, take note of how the projects are placed in relation to the rest of the yard. Does a particular structure seem to fit better snuggled into a corner, or should it be set off as the center of attention? Has a brick or gravel path been laid directly to the gazebo, or does this structure blend more naturally into the rest of the landscape? This is also an excellent time to start noticing which flowers or plants you may want to use around your project.

A PROJECT FOR THE GREAT OUTDOORS

Of course, you want to build a structure that will withstand the extremes of your climate. For example, depending on the severity of your winters, a project may require 36-inch-deep footings to get beneath the frost line. That same project in Florida may require only a 6-inch foundation or it might even rest on concrete pilings. Although building concerns are addressed throughout this book, specific questions can be answered best by your local building inspector.

Other design decisions are motivated by personal preference rather than by structural concerns and, therefore, depend much more on how you intend to use your project. Your choice of roofing material may not significantly affect the longevity of your project, but choosing a composite roof instead of a lattice roof will make a big difference to you when it starts to rain.

Site Considerations

The site you choose for your outdoor structure is one of the most important design decisions you'll make. You can show off the gazebo or pavilion, making it a focal point in the overall plan of your home and grounds. Perhaps you'll want to plan your garden around the gazebo, planting shrubs and flowers to enhance and highlight the beauty of the site. Or you can treat your gazebo as a secluded retreat. Achieving either goal takes careful planning of the site and surrounding plantings.

Do you plan to eat and/or cook frequently in your pavilion or gazebo? If so, you'll want to consider placing the structure near the kitchen. And you'll want to make the structure big enough to accommodate the tables, chairs, and supplies that accompany eating and drinking.

Regardless of the distance from the house, consider building a walkway to your project. Concrete, brick, and treated wood are all good materials for walks. Gravel makes an effective informal walk, but it will need to be bordered with concrete, brick, or treated wood to hold it in place.

Sometimes it's tricky to predict traffic patterns in your lawn. How often have you seen a concrete walkway with a dirt path beaten into the lawn nearby? That's a sure sign that somebody made a wrong traffic pattern prediction. If you are unsure what path your walkway should take, don't build one for a month or two after you complete the outdoor structure. The most popular route will be recorded by the beaten path.

Rain and Moisture

Few things are as enjoyable or refreshing as a gentle summer shower. Unfortunately, it's easy to have too much of a good thing. If you live in an area that's prone to more than a few downpours, you should consider ways of maximizing the time you can spend outdoors and lengthening the life span of your project.

The most obvious accommodation you can make to Mother Nature is in your choice of a roof. As much as you may enjoy the look of lattice, if you live in an area that receives frequent showers, a cedar or composite roof will save you from scrambling for the house at the first hint of rain.

Frequent rainfall can contribute to other water-related problems. One of the most serious concerns is drainage. Even pressure-treated wood will suffer if water is allowed to puddle around the posts. To avoid this problem, provide proper drainage away from your project, either by positioning it on higher ground, elevating the posts on concrete piers, or by crowning the top of the concrete where it contacts the posts. These basic precautions are

covered more thoroughly in the basic construction steps outlined in "Groundwork" on page 49.

Sunlight

If you want climbing plants or vines to eventually envelop your project, you must position the structure on a site that provides at least four hours of direct sunlight daily. Otherwise, it will be difficult to grow much of anything. Southern and eastern exposures are the most desirable. On the other hand, it is possible to have too much of a good thing. Lattice and slat-style roofing are two effective ways of diffusing excess heat while still letting you enjoy the

summer sun. Installing lattice on the sides of your project and encouraging plants to climb up it is another excellent way to create a shady spot.

YOUR PERSONAL PLAN

Building a gazebo, pavilion, or arbor is a great chance to express your own style. Since the project scale is small, you needn't be daunted by fancy details. If want to install fancy frieze boards, you aren't committing yourself to making endless runs of them. On the other hand, you may wish to express your craftsmanship through a simple design.

Lattice and climbing vines provide ample shade from the summer sun.

Before beginning the project, be sure to read the chapters in Part One. Then you can design the structure knowing specifically what kind of trim, lattice, railings, steps, decking, and roof treatment will be used. Don't feel bound by what you see in the projects. As long as you do not alter the structural framework of the design, feel free to mix and match ideas.

Building an outdoor project usually involves two sets of plans—the design of the project and the site plan detailing the yard. These two plans are essential for explaining what your project will be and where it will be built.

Even if you have already selected a site for your project and plan to leave the rest of the yard pretty much as it is, you'll still need some sort of a site plan to show to the building department. If this project is but one step of a bigger landscaping project, which will eventually include adding, removing, or relocating other plants and structures, then it's important to develop a site plan to help you (and the others involved in your project) visualize how the building fits into the overall scheme.

To make a site plan, you'll need to buy some grid paper for a base map (a scale of $1/4$ inch equal to 1 foot is standard) and some tracing paper for overlays. If you have the original map or site plan for your property, this could also serve as your base map. If you don't have the original map, use a 50-foot tape measure to help measure the size of the lot (or the portion being landscaped) and to locate various features within it (house, trees, paths, etc.) Here is how to proceed:

1. Mark Property Lines

On the grid paper, mark the property lines as shown. If only a portion of the property will be affected (for example, the backyard), you needn't include the entire lot. Indicate north and, if you can, the directions of the prevailing summer winds.

At this point, it's a good idea to check with the zoning department to determine setbacks (how close a structure may be to property lines); mark setbacks as dotted lines on your plan.

2. Locate Existing Structures

Starting from a front corner of the house (marked X on the drawing),

measure the dimensions of the house and transfer them to the plan. Again, if only one yard (front, back, or side) will be affected, you need only show the part of the house that faces it. Include the locations of windows and exterior doors that will be facing your project. Measure and mark the locations of other buildings and permanent structures, including patios and decks, fences, and paved walks. Also show any underground

1. Mark Property Lines

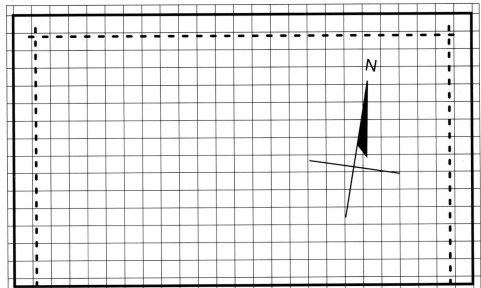

2. Locate Existing Structures

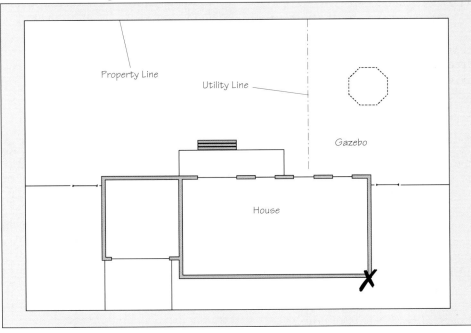

or overhead fixtures, such as utility lines and septic systems. (Most public service companies will locate your utility line for you for free. Their phone numbers should be in your phone book. The site map of your property might also have the utility locations drawn in, especially if you live in a newer home.)

3. *Locate Plantings*

Mark the locations of trees, shrubs, and other major plantings; then specify which ones are to be kept and which ones are to be removed or relocated. If applicable, make notations on the shade cast by trees, tall shrubs, fences, or other structures near the project site.

Give each member of your family a copy of the plan and encourage everyone to sketch anything that may come to mind. There are no bad ideas at this point—brainstorming is the best way of finding new solutions to old problems.

This is also a good time to formulate a "master plan," or at least a "wish list" for the rest of the yard. Even if you are not planning to tackle the entire yard at once, it will save time later if you consider what kinds of improvements you'd like to do over the next few years. For example, if you would eventually like to include a pond on the north side of your gazebo, it would not be smart to invest a lot of money in flowers and shrubs for that spot. Sketch in smaller seasonal projects such as walkways, fences, or outdoor lighting.

4. *Locate Project on Overlays*

On a tracing paper overlay, draw in the exact size and location of the proposed project. Draw the final overlay neatly, and attach it to the base map. Make copies to show to building officials or anyone else involved in the project.

At this point, you should start checking your materials list to see just how much your project will cost. Take your materials list to your local supplier and price it out.

The Stake-Out

When deciding on the final layout of your project, it will help if you can see exactly how it will fit into the real space of your yard. Use some scrap wood for stakes and some string to lay out the perimeter of the project. This will let you get a feel for how much room you will have in the structure and to check the views from the selected site. Staking out the project is also good way to ensure you didn't overlook something when you drew up the site plan.

3. Locate Plantings

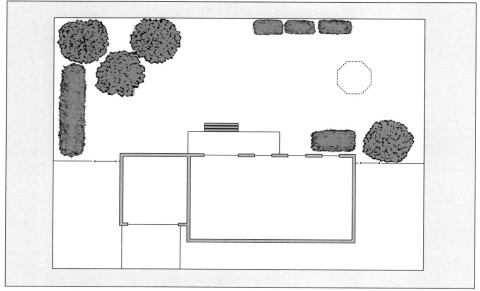

4. Locate Project on Overlays

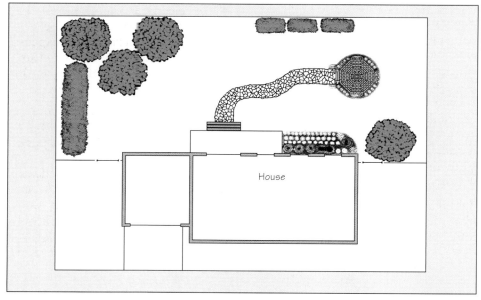

Stake out the location of your gazebo to get a sense of how it will fit in your yard.

COMPLYING WITH BUILDING CODES

Building codes and zoning ordinances apply to permanent structures. In this context, *permanent* means any structure that is anchored to the ground and/or your house. In other words, if you sink posts in concrete or attach support your project on a ledger bolted to your house, the structure is considered permanent. It also means that you'll probably need a building permit. So check with your municipal building inspector before you break ground.

Obtaining a building permit can seem like a real hassle. It's a bunch of paperwork you'd rather not deal with, and it can sometimes delay your work while the paper works

its way through the bureaucracy. Plus you have to pay a fee. As a result, you might be tempted to skip the permit process. Don't do it. Permits are accompanied by visits from the building inspector. If you do any electrical or plumbing work, that will be inspected too. The purpose of the permit and inspections is to make sure the structure is safe and does not infringe on the rights of other property owners.

Building codes regulate building practices and materials. Footing depths, joist sizes, and post spacing are some of the things that must adhere to certain minimum requirements. Zoning codes regulate the amount of setback that must be maintained from the property line. A typical setback would be 10 feet to the sides and 25 feet in the front and back.

Look on your building inspector as an asset. If he or she spots a design problem in your plans, it could save you a lot more money than the cost of a permit.

And think of this: There will probably come a day when you want to sell your home. If you've got a permit and have passed inspections, these will be on record at the town hall. It will be the buyer's guarantee that the gazebo in the backyard was built to code. If there is no record of your structure, its safety is in question. And no bank will approve a mortgage if there is any possible violation of setback requirements.

Neighborhood Regulations

You may also want to check with your neighbors or any local neighborhood committees. Very often, some communities set their own architectural standards, either to preserve local traditions or to beautify the area. Not only will compliance with these standards help maintain good neighborly relations but some communities actually codify these standards; in this case, they carry the full weight of the law.

Tax Effects

Like it or not, there's a good chance that your project will affect your real-estate tax bill. As soon as you apply for a building permit, your tax assessor will know that your house's value is about to increase. Once the project's completed, there's a good chance that he or she will stop by to reassess your property. (Small projects, like a trellis, may not warrant a permit or new assessment.) This is an annual cost, so it would be a good idea to visit the assessor's office to see what effects your project might have on your taxes.

TOOLS

This chapter should not be read as a wish list. For generations, carpenters—skilled craftsmen—managed quite well with little more than a hammer, a saw, some chisels, and a few planes. Except for the additions of the electric drill and circular saw, your toolbox does not need to include more than that same basic cache. Remember that power tools have been created for convenience—no one purchase will ever be able to replace skill, experience, and a little creativity.

Too many carpenters confuse *want* with *need* and end up buying tools that they really have no use for—tools that wind up collecting dust and rust at the bottom of the box. In most cases, one tool can do another's job just as conveniently; which one you use often depends simply on which one you already own. At other times, you will find that, given a little extra time, it's possible to "make do" with what you have. Carpentry is an exercise in improvisation.

Hint

Buying or Renting Tools

Invariably, there will be some tool that you will simply have to have. No matter what the purchase, you first have to understand what you expect the tool to do. For example, if you need a measuring tool, you must first ask yourself questions like: "How large a span will I be working with?" "What kinds of tolerances will I require?" "How much use (abuse) will I expect my tool to take?" A power tool will warrant its own special set of questions: "What kinds of operations will I be expecting from this tool?" "What will I be cutting (or drilling)?" "How much space am I willing to dedicate to this machine?" Of course, your budget will also be a prime consideration.

This chapter outlines the basic tools used in the construction of outdoor projects. The tools fall into three major categories: tools for layout and excavation, cutting tools and joining tools, and everything else.

Purchase the least expensive tool that will meet or exceed all of your criteria and then some. This usually means purchasing the best tool you can afford. (Best does *not* always mean most expensive, so be sure of what you're buying.) A "bargain" tool will not seem to be that great a bargain if its limitations remind you of that fact every time you pick it up.

One-time jobs can be done very professionally and economically with rented tools. Rental shops deal with professional-caliber tools that will perform better than their less expensive counterparts. Renting is a great opportunity to use a more exotic tool at a fraction of its purchase price. And should you eventually decide to purchase that particular type of tool, your on-site experience will better enable you to pick out the model that's right for you.

EXCAVATION AND LAYOUT TOOLS

Marking Out the Site

A tape measure is essential for just about any building project. For this type of work, you'll find that a 25- or 30-foot tape will be the most useful for both long and short measurements. Good tape measures will have the first foot divided into $1/32$ inch lengths for really precise work. Tapes with a 1-inch-wide blade are a little more bulky than $3/4$-inch blades, but the blades are much more rigid and can

be extended farther without folding. This really can come in handy for one-person measuring jobs.

A chalkline is nothing more than that—a roll of string held inside a chalk-filled container. It only takes a couple seconds to "snap a line." Stretch the string against a flat surface and pluck it to produce a straight, chalked layout line. Although red chalk may be a little easier to see, stick with blue. The red pigment is permanent and can stain anything it gets in contact with (hands, wood, etc.).

A plumb bob relies on gravity to enable you to drop a perfectly vertical line from a given spot. The heavy pointed bob is suspended on a string and is useful for aligning posts with pinpoint accuracy. Some chalklines can also be used as plumb bobs.

Digging Holes

If you have to sink only a few posts or if you have a really strong back, you can dig holes by hand with a posthole digger. This double-handled tool is designed to cut deep narrow holes and scoop out the dirt with its clamshell-like blades.

For larger projects, you'll thank yourself for renting a power auger to speed up the job. Power augers are powered by a gasoline engine and work just like a giant drill. Some models can be handled by one person, others require two. You will still need a posthole digger to clean out the holes when you're finished with the auger.

Whether you are using the auger or a posthole digger, if you run into rock, you'll need a wrecking bar (also referred to as a breaking bar) to break up the stone or to wedge it loose. Roots can also slow down

Tools for Excavation and Layout

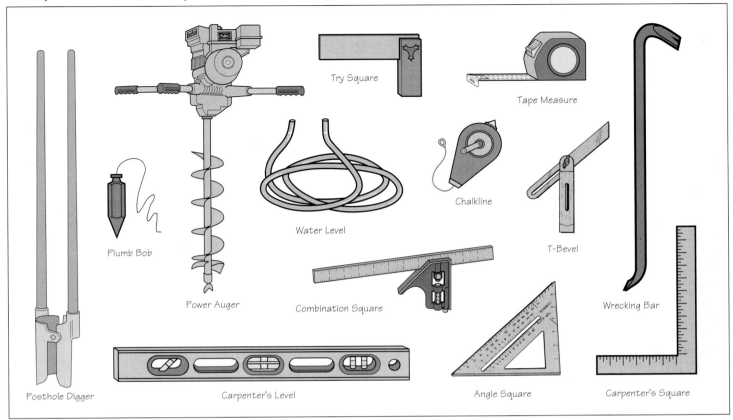

Try Square

Tape Measure

Plumb Bob

Water Level

Chalkline

T-Bevel

Power Auger

Combination Square

Wrecking Bar

Posthole Digger

Carpenter's Level

Angle Square

Carpenter's Square

your progress; cut them out with either a hand ax or branch pruners.

Levels

There are two levels that can assist you in making sure that the longest spans are "on the level": a water level and a line level.

A water level consists of a pair of clear graduated vials fitted onto a long tube (your garden hose will do nicely). Water naturally seeks its own level; when the water levels in the two tubes are even, the points are level with each other. This is the most accurate method for measuring over long distances. A line level consists of only a single vial. It's designed to be hooked to a string for leveling long spans. Make sure that the string is taut to ensure an accurate measurement.

The carpenter's level is a workhorse on any construction site. Available in 2-foot and 4-foot lengths, you will use one for leveling beams, ledgers, and making sure posts are plumb. Take special care of your level; all it takes is one good drop to make it inaccurate. One way to test your level is by setting it on top of a level surface. Now flip it over. The bubbles should still be in the center; if they've moved, then your level is off.

A torpedo level is a good tool for plumbing up concrete forms and J-bolts as you set them in wet concrete. Its compact size makes it a handy addition to your toolbox.

Squares

A carpenter's square is made from a single piece of steel or aluminum and is useful for laying out stair stringers and rafters. Its large size makes it good for squaring up large boards and calibrating your other squares, but when you're setting individual tools, such as your circular saw, you will probably find it's more convenient to use a smaller square.

A combination square is adjustable. The body of this square contains both 90- and 45-degree ends and can slide up and down the blade if you unlock the thumbscrew. The moveable body makes this tool ideal for transferring depth measurements or running a line along a board.

Angle squares are thick, strong, triangular castings of either aluminum or plastic that are tough enough to withstand the rigors of general construction without losing their accuracy. The angle square's triangular shape enables you to lay out a 45-degree angle as quickly as a 90-degree angle. Using markings on the body, it is also possible to lay out angles other than 90 degrees, as when laying out rafters. The edges of this square can also be used as an accurate cutting guide.

Probably the best tool for gauging and transferring angles other than 45 and 90 degrees is a sliding T-bevel (also known as a bevel gauge). A bevel gauge has a flat metal blade that can be locked into a wooden or plastic handle at any angle. A bevel gauge is great for transferring an existing angle on the actual project, it can also be used in conjunction with a protractor to record a specific angle (for example, if you wanted to draw a 25-degree angle).

CUTTING AND JOINING

Most people consider cutting and joining to be the most enjoyable part of carpentry. This feeling and accomplishment is the result of actually working with the wood, cutting and shaping it to fit your design. That feeling of enjoyment will be enhanced if you work with the correct tools. More important, having the right tool for a specific job and knowing how to use it are the best ways to avoid wasting material and to prevent injuries.

Cutting

The circular saw has replaced the handsaw in almost every situation. That's because a circular saw is capable of crosscutting, ripping, and beveling boards or sheets of plywood quickly and cleanly. It can be used to create a variety of common joints, such as miters, laps, and dadoes.

The most popular saws with carpenters and do-it-yourselfers alike are the models that take a 7¼-inch blade. This blade size will enable you to cut to a maximum depth of about 2½ inches at 90 degrees. (Larger saws are available for cutting thicker material, but they're generally too bulky for this type of use.)

Choosing a Circular Saw

There are many options that distinguish one saw from another, the most important of which is its power. Don't judge a saw's performance by its horsepower rating, but by the amount of amperage that the motor draws. Low-cost saws may have only 9- or 10-amp motors with drive shafts and arbors running on rollers or sleeve bearings. A contractor-grade saw is rated at 12 or 13 amps and is made with ball bearings. This extra power will enable it to better withstand the wear it will receive cutting through a lot of tough pressure-treated lumber.

Plastic housings are no longer the mark of an inferior tool; however, a thin, stamped metal foot is. A thin, stamped steel base won't stay as flat as a thicker base that is either extruded or cast.

For safety's sake, be sure that your saw is double insulated, to minimize any chance of electric shock. Some saws have an additional safety switch that must be depressed before the trigger will work. Another feature to look for on a saw is an arbor lock. The lock secures the arbor nut and prevents the blade from turning while you are changing blades.

Choosing a Blade

For general all-purpose use, carbide blades are the best for achieving smooth, precise cuts. Carbide blades may cost a few dollars more than a comparable blade made from high-speed steel, but you can expect it to cut five times longer before it needs to be resharpened.

A 24-tooth blade is usually adequate for deck construction and general use. (There is a trade-off between the number of teeth and cut rates and cut quality. For example, a blade with less teeth will cut faster, but the cuts will tend to be ragged. More teeth will produce a finer cut, but your saw will also have to work harder to move more teeth through the wood, and it will cut slower.) It's a good idea to have

Tools for Cutting and Joining

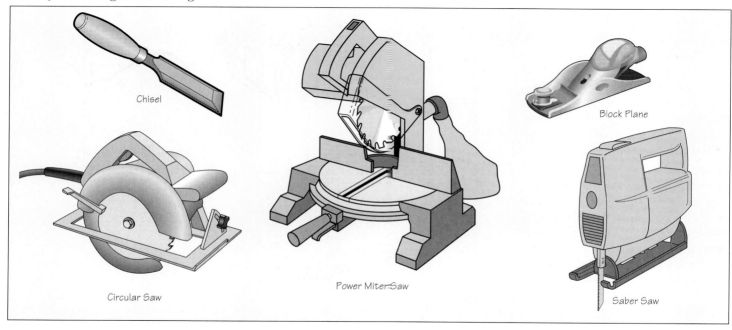

Chisel

Block Plane

Circular Saw

Power Miter Saw

Saber Saw

an extra blade or two on hand; wet wood and dense pressure-treated wood will dull your saw's blade relatively quickly.

For angle cuts, you'll want to use a motorized miter box. These tools (also called chop saws or cutoff saws) are simply circular saws mounted on a pivot assembly and are designed to make precise crosscuts in boards, planks, and pieces of trim. Chop saws are more expensive than circular saws, but they make it possible to cut difficult angles precisely and quickly.

A saber saw is a good choice for cutting decorative curves on the ends of rafters and for making elaborate pieces of trim. A saber saw can cut curves, make cutouts, and finish cuts started by a circular saw.

For certain types of cuts, nothing will completely replace a good handsaw. A handsaw is just the thing whenever you have just a few cuts to do, for those spots where a circular saw can't reach, or when you want to finish off a circular saw cut. A 15-inch saw with 10 to 12 teeth per inch (tpi) will cut well and still fit into your toolbox.

Joinery Tools

No matter how adept you become with your power tools, sooner or later you will end up falling back on certain old reliables to achieve close-fitting joints. A block plane is great to carry along with you on the site. A properly set plane will trim a shaving off at a time, until the joint matches up perfectly. A plane is also handy for softening hard edges that might splinter or catch someone's clothing.

A set of three chisels, 3/4 inch, 1 inch, and 1½ inches, will also be useful for close paring. The blades must be kept as sharp as possible for these tools to work safely and smoothly. Pressure-treated wood will dull steel edges more quickly than other types of wood.

Safety Equipment

Common sense should tell you not to do carpentry without first having some basic safety equipment, such as eye and ear protection.

Wear safety goggles or plastic glasses whenever you are working with power tools or chemicals . . . period. Make sure your eye protection conforms to American National Standards Institute (ANSI) Z87.1 or Canadian Standards Association (CSA) requirements (products that do will be marked with a stamp). Considering the cost of a visit to the emergency room, it doesn't hurt to purchase an extra pair for the times when a neighbor volunteers to lend a hand or when you misplace the first pair.

The U.S. Occupational Safety and Health Administration (OSHA) recommends that hearing protection be worn when the noise level exceeds 85 decibels (db) for an 8-hour workday. However, considering that a circular saw emits 110 db, even shorter exposure times can contribute to hearing impairment or loss. Both insert and muff-type protectors are available; whichever you choose, be sure that it has a noise reduction rating (NRR) of a least 20 db.

Your construction project will create a lot of sawdust. If you are sensitive to dust, and whenever you are working with pressure-treated wood, wear a dust mask. Two types of respiratory protection are available: disposable dust masks and cartridge-type respirators. A dust mask is good for keeping dust and fine particles from being inhaled during a single procedure. Respirators have a replaceable filter. Both are available for protection against nontoxic and toxic dusts and mists. Whichever you purchase, be sure that it has been stamped by the National Institute for Occupational Safety and Health/Mine Safety and Health Administration (NIOSH/MSHA) and is approved for your specific operation. When you can taste or smell the contaminate or when the mask starts to interfere with normal breathing, it's time for a replacement.

Work gloves are also nice for avoiding injury to the hands—catching a splinter off a board or developing a blister when digging post holes is not a good way to start a workday. Similarly, heavy-duty work boots will protect your feet. Steel toes will prevent injuries from dropped boards or tools. Flexible steel soles will protect you from puncture by a rogue nail.

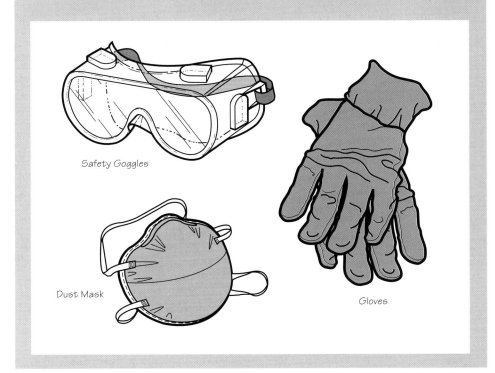

Safety Goggles

Dust Mask

Gloves

OTHER CONSTRUCTION TOOLS

There are a few tools that don't really fit into one specific category or that seem to apply to more than one category, and for that reason, they warrant their own special mention.

For every project in this book, it is assumed that you have an electric drill. (If you don't, you should pick up one with a 3/8-inch chuck, variable speed control, and a reverse switch.) Make sure that your drill is sufficiently powered (at least 3 amps) to handle the kind of abuse that it will receive on the job. You will discover that by inserting the proper bit in the chuck, your drill is also able to drive screws faster than you could ever do by hand.

If you're in the market for a second drill, a cordless drill will provide you with all of the attributes of an ordinary drill, but without the hassle of having to drag around a cord. An adjustable clutch is a desirable option, because it will allow you to drive screws to a set depth without overloading the motor or stripping the screwhead.

And how can you build anything without a hammer? You can manage quite well with a standard 16-ounce hammer; a lighter hammer is ideal for fastening railings, trim, and other light members when you are concerned primarily with control. When driving 12d or 16d nails into the beams, or joists, you will quickly learn to appreciate the way a 20-ounce framing hammer can sink a nail in just a few blows. If you are considering roofing your project with wood shingles or shakes, you may find that with practice, a roofer's hatchet is handy.

One problem with driving nails with a hammer is the "rosettes" that seem to spring up when you are trying to drive the nail flush with the wood. A nail set picks up where most hammers leave off. A nail set is a small shaft of metal with one square end and the other tapered to a point. The tapered point is sometimes cupped to hold the nailheads. With a nail set, not only can you drive a nail flush with the surrounding wood but you can also countersink nails so that they can be filled with putty to produce a nail-free finish. Nail sets come in various sizes to match different types of nails; use the nail set sized to the nailhead being driven to avoid enlarging the hole.

Unless you want to spend most of the day trying to remember where you left everything, a tool belt or work apron is a must. A good tool belt will have a spot for your hammer, tape measure, chalkline, and block plane, and still have a pocket left over for nails and screws.

A utility knife will probably be the most reached for tool in either your toolbox or pouch. You will use your utility knife for everything from sharpening your pencil to marking cut lines to cutting shingles to shaving off wood to ease in a close-fitting joint. For general use, you should invest in a fairly heavy-duty knife that has a large angular blade held in place within a hollow metal handle. As with all cutting tools, sharp blades are safest because they provide the most control with the least amount of effort. Discard blades as soon as they're dull.

And there's one thing that a carpenter can never have enough of—pencils, pencils, pencils.

Additional Tools

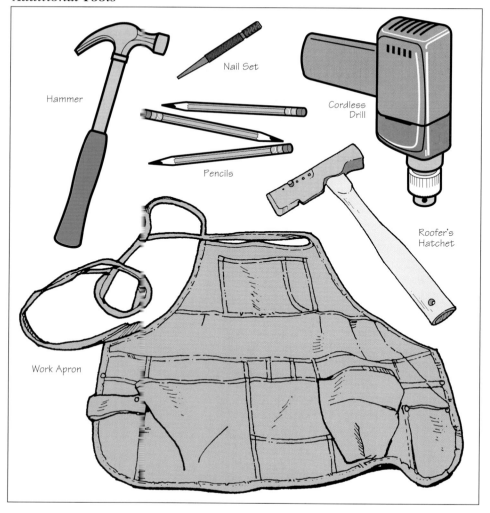

Hammer

Nail Set

Pencils

Cordless Drill

Roofer's Hatchet

Work Apron

FASTENERS

Regardless of the type of outdoor structure you're planning to construct, you'll need a variety of nails, bolts, or screws, and some framing hardware to join materials and strengthen joints. Metal fasteners will free you from having to cut and fit complex joints. And considering that cuts made on site are sometimes less than perfect, metal fasteners offer some leeway while still ensuring that the joint will be strong and secure. Some metal fasteners are essential for joining different materials together—no amount of nails can replace a post tie for joining a wooden post onto a concrete footing.

But metal fasteners do have some disadvantages. Large fasteners, such as rafter ties and decking cleats, can save time, but the job will cost you more than if you simply use nails. This price difference can be significant if your project incorporates many metal fasteners into its design. Sometimes metal connectors, even nails, can be visually obtrusive and take away from the overall appearance of a carefully crafted project.

Remember, some local building codes may require structural fasteners in addition to nails. Be sure to check before building.

NAILS

The most basic of metal fasteners is the nail. As commonly used, the term *penny* (abbreviated as *d*) indicates a nail's length. The number did not originally refer to the length of the nail but to the cost of 100 nails of that size. The length of the various penny sizes of common and finishing nails are listed in the table on the inside back cover of this book.

The best overall choice for outdoor use is hot-dipped galvanized nails. These nails should be used where rust staining could become a problem. But even though they are coated with a layer of zinc, galvanized nails will rust over time, especially at the exposed nailhead where the coating has been damaged by hammering. You must also be wary of "galvanic corrosion," which can happen any time galvanized nails are used to join a dissimilar metal, particularly in a humid environment. Galvanic corrosion is a reaction between the two metals that creates accelerated weathering at the point of contact. Always select nails that are compatible with any metal being attached to the wood (i.e., use aluminum nails to attach aluminum gutters, copper or brass nails for copper flashing, etc.).

Since they will not rust, stainless-steel and aluminum nails are also suitable for exterior use. Aluminum nails are softer and tend to bend easier than steel nails. Both types of nails are usually more expensive than galvanized nails (stainless-steel nails can be twice as expensive as hot-dipped galvanized), but where excessive corrosion could be a problem, like for a deck near the ocean, it might be the best investment.

Fasteners

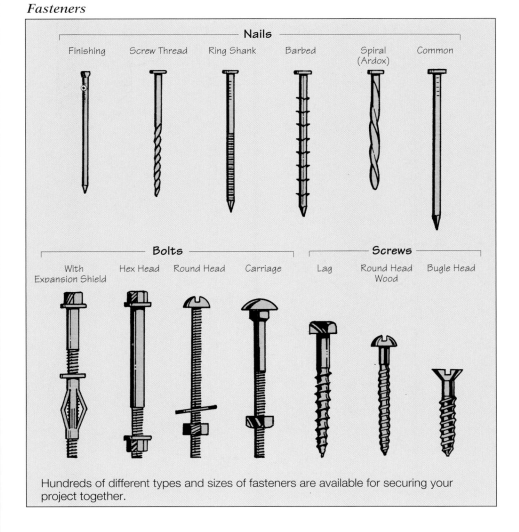

Hundreds of different types and sizes of fasteners are available for securing your project together.

Common nails are preferred for general construction because they have an extra-thick shank and a broad head. You can also purchase common nails that have been cement-coated (actually nylon coated) to increase their holding strength. Their coating is melted by the friction of being driven through the wood and quickly resets. Try to drive cement-coated nails home in a few quick blows.

"Deformed" nails, such as helical, barbed, or ridged nails, also exhibit greater withdrawal resistance. These nails' shanks have been adapted to increase friction (helical nails are actually threaded like a screw) and have a 40 percent greater withdrawal resistance than common nails. These nails are harder to drive.

If you don't want the nail's head to show, choose a finishing nail. Casing nails are similar to finishing nails but have a duller point and thicker shank; they have more holding power than a finishing nail of the same size. After the nail is driven nearly flush, both types can be sunk with a nail set. You can fill the hole with wood putty.

Holding Power

Several characteristics determine the holding power of a nail—its shape, diameter, point (pointed, chisel, or blunt), and the coating of the shank. Think of a nail as a small wedge being driven against the fibers of the wood; anything that would enable this wedge to contact more wood fibers without damaging them or that can attach the wedge more securely to the existing fibers will increase the nail's hold. And holding power is a key part of keeping framing square, plumb, and level.

A thicker nail, for instance, will be more difficult to remove than a thinner nail. The resistance of nails to withdrawal increases almost directly with their diameter; a nail's holding power is doubled with a proportional increase in diameter,

because more wood fibers are acting against the wider wedge. A pointed nail will have a greater resistance because it is driven between wood fibers that a dull nail would tend to sever. And a deformed or textured nail, such as a ring-shank or a coated nail, will have greater withdrawal resistance than a smooth shank because the wood fibers have a textured surface to grip.

The characteristics of the wood also contribute to overall resistance. Hard, tight-grained woods, such as oak, will grip a nail tighter than a softer wood such as pine. Oak and other hardwoods offer so much resistance that you'll usually have to drill before nailing to drive the nail without bending it. Dry wood will hold a nail better than wet wood. Withdrawal resistance is also determined by how a nail is driven in relation to the wood's grain.

Using more nails will also increase overall holding strength, just make sure that the nails do not end up splitting the wood. Staggering a row of nails will help. Even slight splitting will greatly affect holding power.

SCREWS

Bugle-head screws are commonly known as drywall screws because they were originally developed for installing wallboard. These handy screws have become popular for all kinds of woodworking and carpentry projects. Drywall screws have an aggressive thread and do not require a pilot hole. "Bugle-head" refers to the taper beneath the flat head of the screw that allows you to drive them flush in softwood and drywall without drilling a countersink hole.

Screws have greater holding power than nails and can actually pull two boards tightly together. They also create a clean finished appearance by eliminating the possibility of hammer dents and scuffs, and unlike nails, screws will not "pop,"

or work themselves loose, after a couple of seasons. And since screws can be removed cleanly, they facilitate disassembly or the removal of a damaged board. But, while screws can be used anywhere nails are used in outdoor construction, they cost considerably more than nails. As a result, screws are usually limited to two applications—installing deck boards and finish trim work.

In the United States, drywall screws are most readily available with Phillips heads. Some woodworking supply catalogs offer them with a square recess for driving the screws. Square drive screws are more readily available in Canada. You'll need a power drill or driver to install drywall screws. The square drives are superior because you can't easily strip the drive hole or the bit.

Drywall screws are available in a black oxide finish, suitable for interior work, and in a hot-dipped galvanized finish, for exterior projects. You'll usually find the exterior version sold as "deck screws." The most common lengths are 1, $1^1/_2$, 2, $2^1/_2$, and 3 inches.

If you need to toe-fasten pieces in an area of your project that will be highly visible, you can avoid ugly hammer dents by toe-screwing instead of toe-nailing. Position the boards in place and drill a starter hole with a bit approximately equal in diameter to the shank of the screw.

Planning Ahead

Keeping a few spare pounds of screws around can come in handy for a difficult job. Purchase a pound each of $1^1/_2$-, $2^1/_2$-, and 3-inch screws for those situations where you need additional strength or for those spots that are too tight to swing a hammer.

Sizing

When determining nail or screw length, the general rule for softwoods is the nail penetration into the bottom piece should be equal to or greater than the thickness of the top piece. For example, if you are nailing 1-inch-thick ($^5/4$) decking boards to joists, 8d nails would do the job. You'll get even better holding power with 10d nails.

When fastening plywood, the choice of the nail depends on the thickness of the panels. For $^3/4$- and $^5/8$-inch plywood, use 8d common nails. For $^1/2$- and $^3/8$-inch panels use 6d common nails. Space nails every 6 inches along the edges and 12 inches in the field. Ring- or screw-shank nails are recommended for this application to prevent the nails from working their way loose when the wood expands and contracts with moisture changes.

The chart "Nailing Schedule for Light Outdoor Structures" tells you what kind and how many nails to use in the various connections you'll make.

Although not recommended for framing, screws can be used effectively for installing sheathing. For $^3/4$- to $^5/8$-inch plywood use a $1^1/2$-inch screw. For $^1/2$- to $^3/8$-inch plywood use a $1^1/4$-inch screw. Space screws 12 inches along the edges and 24 inches in the field.

BOLTS AND RODS

The most rigid joint fasteners are bolts and lag screws. These heavy-duty fasteners are recommended for connections that must be extremely strong, such as post-to-beam connections or where a ledger joins to the house. For strength and appearance, a single lag screw or bolt can replace three or four bugle-head screws.

Bolts pass all the way through the pieces they join (or are "through-bolted") and are secured with washers and nuts. The bolt hole diameter should equal the stated diameter of the bolt. Two types of bolts are commonly used in outdoor construction: machine bolts and carriage bolts. Machine bolts resemble lag screws in that they have a hexagonal-shaped head that remains above the surface of the lumber.

Carriage bolts work just like machine bolts, but they have a round head instead of a hex head. Just beneath the head, the shank is square. When tapped into a tight-fitting hole, the square shank seats the bolt into the wood, so that the nut can be tightened. A carriage bolt does not always require a washer beneath the head, but a washer is needed beneath the nut. Because the head is pulled almost flush to the surface of the lumber, carriage bolts are typically used on railing posts or in other places where a lag bolt might be visually obtrusive or snag clothing.

Bolt lengths range from 3 to 12 inches, and diameters range from $^1/4$ to $^3/4$ inch in $^1/16$-inch increments. For longer lengths, you

NAILING SCHEDULE FOR LIGHT OUTDOOR STRUCTURES

Area	Application	Method	Number	Size	Nail Type
Frame	Header to joist	End-nail	3	16d	Common
	Header to sill	Toe-nail	16" oc	10d	Common
	Joist to sill	Toe-nail	2	10d	Common
	Ledger to beam	Face-nail	$^3/16$" oc	16d	Common
	Double top plate	Face-nail	16" oc	10d	Common
	Ceiling joist to top plate	Toe-nail	3	8d	Common
	Rafter to top plate	Toe-nail	2	8d	Common
	Rafter to ceiling joist	Face-nail	5	10d	Common
	Rafter to hip or valley	Toe-nail	3	10d	Common
	Ridge board to rafter	End-nail	3	10d	Common
	Rafter to rafter	Toe-nail	4	8d	Common
	Collar tie (2") to rafter	Face-nail	2	12d	Common
	Collar tie (1") to rafter	Face-nail	3	8d	Common
Roof	Asphalt, new	Face-nail	4	$^7/8$"	Roofing
	Asphalt, reroof	Face-nail	4	$1^3/4$"	Roofing
	Wood shingle, new	Face-nail	2	4d	Shingle
	Wood single, reroof	Face-nail	2	6d	Shingle
Sheathing	$^3/8$" plywood	Face-nail	6" oc	6d	Common
	$^1/2$" and thicker plywood	Face-nail	6" oc	8d	Common
	$^1/2$" fiberboard	Face-nail	3" oc	$1^1/2$"	Roofing
	$^3/4$" fiberboard	Face-nail	3" oc	$1^3/4$"	Roofing
	$^3/4$" boards	Face-nail	6" oc	8d	Common

can purchase threaded rod. Bolts should be approximately 1 inch longer than the thickness of the combined pieces to accommodate washers and nuts. Threaded rod uses washers and nuts on both ends, so size it 2 inches longer than the combined thickness. Plan to drill bolt holes using a bit of the same diameter as the bolt. When setting or removing lag or carriage bolts, try not to damage the threads by striking them with a hammer or against a metal surface; damaged threads will make it impossible to thread on the nut. If you must tap the threaded end, protect it with a scrap of wood or hit it with a plastic mallet.

LAG SCREWS

Lag screws are available in the same size and length as machine or carriage bolts. Because they have a bolt-shaped head, lag screws are sometimes confused with lag bolts, but unlike bolts, they do not protrude through the objects being joined. They're particularly useful in tight spots where you can reach only one side of the connection with a wrench (a socket wrench is easiest). Drill a lead hole about two-thirds the length of the lag screw, using a bit $1/8$ inch smaller than the lag screw's shank. Place a washer under each lag screw's head.

It is a better idea to make connections with several small-diameter bolts or lag screws instead of fewer large-diameter bolts. See "Bolt and Lag Screw Schedules" to help you estimate the sizing and spacing for joining boards with lag bolts or screws.

FRAMING HARDWARE

You'll find many types of framing connectors in sizes to fit most standard-dimension rough and surfaced lumber. There are several major manufacturers of structural wood fasteners. Their basic product lines cover nearly all applications, but you may need to ask about special fasteners such as the gazebo roof peak fastener, hip rafter ties, or truss plates. Explain your needs to the salesperson. While an effort has been made to select the generic name for the fasteners described in this book, one manufacturer's hurricane clip may be another's storm tie. The fasteners you do buy may also look a little different from those illustrated. Just make sure they are designed to do the same job.

Remember that most of these fasteners are simply metal accessories designed to assist with, or replace, other traditional joinery techniques. If you cannot find a particular fastener or wish to maintain a metal-free appearance, consider other options.

Nails for Fasteners

Most structural fastener manufacturers also supply nails sized and designed to provide maximum load performance when used with their fasteners. Since they are connecting sheet metal to wood, the nails can be shorter than if you were using a common nail to fasten together two boards of the same thickness. Fastener nails are typically blunted to help eliminate wood splitting. Their surface finish can be galvanized or cement coated to prevent rust.

Use the number of fasteners and nails and the nailing pattern specified by the fastener manufacturer. If specialty nails are not available, use the thickest common nails that will fit through the nailing flange holes. You may have to clinch the nails if they protrude. In the descriptions below, letters refer to the chart on page 33.

A. Post Anchors. These connectors secure the base of a load-bearing post to a concrete foundation, slab, or deck. In areas where there is a lot of standing water or rain, choose an elevated post base that raises a post 1 to 3 inches above the surface.

B. Joist Hangers. Joist hangers are used for butt joints between deck joists and beams. Single- and double-size hangers are available. Rafter hangers are similar to joist hangers but are used to hang roof rafters from a ledger board.

C. Saddle Hangers or Purlin Clips. Available in single and double designs, these clips are ideal for installing crosspieces between joists or rafters.

D. Rafter Ties. These ties are used to provide wind and seismic ties for trusses and rafters.

E. Ridge Rafter Connector. These connectors resemble joist hangers with an open bottom. Use them to fasten 2x6 rafters to ridge boards or ledgers. The open bottom can accommodate slopes up to 30 degrees.

F. Truss Plates. These plates are used in the construction of roof trusses. They can be designed with

Bolt & Lag Screw Schedules

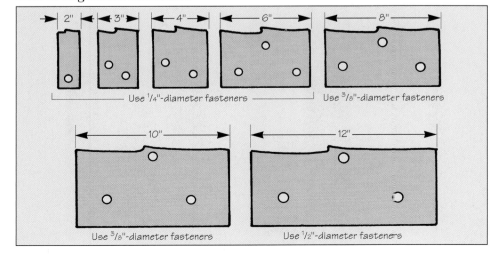

or without a lip. Various sizes are available.

Caution: Not all plate type fasteners are designed for truss applications. Be sure the plates you buy are specified for roof truss construction. Special truss nails may also be required.

G. Twist Tie. These straps are ideal for tying pieces that cross at 90 degree angles, such as joists, rafters, and beams.

H. Hip Corner Plate. A hip corner plate connects a rafter or joist to double top plates at a 45 degree angle.

I. Gazebo Roof Peak Tie. Two of these connectors are used at the peak of a six-sided gazebo roof to tie together all rafters. A key block is not needed.

J. Hip Rafter Gazebo Tie. Similar to a hip corner plate, this connector is angled to tie roof rafters to the top plate of a six-sided gazebo.

K. Hurricane Ties. Use these ties to secure rafters and trusses to top plates.

L. Post Caps. These fasteners can be used at the top of a post to join

it to a beam or to strengthen a splice connection between two beams.

M. Panel Clips. These clips are slipped between the edges of plywood panels to lock them together where they span between rafters. Panel clips will also help maintain a sufficient gap between panels to allow for thermal expansion.

N. Stair Angles. These clips support treads, eliminating the need for notching stringers.

Framing Hardware

WOOD

Once you've decided on a design for your gazebo, arbor, or pavilion, the next important decision is selecting a wood for your project. The wood you choose must fulfill many requirements. Your project must weather years of exposure without losing its strength or stability. It must resist the combined effects of sun, rain, mold, and wood-boring insects. In addition, the wood you use should be easy to work with, attractive, and reasonably priced.

Trying to find wood at your local lumberyard that will best meet all of these requirements should not be intimidating. This chapter is designed to introduce you to the types and grades of woods typically used in exterior construction. After reading this chapter, you will be able to select the wood that is best suited for your particular project. This chapter will also guide you through the purchase of your lumber.

CHOOSING WOOD

Lumber is divided into softwoods and hardwoods. Softwood comes from coniferous trees (evergreens), while hardwood comes from deciduous trees (those that loose their leaves in the fall). While most hardwoods are harder than most softwoods, this is not always the case. Southern yellow pine, which is a softwood, is harder than poplar, which is a hardwood.

Nearly all outdoor construction today is done with softwood lumber, because it is more readily available, easier to work, and generally less expensive than hardwood. Although more costly, hardwoods are typically used in smaller decorative elements because they can be cut or milled more sharply and because they have attractive grain patterns. (Premade cornice pieces and frieze boards are typically made of poplar, because this hardwood cuts cleaner and weathers better than pine.)

Of the softwoods, redwood, cedar, and cypress are considered the most highly desirable outdoor building materials because of their beauty and natural resistance to decay. These woods are used for decks, gazebos, lathe- or lattice-style roofing, shingles, siding, and shakes. Unfortunately, due to their popularity, they are also the most expensive of all softwoods and may not be available in all regions.

But don't think that you have to use higher-priced redwood or cedar for a great looking outdoor project. Other softwoods are available in various regions of the country—for example, pine, fir, spruce, and larch. Granted, these woods will require additional weather protection, but the extra care will enable you to build the same beautiful project for a lot less money.

Redwood

The redwood trees of the Pacific Northwest are legendary for their size and the quality of the lumber they provide. Redwood's beautiful straight grain, natural glowing color, and weather resistance have traditionally marked it as the Cadillac of all outdoor building materials. Unfortunately, past overlumbering has affected the availability (and price) of redwood today.

There are two "types" of redwood in each log. The younger, outer portion of the wood is called sapwood; the older, denser center is referred to as heartwood. The sapwood is lighter in color and less weather resistant than the heartwood. Redwood heartwood is extremely stable and can be milled to produce very smooth surfaces. When it is sawn, the reddish heartwood produces a wonderful fragrance, releasing the same chemicals that discourage wood-boring insects. If you like, you can let redwood age naturally to a light gray patina; however, it will also accept paint or stain readily.

There are several grades of redwood. The two grades preferred for outdoor construction—because they consist entirely of heartwood—are Clear All Heart and Construction Heart. Of the two, Clear All Heart is more expensive because it is knot free. Its price will probably limit its use to railing and other important trim pieces that must be smooth and clear. In comparison, Construction Heart, or Con-Heart, does contain some minor imperfections, but should be ideal for almost every other element of your outdoor project. Because they contain some sapwood, Clear, B Grade, Construction Common and Merchantable are not recommended for deck framing or decking. They can be effectively used for accessories around your project, such as fences, planters, or trellises.

Although it is weather and rot resistant, redwood does not last as long as pressure-treated lumber under ground-contact conditions.

GRADES OF REDWOOD

Grades Containing Only Heartwood
Clear All Heart
Select Heart
Construction Heart
Merchantable Heart

Grades Containing Some Sapwood
Clear
B Grade
Construction Common
Merchantable

It's a good idea to raise the deck of your project several inches above the ground by setting your posts on concrete pillars. Another popular and attractive (and cost-effective) option is to build the understructure from pressure-treated wood and to use redwood for the parts that will be visible.

Western Red Cedar

Western red cedar is more decay resistant than eastern cedar varieties. Western red cedar trees are also significantly larger and yield a reasonable selection of dimension lumber. Like redwood, cedar is a fragrant, dark-colored wood that is extremely stable and rot resistant. It can be left to develop a gray patina, or it can be painted or stained.

Cedar does have some drawbacks. Because it is softer and weaker than other species, cedar is not the best choice for framing members. The popularity of cedar shingles, clapboards, and shakes limits the use of cedar for other applications by driving up the price.

RETENTION LEVELS AND RECOMMENDED USES FOR PRESSURE-TREATED WOOD

Retention (lb/ ft³)	Recommended Use
0.25	Aboveground exposure
0.40	Ground contact
0.60	Permanent wood foundation
0.80	Marine use: freshwater contact
2.50	Marine use: saltwater contact

Cypress

Bald cypress is the South's answer to redwood. Native to the swamps and lowland areas throughout the southeast, bald cypress is extremely resistant to decay and insect attack. Cypress is similar to redwood in hardness and strength, although it's not as stable. In the southern United States, local sawmills can be a very economical source for your building materials. Cypress isn't usually stocked outside of its native region, but it can be custom ordered by northern consumers.

Other Decay-Resistant Woods

Depending on where you live, you may have some local woods that are quite resistant to rot. Osage orange, black locust, and white oak are all excellent for outdoor projects. However, most of these species will not be readily available through a home center. Availability is limited, you'll have to get them from a local sawmill.

Pressure-Treated Lumber

Pressure-treated lumber (typically southern yellow pine, Douglas fir, ponderosa pine, or Engleman

PRESSURE-TREATED LUMBER'S STAMP

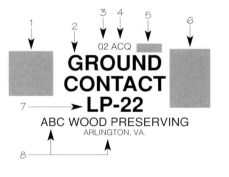

1— Trademark of building code–approved quality-control agency
2— Proper exposure conditions
3— Year of treatment
4— The preservative used for treatment
5— Drying procedure, if applicable
6— Trademark of agency supervising the treating plant
7— Preservative retention level and/or the quality-control agency procedure indication
8— Treating company and plant location

Redwood Grading

From left to right, Clear All Heart, Select Heart, Construction Heart, Merchantable Heart, B Grade, Select, and Construction. Use heartwood for outdoor construction.

spruce) is wood that, in addition to being graded, has been factory treated with preservatives to repel rot, insects, and other causes of decay.

Pressure-treated (PT) lumber is almost always the best choice for building decorative outdoor structures without spending a lot of money. There is much to recommend it: the cost is comparatively low and a good deal less expensive than redwood or cedar—and if you choose the right kind of lumber, it will most likely last longer than redwood or cedar. But consider this choice carefully because there are some drawbacks: PT lumber will often check and splinter over time as it dries out. Left unfinished, PT lumber will turn gray, but not the same pleasing color and sheen that you will get with redwood and cedar. And PT lumber sometimes has a series of incisions left over from the treatment process; these will not go away over time but can become little collectors of dirt.

For nearly 70 years, chromated copper arsenate (CCA) has been used to treat lumber, making it decay- and insect-resistant. Wood used outdoors that has a characteristic greenish hue is treated with CCA. Over the years, complaints about the toxicity of the chromium and arsenic used in CCA have plagued the manufacturers of treated lumber. Now they have done something about it, implementing a voluntary phase-out of CCA-treated lumber. After December 2003, you will no longer be able to buy the lumber for use in residential projects such as gazebos and trellises.

However, alternative treatments said to be just as effective as CCA but less toxic will take the old treatment's place, ensuring that PT lumber will still be available for use outdoors. Two replacements for CCA are copper azole and alkaline copper quaternary (ACQ), both of which are alkaline copper compounds.

Working with Pressure-Treated Wood

Pressure treated lumber has traditionally been judged safe for all types of outdoor building projects (except for those that would place it in direct contact with food). But even so, experts say that the new chemical treatments for PT lumber are less toxic than the familiar green CCA. Still, it's wise to take precautions. Use gloves when you handle the lumber, especially when moving or stacking it. This is a good idea with any lumber. Wear safety glasses and a dust mask or respirator when you create lots of dust—again, good advice when working with any lumber.

After you complete your project, make sure that you clean up all scraps and sawdust. You should either bury these scraps or discard them in the trash. Do not burn pressure-treated wood. Burning will cause the wood to release treatment chemicals.

It's not a bad idea to hose down your completed project or to let it sit through a few rainstorms before allowing small children or pets to use it.

BUYING LUMBER

Dimension softwood is sold by the lineal foot, in lengths of even 2-foot increments from 6 to 24 feet. Many of the projects in this book call for standard lengths, such as 8, 10, or 12 feet, to minimize the amount of cutting (and waste) involved.

You cannot always count on the lumberyard to provide square ends, particularly on lower grades of lumber. Examine the ends of any critical-length lumber to make sure that it is not slanted or damaged. Take a measuring tape with you to make sure that the boards measure up to (preferably, a little over) their specified lengths. If you have to square cut the ends yourself, plan on losing $1/2$ to 1 inch on both sides.

You can also move up to the next available length and trim to exact plan dimensions. But, unless there's some use for all the generated scrap, you'll save a lot of money by adapting the plan to the material.

Not all suppliers stock every lumber grade in every possible length, so you might have to make adjustments. Make sure that the critical support members (posts, beams,

---

Hint

Retreating Pressure-Treated Wood

Even after pressure treating, the chemical preservatives may not penetrate throughout the entire depth of a board. The Western Wood Products Association (WWPA) does not recommend ripping for width or resawing for thickness, because these operations can expose large untreated sections of wood on the treated board. Of course, some cutting is inevitable. The WWPA suggests brushing or dipping on additional preservative on all freshly cut surfaces until the wood is saturated.

Hint

Wet vs. Kiln Dried

Pressure-treated wood is available as "wet" or "kiln dried after treatment" (KDAT). The specific treatment should be indicated on the wood's stamp.

If paintability and product stability are your primary concerns, you might want to invest a little more and use KDAT. For example, KDAT wood would be a good choice when building the rails, since they would not tend to bow or cup and would be ready for painting as soon as you nail them in. Wet-treated wood also will dry out within a few weeks of exposure, and unless it is used immediately or properly stickered, it may begin to warp or cup.

NOMINAL AND ACTUAL SIZES OF LUMBER

Lumber	Nominal Size (inches)	Common Actual Size (inches)
Boards	1x3	$^3/_4$x2$^1/_2$
	1x4	$^3/_4$x3$^1/_2$
	1x6	$^3/_4$x5$^1/_2$
	1x8	$^3/_4$x7$^1/_4$
	1x10	$^3/_4$x9$^1/_4$
	1x12	$^3/_4$x11$^1/_4$
Dimension lumber	2x2	1$^1/_2$x1$^1/_2$
	2x3	1$^1/_2$x2$^1/_2$
	2x4	1$^1/_2$x3$^1/_2$
	2x6	1$^1/_2$x5$^1/_2$
	2x8	1$^1/_2$x7$^1/_4$
	2x10	1$^1/_2$x9$^1/_4$
	2x12	1$^1/_2$x11$^1/_4$
Posts	4x4	3$^1/_2$x3$^1/_2$
	4x6	3$^1/_2$x5$^1/_2$
	6x6	5$^1/_2$x5$^1/_2$

joists, and rafters) are lengths that match or exceed those required. For lumber that will be sized to smaller pieces, it is more economical to buy several smaller lengths than a single long length. For example, it's cheaper to buy two 6-foot 2x4s than a single 12-foot length.

Nominal vs. Actual Dimensions

When a 2x4 is sawn from the log, it really does measure 2 by 4 inches. But then the piece of lumber is surfaced to make it flat and smooth and left to dry, its dimensions begin to change. As a result, the 2x4 actually measures 1$^1/_2$x3$^1/_2$ inches by the time it gets to you. A 1x4 actually measures $^3/_4$x3$^1/_2$ inches while a 2x8 is only 1$^1/_2$x7$^1/_4$ inches. See the chart "Nominal and Actual Sizes of Lumber."

Lumber Grades

Lumber is sorted and marked at the mill with a stamp that identifies the quality, moisture content, grade name, and in many cases, the species and the grading agency. Grade is determined by natural growth characteristics (such as knots), defects that result from

Lumber Grades

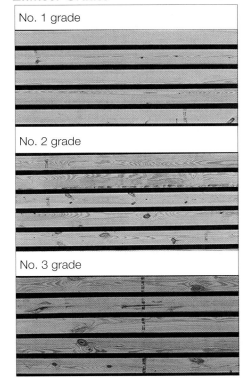

No. 1 grade

No. 2 grade

No. 3 grade

milling errors, and manufacturing techniques used for drying and preserving the wood (they affect the strength, durability, and appearance of the wood).

Surfaced lumber is the standard material for most construction and is available in nearly all grades. Lumber that is surfaced on all four sides is termed S4S. If you want your project to have a rustic final appearance, rough-sawn lumber may be just what you need. Since rough-sawn lumber is not reduced by surfacing operations, the actual dimensions will be quite close to nominal. And rough-sawn is cheaper than S4S because you don't have to pay for surfacing. Most lumberyards don't carry rough-sawn lumber, so you'll need to buy it directly from the sawmill.

The two major grades of softwood are select and common. Select softwood has two good faces. Select grades are further broken down into B and Better, C, and D. Select lumber, classified as "clear," is free from knots and other surface imperfections. You will usually have

to hand pick select clear lumber at a slight extra charge per piece.

Common grade softwood is lower in quality than select grades. Common grades include 1, 2, 3, Const, Stand, Util and Stud. You'll find that number 2 is most readily available in lumberyards and home centers and is suitable for most general construction. You can save some money by planning where each board is to be used in relation to the project. Use lower-grade (number 2) wood for the less visible areas, like the floor framing. You'll want to spring for number 1 for the railing.

When purchasing lumber, you want to avoid as many defective boards as you can. A defective board not only is unsightly but can affect the structural integrity of your project. Some defects can be avoided by planning around the defect or by cutting it out of an otherwise good board.

However, if you encounter a significant percentage of defects, you should probably invest in a better grade of lumber. It is also a good idea to inspect several lumberyards, since one may have superior wood, even though it is advertised at the same grade.

LUMBER GRADING STAMP

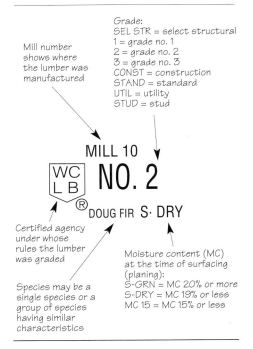

Mill number shows where the lumber was manufactured

Grade:
SEL STR = select structural
1 = grade no. 1
2 = grade no. 2
3 = grade no. 3
CONST = construction
STAND = standard
UTIL = utility
STUD = stud

MILL 10
WCLB® NO. 2
DOUG FIR S·DRY

Certified agency under whose rules the lumber was graded

Species may be a single species or a group of species having similar characteristics

Moisture content (MC) at the time of surfacing (planing):
S-GRN = MC 20% or more
S-DRY = MC 19% or less
MC 15 = MC 15% or less

Lumber Defects

Bow is a deviation from a flat plane of the wide face, end to end. It has no effect on strength and can be used as long as you can nail it back to a flat plane.

Cup is a deviation from a flat plane of the narrow face, edge to edge. Cupping tends to loosen fasteners.

Crook is a deviation from a flat plane of the narrow face, end to end. It makes wood unsuitable for framing. Small crooks can be pried straight and nailed in place.

Twist is a deviation from a flat plane of all faces, end to end. Twist makes lumber unsuitable for framing or decking.

Check is a rift in the surface caused when the surface of the timber dries more rapidly than the interior. Checks are generally cosmetic; they do not affect structural strength. Checking can be avoided by using kiln-dried wood.

Split is a crack that passes completely through the wood. It constitutes a serious structural weakness. Lumber with splits should not be used for any structural members, such as joists or posts.

Wane is the presence of bark, or lack of wood at an edge. It is the result of the sawyer maximizing the amount of wood milled from a tree. Wane has very little effect on strength. Any remaining bark should be removed, since the bark will promote rot.

Knots are the high-density roots of limbs. The knots themselves are very strong, but they are not connected to the surrounding wood. The rules for knots in joists and rafters are (1) tight knots are allowed in the top third, (2) loose or missing knots are allowed in the middle third, and (3) no knots at all over 1 inch are allowed in the bottom third of the board width.

Decay is the destruction of the wood structure by fungi or insects.

Although it may enhance the decorative nature of the wood, it severely prohibits any structural applications.

Pitch Pockets are accumulations of natural resins. They have little effect on strength but should not be allowed in lumber that will be painted because the pitch will bleed through.

PLYWOOD

Standard softwood plywood is commonly used for roof and wall sheathing. Plywood panels measure 4×8 feet, their thicknesses range from $1/4$ to $3/4$ inch.

The appearance of the two sides of the panel determine its grade. Letters A through D designate the grades, A being the highest and D, the lowest. A/C (exterior) panels are an economical choice for projects where only one side will be visible. Face and back grades, glue type, and group number should be stamped on each panel, along with an association trademark that ensures quality.

When plywood is used as sheathing that will be covered on both sides, the most commonly used grade is CDX. As mentioned, the *C* and the *D* indicate the grade of the two sides. The *X* stands for "exposure" not for "exterior" as many people assume. This means that the plywood is designed to weather a few rainstorms until you get around to applying siding over it. It doesn't mean that the plywood is intended to be used as permanently exposed siding. Siding grade plywood will have a designation such as AC ext.

Lumber Defects

Defect	End View	Long View
Bow		
Cup		
Crook		
Twist		
Check		
Split		
Wane		
Knot		
Decay		
Pitch Pocket		

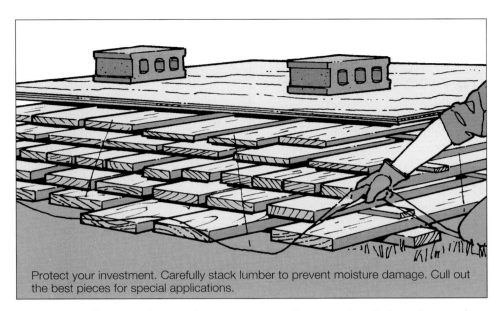

Protect your investment. Carefully stack lumber to prevent moisture damage. Cull out the best pieces for special applications.

The *ext.* marking on the panel is an abbreviation for "exterior."

When CDX plywood is used for house sheathing, the C side is set facing out because that grade makes a fine nailing base for siding or shingles. However, in sheathing outdoor projects, the inside face is often left exposed. For example, you might sheathe and shingle the roof of a gazebo, leaving the rafters and inside face of the sheathing exposed. For this application, ACX would be a good choice. Face the C side out for a good nailing base with the A face in for appearance. Exposure grade is fine here, since the inside face is protected from the weather.

DELIVERY

If you don't have access to a truck, you'll have to arrange for delivery to the site. Find out if there will be a delivery charge for your order. Make sure that the supplier will be able to deliver the wood when you need it.

It's also important to establish the dealer's policy regarding the return of unusable material. You should not have to pay for boards that are cracked, warped, or otherwise too defective to be used. For this reason, it's a good idea to be on hand when the delivery arrives so that you'll be able to give the wood a quick inspection before the truck leaves you with the defective wood.

DRYING AND STORING WOOD

Some of the wood used in exterior projects, especially wet pressure-treated lumber, will still be fairly saturated with water when it is delivered to your construction site. Wet wood is not that enjoyable to work with; it will dull your saw's blade in record time and some boards will even seem to "bleed" every time you sink a nail.

What's worse, wet wood will continue to shrink or otherwise distort until its moisture content matches that of its surroundings. The wood you are using can change shape as you are working with it; the parts that you carefully fitted one weekend may not fit by the next.

If you have to store your lumber for even a short time, you must also consider the effects of moisture damage. It takes only a little water to promote mold and mildew, not to mention insects. The extra money you spent on kiln-dried wood will be wasted after the first rain unless the wood is protected and stacked in such a way as to dry uniformly. When wood is stacked incorrectly, moisture absorption will be uneven, causing the boards to cup or warp.

You can protect your investment by following a few simple steps. Store the wood in a protected, well-ventilated location. Stack wood a few inches off the ground so that your boards will not wick up extra moisture. Stacking the boards neatly on top of each other will help keep the lower boards straight. Stones, bricks, or other weights placed on top of the pile will help to stabilize the uppermost pieces. Remember to cover your pile to protect it from a heavy rain.

Restacking lumber also offers you the opportunity to pick out the best pieces of wood to use in the most visible elements of your project. For instance, you may end up making the railing from the beautiful straight 2x4s that you found on the bottom of the delivery. The warped 2x4s that were originally piled on top can be cut to shorter lengths.

Storing Plywood and Siding

Plywood and siding should also be kept as protected from direct exposure as possible. If you have the room, stack plywood flat; rest the bottom sheet on cinder blocks or some sort of frame to avoid ground contact. Plywood can also be stacked on edge. Rest the edges of the sheets on runners made from scrap dimension lumber so they don't touch the ground. Try to keep the sheets perpendicular to the ground to reduce the tendency of the wood to bow. In both cases, the sheets should be kept within a roofed enclosure, such as a shed or garage, or at least covered with a tarp, so they won't get saturated by every rainstorm.

Hint

Wet Wood Field Test

To determine if your lumber is dry enough to use, make a test cut. Rub the sawdust between your fingers. If the sawdust is dry, then the board is ready to use.

TECHNIQUES

Every carpenter has his or her own approach to a job. However, if you were to watch several people, you would start to notice similarities in the ways they get the job done. Many of these similarities evolve through trial and error. By working on your own, you too will eventually learn that certain systems work better than others.

But you don't need to learn everything from the school of hard knocks. Starting off with a few basic techniques will provide you with a solid foundation to successfully (and enjoyably) build your project right on the first try, with a minimum of wasted time and materials. Some of these suggestions may seem to be

common sense—the point is to learn to think like a carpenter. In time, you will come to use some of these suggestions reflexively.

PLANNING A WORK SPACE

The phrase *a place for everything and everything in its place* is not reserved solely for the Shakers. Good carpenters appreciate and abide by this well-worn saying.

Think back to your last project. Chances are you probably wasted far too much time looking for a screwdriver, trying to find a free receptacle to plug another tool in, or carrying wood from one side

of the yard to the other. And then there were the half dozen trips to the hardware store. When you work this way, even the smallest project will devour the entire weekend. Planning out your project in relation to your tools and work space is an excellent way of making more efficient use of your time.

A well-planned work site is a lot safer, too. For example, placing a few sawhorses or a chop saw right next to the stack of lumber will take the strain off of your back by minimizing the times you have to drag those 16-foot boards across the length of the site. Centralizing power tools in one corner also centralizes power cords, which

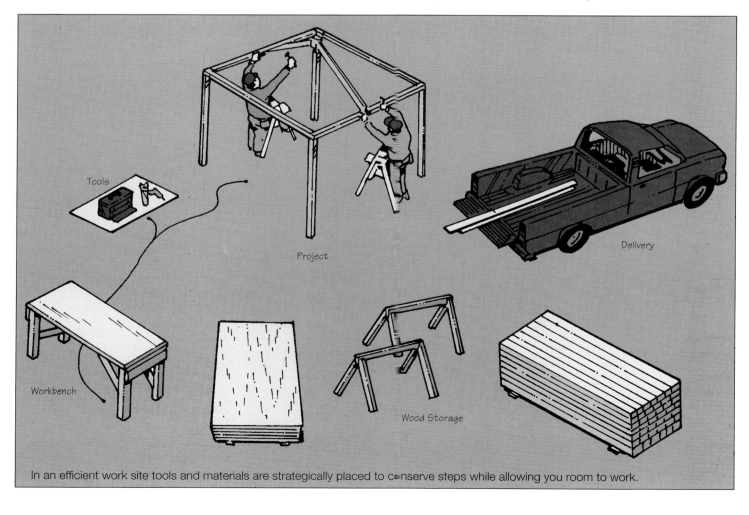

In an efficient work site tools and materials are strategically placed to conserve steps while allowing you room to work.

Hint

Corraling Tools

Tools have an annoying habit of walking away from a work site (even when you're working by yourself). One way to prevent your tools from sprouting legs is to mark off a spot where each item should be returned whenever it is not in use. (An old blanket or scrap sheet of plywood works fine.)

At the end of the day, make it a point to put away your tools on your own. That way, you'll know exactly where something is because you're the person who put it there. This is also a perfect time to give everything a quick inspection, to check for dull blades, dead batteries, or other damaged or missing parts.

could save you from tripping over the one that you "don't know how it got there in the first place."

Sometimes a quick sketch is all that it takes to visualize how everything will be able to work best on a given job. Plan how you want your site to work. Include all the major elements of construction: where you can park your car or truck, where the wood will be delivered, where the electrical cords are running from, and of course, the location of your project's foundation. Try to imagine how these elements will work with each other, and plan the work space accordingly. For example, if you are handling delivery of wood on your own, you will naturally want to keep wood-toting to a minimum. Make preliminary cuts near the side of the stack before carrying the boards to the foundation. Make sure that you'll be able to supply enough electricity at the cutting site. If you are working in an area that's inaccessible to extension cords, you might have to rent a generator for a few days. Planning out the site this way is an excellent way of identifying and solving problems before you begin.

Besides your time, your greatest investment in this project is wood. Be sure to stack your pile neatly to avoid unnecessary damage to the material as well as to your workers. The weight from a properly stacked pile will prevent boards from cupping and warping. Centralizing all the material in one corner will prevent a lot of accidents throughout construction. Cutoffs and sawdust will also be centralized in one corner, which should make cleanup a little easier. Restacking your material gives you an opportunity to select pieces for special applications, such as railings and trim.

NAILING AND DRILLING

There's a little more to nailing than just a well-aimed blow. The structural strength of your project depends on using the right size and number of nails in the right locations.

Splitting

Splitting is not a major problem with softwoods. But woods without a uniform texture, such as southern yellow pine and Douglas fir do split more than the uniformly textured woods such as northern and Idaho white pine, sugar pine and ponderosa pine. And all boards have a tendency to split near the end. Even a minor split will affect the holding power of the nail and the overall strength of the joint.

Skewed nails are driven in at opposing angles to hook the boards together.

If you use several nails at a single joint, stagger their positions. Another way to avoid splitting is to drill holes 75 percent of the nail diameter or to switch to a smaller diameter nail. You can also reduce the chance of splitting by blunting the tip of the nail. Remember that a blunt point destroys wood fibers and will result in a reduced withdrawal resistance.

Skewing

Skewing creates a sounder connection by "hooking" the boards together as well as by reducing the possibility of splitting. You can do this by simply driving the nails in at opposing angles.

Clinching

If nails go completely through both boards, you have three possible options. You could simply use shorter nails, or you could try driving the longer nail at an angle, to make it travel through more wood. A third alternative is to "clinch" the nails, or to bend over the exposed tip. Although it's not the most attractive option, clinching increases holding strength as much as 170 percent over unclinched nails.

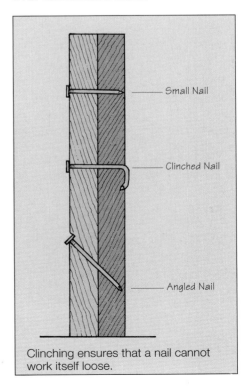

Small Nail

Clinched Nail

Angled Nail

Clinching ensures that a nail cannot work itself loose.

Toe-Nailing

Most of the time, when two boards need to be joined at a right angle, you can nail through the face of one board into the end of the other. But sometimes, the face you would prefer to nail into is inaccessible or the piece you have to nail through is too thick. For example, you can't nail through a 4x4 post to attach a handrail. In cases like this, you need to toe-nail the pieces together. Toe-nailing means joining two boards by nailing at an angle through the end, or toe, of one board into the face of another. Position the nail on the first piece at least 1½ inches from the second piece. Start the nail at a 60- to 75-degree angle. When it is started, adjust it to a 30- to 40-degree angle. Move your hand and drive the nail home. If it is possible, drive another nail on the other side of the board as well to increase holding power.

Screwing

Considering the popularity of cordless drills and drivers on today's construction sites, you probably will be using a few screws in addition to

Starting a Toe-Nail

To prevent a nail from slipping when toe-nailing, place the nail upside down on the spot where you want to start your toe-nail and give it a few light taps. Not only will this method give you a flat spot to start driving but it will also blunt the nail, reducing its chance of splitting the wood.

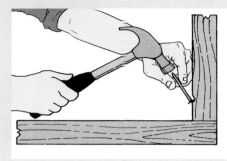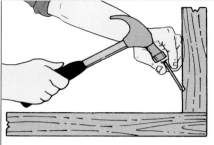

nails to put your project together. Screwing boards together does have its advantages. First, screws have a way of "pulling" two boards together to make a tighter-fitting joint if one board clears the threads. Using a driver also enables you to drive screws accurately in spots where you don't have the room to swing a hammer. Also, because of their threads, screws grip better than nails. At the same time, screws are easier to remove.

It does take a little practice before you can drive a Phillips head screw at high speeds without stripping the screw head or the driver bit (buy a couple of #2 Phillips head bits just in case). When driving screws with a driver, start at a slow speed until the screw takes hold and increase the speed until the screw is set. Maintain constant pressure parallel to the screw and avoid stopping before it is in all the way. Friction exerted on these fasteners can sometimes catch the screw and you may snap it if you allow the wood fibers time to bind. When the head has countersunk itself into the wood, lift the driver as you take your finger off the trigger. If your driver has an automatic clutch, you don't have to worry as much about stripping or snapping the screw, the clutch will disengage the driver when the screw is at the correct depth.

Toe-Nailing

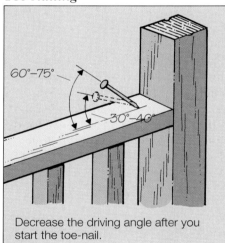

Decrease the driving angle after you start the toe-nail.

Using a Power Driver

Maintain pressure through the screw to prevent slippage.

Nailing Rule of Thumb

For a strong connection, always try to nail a thinner member to a thicker member. The nail should be three times the thickness of the thinner member.

CUTTING WITH A CIRCULAR SAW

You'll probably pick up the circular saw almost as frequently as your hammer. The tool is capable of performing very straight, precise cuts suitable for all types of joinery as well as decorative ornamentation. The most elaborate effects are simply variations of a few basic cuts.

Choosing the Blade

It goes without saying that carbide-tipped blades are far better than steel blades. Although they cost a bit more, carbide stays sharp five times longer than steel—a definite advantage when cutting dense (and usually wet) wood like pressure-treated southern pine. A sharp blade also puts less stress on your saw's motor and reduces the chance of binding or kickback.

But which type of carbide-tipped blade should you buy? For these projects, you should be able to do all of your cutting with an 18- to 24-tooth combination blade. *Combination* means that it cuts well perpendicular and parallel to the grain. This blade also works fine when cutting posts and plywood. A coarser blade is designed for rough work, like demolition, and will produce a splintery cut. A blade with 36 or more teeth is too fine for this kind of construction and may tend to bind in wet wood.

Although a top-of-the-line blade may cut cleaner and stay sharper than a less expensive blade, and unless you are willing to have the blade professionally resharpened, you might be better off with a middle-of-the-line model. A new less expensive carbide blade will out perform even the best blade after it has chewed through a whole stack of wet wood or snagged a nail. Some very good 24-tooth blades can be purchased for less than half of the price of the premiums. And why pay for a sharpener (if you can find one) when it's cheaper and easier just to buy a new blade?

Kickback

Kickback is the term describing that dreaded action when the saw suddenly kicks backward in the middle of a cut. What happens is that the teeth on the rear part of the blade catch the edge of the saw cut, causing the saw to jump out of the kerf. The threat is that the saw could buck up or perhaps even run backward toward you before you could release the switch. As soon as you feel the saw start to kick back, stop and correct the problem before continuing.

Leading Causes of Kickback:

■ **Binding Board.** Sometimes the stresses in the wood cause the kerf to close. Binding also will occur if the cutoff is not falling free and is pinching the blade.

■ **Twisting Blade.** A circular saw is not a jigsaw. If for whatever reason you started your cut off the line, do not try to correct your error in midcut. Stop the saw and start the cut over.

■ **Backing Up the Blade.** Don't do it. Always stop the blade before backing up the saw.

■ **Dull Blade.** A dull blade will heat up and bind, which could cause it to kick back. It pays to have a spare blade handy.

Unfortunately, kickback is the nature of the beast, and it happens even to experienced carpenters. For this reason, it's important always to keep your hands well away from the blade or cut path and position yourself to one side of the cut—never directly behind it.

Anatomy of a Kickback

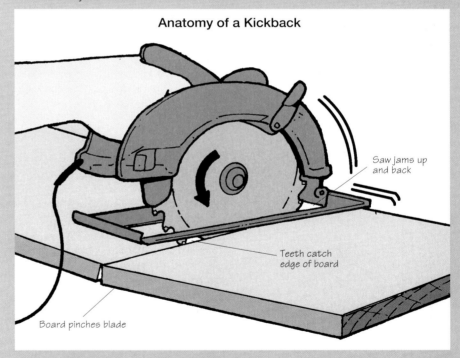

Saw jams up and back

Teeth catch edge of board

Board pinches blade

Your saw will tell you when it's time to switch blades. Some indications of a dull blade include a slower cut speed, a "strained" motor sound, splintery cuts, and even smoking or burned cuts.

Squaring the Blade

No matter what circular saw you have, you can't expect the angle markings stamped on the saw to be accurate. To ensure square cuts, use a square to set the blade.

1. Square Blade to Base

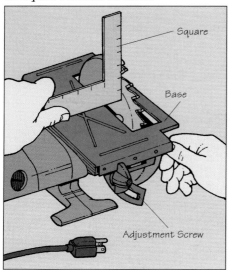

1. Square Blade to Base

2. Test for Squareness

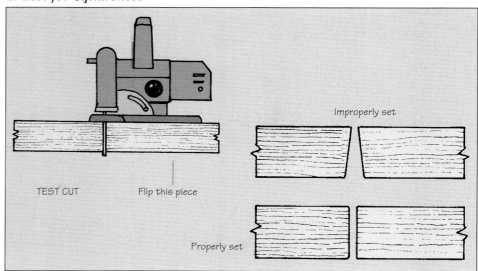

2. Test for Squareness

1. Square Blade to Base

Unplug the saw. Now turn the saw over and loosen the angle adjustment. Set an angle square or try square against the blade and the base. Make sure you hold the square against the body of the blade without touching the teeth. The teeth are offset from the body and will throw off your adjustment. Tighten the angle adjustment when the blade and base bear evenly on the square.

2. Test for Squareness

Crosscut a small block off a scrap piece of 2x4. Flip the block and match the piece, cut edge to cut edge, with the 2x4. If your blade is not square to the base, you'll see a gap equal to twice the amount your blade is out of square. If you see a gap, repeat Step 1 and try again. When the cut edges meet

squarely, the blade is square to the base. Check the stamped markings on your saw. You might want to make your own square mark with a scribe or small file.

Making Square and Accurate Cuts

1. Position Workpiece

Before making the cut, your workpiece must be well-supported on a stable surface that won't move during the cut. To avoid dangerous kickback, you must ensure that the piece you are cutting off can fall away without binding. If you are trimming a small piece off a board, position the board across two sawhorses and make the cut to the outside of one of the horses, never between the horses.

When the piece being cut off is too long to let fall on the ground, you can do your cutting right on top of a stack of wood, as long as the stack is neat and stable.

2. Align Blade to Line

Use a square to strike a line where you want to cut the board. Make sure the workpiece is well-supported on a stable surface and that the waste piece will be able to fall away without binding the blade at the end of the cut.

As mentioned, the teeth on a circular saw blade are offset. One tooth is offset to the left, the next to the right and so on in an alternating pattern. Position the saw blade along the waste side of your cut line. Select a tooth that's offset toward the cut line and align the saw so that tooth just touches the line.

1. Position Workpiece

2. Align Blade to Line

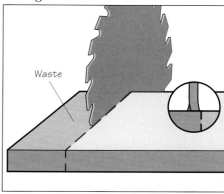

3. Make the Cut

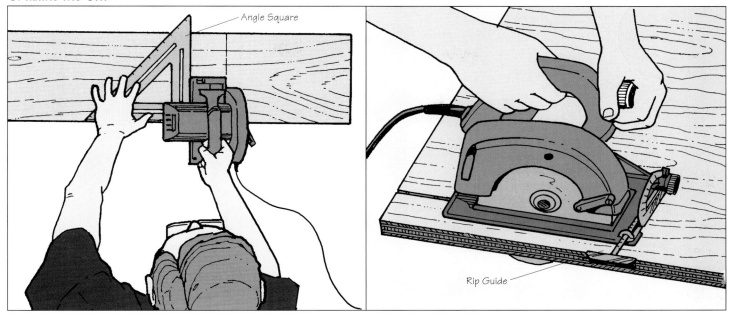

Angle Square

Rip Guide

3. *Make the Cut*

With just a little bit of practice you'll be able to cut squarely by following a pencil line. Get in the habit of keeping your eye on the leading edge of the blade, not the little notch or mark on the front of the saw base.

If you are new to using a circular saw, you might want to use your angle square as a guide until you get a feel for the saw. Even when you gain confidence, this is a useful technique for joinery cuts that will show in the final project; for example the end cut on a rail that will meet a post. You can also use the angle square to make accurate 45 degree miter cuts with the circular saw.

First, use the square to mark the cut line. Slide the square back onto the piece you mean to use and hold it firmly with one hand against the edge of the stock. Set the base of your saw so that its edge bears against the square edge of the angle square. Adjust the saw and the square's position until the saw blade lines up with the cut line. Brace the square against the stock and make the cut, using the square's edge as a guide. Saw with a light, steady pressure, allowing the blade to set the feed rate.

Ripping Lumber. When ripping lumber, you should use a rip guide. This is a steel guide that attaches to the base with a thumbscrew. The guide has a shoe that runs along the side of the board as you cut it along its length.

Cutting Plywood. Cutting plywood is the exception to the free-fall rule.

Hint

Unless it is properly supported, the cutoff always binds as it falls away. The easiest way to avoid this is to cut large sheets of plywood right on the floor. Support the sheet with 2x4s. This way, you can stand on the plywood and "walk-through" the cut. It is also a lot safer; a long cutoff section can't fall, splinter, bind, or cause kickback.

Setting the Depth of Cut

To use a circular saw safely and produce the cleanest possible cut, you want to set the blade so that it just penetrates the other side and clears itself of wood chips with the least amount of blade. The deeper the blade is set, the more heat it generates and the greater the risk of binding and kicking back, especially when cutting tricky materials like plywood. Set the saw blade depth about 1/4 inch deeper than the thickness of the wood.

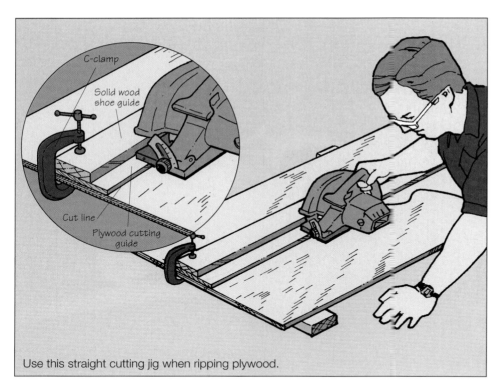

Use this straight cutting jig when ripping plywood.

One way to guide a saw through an accurate rip is to use a straight cutting jig. Simply tack a thin strip of hardboard or plywood to the bottom of a straight length of 1-by stock. Using the 1-by as a guide, cut off the excess plywood to determine the exact cut line. Clamp or tack nail the jig directly to the sheet you are cutting.

Circular Saw Joinery

One way to gauge the level of craftsmanship used in a project is to inspect the ways the builder joined one board to another. Skillful joinery has been used for many hundreds of years to join wood members—long before the invention of nails and screws. Besides being visually attractive, these techniques produce joints that are stronger than simply

Circular Saw Joinery

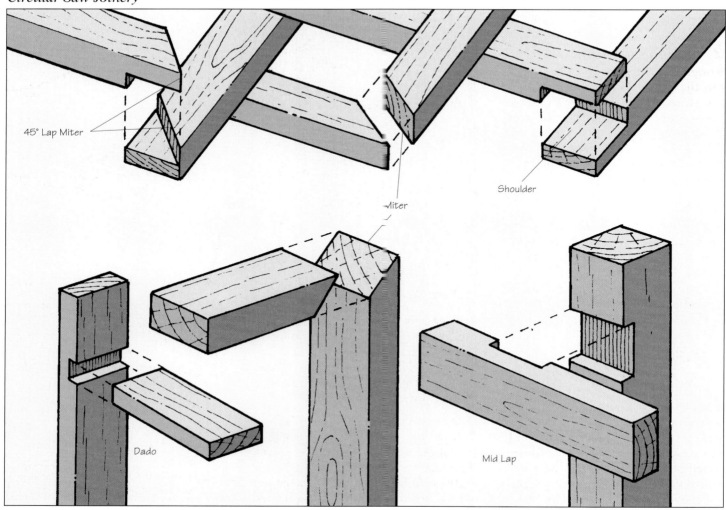

nailing one board to another. These joints will take some time to produce, but by working with a circular saw, you should have no problems cutting them quickly and consistently.

Miter joints can be cut in one pass. Notches, lap joints, and dadoes require three separate steps: kerfing, roughing out, and paring.

1. Kerf the Joint

Lay out the shoulders of the notch, lap joint, or dado you wish to cut. Adjust the saw to the depth you want the joint to be. (It's a good idea to make a test cut to make sure your setting is right.)

Make a series of closely spaced kerfs in the waste area of the joint. The first and last kerfs should be made with a angle square to ensure that the shoulder is square, all the other kerfs need not be precise since you are just cutting wood out of the notch.

2. Rough Out Joint

Rough out the joint by chiseling out the waste. At this point, hit the chisel with a hammer to break the pieces free, but keep the chisel bevel pointing down to control the depth of cut. Chisel to the bottom of the joint in the center, leaving the edges high.

3. Pare Out Joint

With the chisel's bevel pointing up, pare away leftover ridges. Work from the outside edges in to the center. Use one hand to push the chisel into the waste and use the other to keep the back of the chisel flat against the wood.

FIGHTING CROOKED STOCK

The challenge of carpentry is that you are trying to make something straight and square out of a natural material that resists our best efforts to make it regular. Almost every board you use will be at least slightly crooked, cupped, or twisted.

1. Kerf the Joint

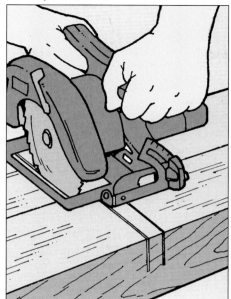

2. Rough Out Joint

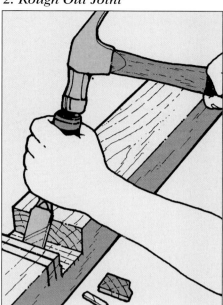

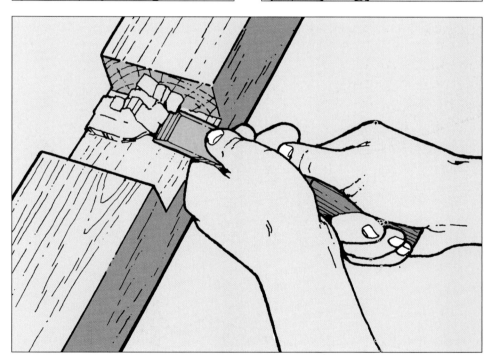

3. Pare Out Joint

Carpentry is a constant battle to wedge and nail pieces of wood into the position and shape you want them to take. A smart carpenter uses the forces within the board to his or her advantage.

The most common example is "crowning" horizontal structural members such as beams and joists. This means to sight along the edges of a board to decide which way it bows. Then install the board

Look down one edge of the board to see if it is straight, bowed, or crooked.

Spacer Jig

When you use lumber decking boards, you need
to leave a small space between each board for
appearance and to let water through. One way
to gauge the space is with the body of a 10d or
16d common nail. The problem with this method
is you wind up spending a lot of time fetching
nails that fell through the spaces. Here is a handy
spacer jig that will eliminate that problem.

All you have to do is rip a strip of wood at the
desired gap thickness (about ⅛ inch). Tack the
strip to a wider piece of scrap as shown.

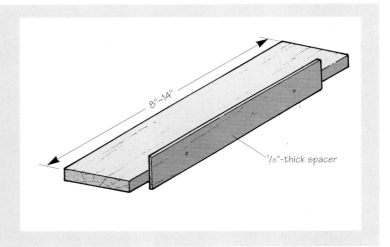

8"–14"

⅛"-thick spacer

with the convex edge facing up.
This gives the board a head start in
resisting sagging from the weight
bearing on it.

If you are installing decking boards,
there is no way to use crook to your
advantage. If a board is badly
crooked, use it to make short pieces.

But if the crook is mild, there are a few
ways to force it into place.

Maximize your straightening leverage
by first fastening the straightest end
of the board to at least two joists. Position the board so that the curve bends
out away from the decking boards that
have already been installed.

One method is to use a pipe clamp
to pull the board straight. Concentrate on straightening the board on
a joist-by-joist basis. As soon as the
board is properly positioned, nail it
into place and reposition the clamp
as necessary to gain more leverage.

Another way of doing the same
thing is to screw a temporary plank
onto the joists in front of the
crooked board. The brace should be
positioned at an angle that approxi-
mates that of the wedge. Use a
wooden wedge to force the plank
into position. It is also possible to
lever the board straight with a
length of 2x4. Never use a pry bar
to force a board into position. The
metal can dig into the wood or dent
the edge of the decking.

Good Side Up

Some carpenters believe that deck
boards will shed water better if
installed with the bark side down
because boards will cup to shed
water that way. Others prefer bark
side up because boards installed
bark side down will suffer more
from grain raising and splitting
along the annular rings.

The U.S. Department of Agricul-
ture's Forest Products Laboratory
has tested both these theories. Their
conclusion is, it doesn't matter
which way the boards are laid. The
laboratory's recommendation is
simply to place the most attractive
side of the board up.

Fighting Crooked Stock

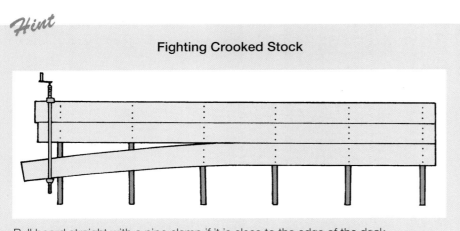

Pull board straight with a pipe clamp if it is close to the edge of the deck.

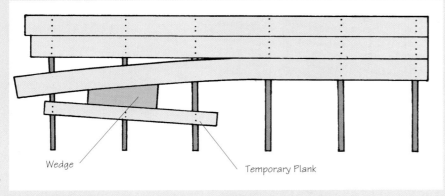

Wedge

Temporary Plank

Wedge crooked boards in place with a temporary plank and a tapered piece of scrap.

GROUNDWORK

Begin your project with foundation work that is accurate and strong, and the rest of the construction process will be a pleasure. For the projects in this book, accurate foundation work means getting support posts firmly set in exactly the right positions. If you get the post support positions wrong, you'll spend the rest of the project compensating for it. Strong foundation work means the posts must be firmly anchored either in the ground or in concrete. If you decide instead to rest your project on a slab, the post anchor bolts must be accurately placed and the concrete surfaced to a smooth, hard finish.

PREPARING THE SITE

Clear the construction area. Remove all shrubs, rocks, and other obstacles that are not part of your design. Rake up all loose twigs and leaves.

It is not always necessary to strip away low grass and ground cover before building wood deck projects, such as a gazebo. Any grass covered by the deck will die from lack of sun. However, a little landscaping now will ensure a better looking site that will be easier to maintain later. Once the footings are in place, lay down a layer of landscaping fabric right on top of the grass and cover it with 2 to 4 inches of gravel or wood chips. Landscaping fabric is preferable to covering the ground with 6-mil polyethylene. Both materials will keep weeds from sprouting and will provide a clean, finished appearance, but the fabric will also allow water to percolate through to the soil, preventing puddling or washout.

If you plan to set your project on a concrete slab, you will have to strip away grass and other ground cover and excavate to the necessary depth. Concrete must be placed on firm, compacted soil.

Cover the ground under your project with landscaping fabric and wood chips to discourage weeds and prevent washout.

Remove sod and soil and level out the excavation before pouring a concrete slab.

SLOPE AND DRAINAGE

You don't need to worry about slope when building a project that has a wood deck. That's because water drains through the cracks between deck boards or is shed by the roof. A concrete slab, however, should slope slightly, or have a slight crown, to ensure proper drainage. On attached projects, slope the deck away from your home. Slope is equally important for freestanding projects to prevent water from puddling and possibly causing damage to the concrete itself. A slope of $1/8$ inch per foot is sufficient. To determine just how the pitch will affect the overall layout of your slab, multiply the length of the run in feet by 0.125. That number indicates in inches how much your slab must vary from level over the course of the entire run.

Some carpenter's levels have two sets of lines on each vial. The second set of lines is used by plumbers to ensure proper drainage when

Hint

Checking Slope

One way to determine slope is to first string a level line with the top of the form. At the far side of the board or form measure down from the string to the desired slope. (For example, you would have to measure down $2 1/2$ inches from level to give a 10-foot span a slope of $1/4$ inch per foot.) Mark the desired slope with another string.

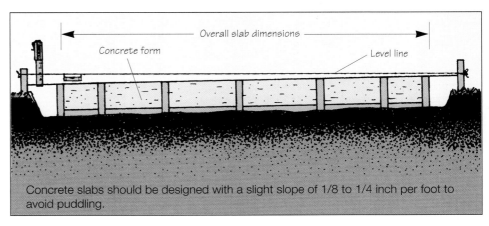

Concrete slabs should be designed with a slight slope of 1/8 to 1/4 inch per foot to avoid puddling.

Laying Out the Site

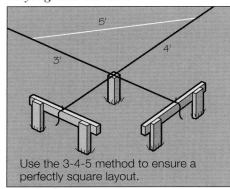

Use the 3-4-5 method to ensure a perfectly square layout.

running pipes; when the bubble touches the outside line, the slope is at $1/4$ inch per foot. You can also use this tool to determine the correct pitch for your project. First string a level line starting from the highest point of the form. Next, use the level to determine the slope. Hold one end of the level against the high side of the form next to the string and lower the other end until the bubble touches the outside line. Mark this slope with another string.

1. Rough Out Dimensions

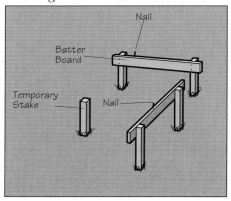

This method is not as accurate as measuring the slope off of a level line, but it is a quick way of double-checking your calculations.

If any roof gutters empty into or near the project area, try to angle the downspouts to direct the runoff away from the deck. If that is not practical, you might have to install an underground line to drain water away from the area.

LAYING OUT THE SITE

All of the projects in this book, including the six- and eight-sided gazebos, begin with either a square or rectangular layout. You can easily check a project for square using the 3-4-5 layout method. Simply remember that if one side of a right triangle measures 3 feet and another measures 4 feet, the hypotenuse must measure 5 feet. If any of these measurements are off, the corner is not a true right angle. The same rule holds true for multiples of these dimensions. A right triangle with sides measuring 6 and 8 feet will have a hypotenuse of 10 feet.

1. Rough Out Dimensions

Use a tape measure to rough out the perimeter dimensions of the project. Drive in temporary stakes at each corner.

Erect batter boards at right angles to each other about 2 feet outside

the rough corner locations of the slab foundation or deck. These batter boards provide support for guide strings and a location to mark out key dimensions. The batter boards can be any scrap stock as long as they are about 2 feet long. Support each batter board with two short stakes. Use a line level to set the batter board crosspieces at the same height.

2. String the Lines

Set up guide lines to outline the entire slab or deck. Check that the line is level and secure it to the batter boards.

Make right angles at each corner by using the 3-4-5 triangle method. Measure from point A on the first stake along the line 3 feet and mark point B. Run a second line perpendicular to the first across point A. Mark point C 4 feet from point A. Move line AC so that the distance BC is exactly 5 feet. Angle BAC is now a 90-degree angle.

With all four string lines in place, double-check squareness by measuring the diagonals between opposing corners. The measurements should be equal. If they are not, recheck your layout.

3. Reposition Corner Stakes

Accurately reposition the temporary corner stakes using a plumb bob to transfer the point of intersection to the ground.

2. String the Lines

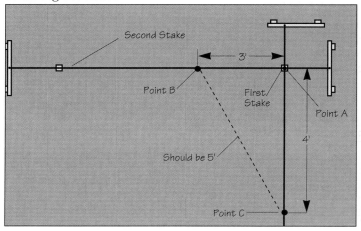

3 Reposition Corner Stakes

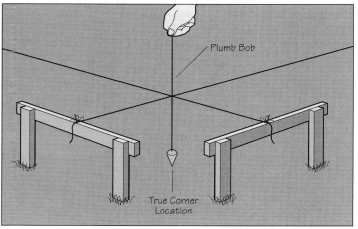

SETTING POSTS

Projects that do not use a slab foundation require the setting of posts firmly in the ground or on concrete footings. You can use a clamshell-type posthole digger to dig holes for the footings or posts. If many holes are needed, renting a gasoline-powered auger-type digger will certainly speed up the work. You can rent either one- or two-man models; the size you choose depends on the number of holes that you have to dig and the soil conditions of the area. The manager of your rental store will be able to suggest which one will best meet your specific needs. Be sure to read and follow safety directions for all power machinery, and be aware of any hidden utility lines, such as gas and water.

To prevent frost heave, your footing should extend below the frost line. Follow local building codes concerning the depth and diameter of the footing or post placement.

PLACING POSTS DIRECTLY IN THE GROUND

As a general rule, when setting posts directly in the ground, the post hole should be about three times the width of the post. It should also extend into the ground at least one-third the overall post height. For example, if you need 8 feet of post above ground level, you should buy a 12-foot post and dig the holes 4 feet deep. These are only general guidelines; always check with your building inspector before deciding how deep to sink your posts.

Compact the base of the hole and add 6 inches of gravel to help drainage. Place the post in the hole. For posts set in the ground, you should always use pressure-treated wood.

Premixed bag concrete is the most convenient method of setting posts in the ground. Fast-setting

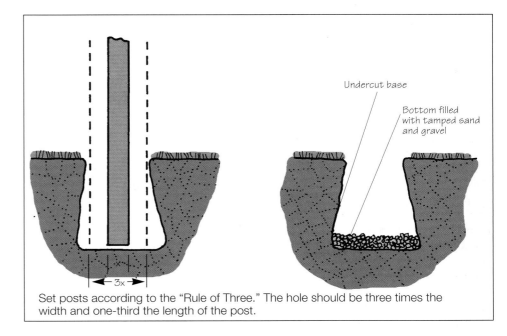

Set posts according to the "Rule of Three." The hole should be three times the width and one-third the length of the post.

mixes are available that set up in minutes and reach final set in several hours. With some brands, installation can be as simple as positioning the post and adding layers of dry mix and water until the hole is filled. Follow the concrete manufacturer's directions.

Slope the top of the concrete away from the post to drain water. Use a level to check for plumb and brace the post firmly with lengths of scrap lumber, and recheck.

POST FOOTINGS

Another method of securing posts is to use metal post anchors set in concrete footings. Metal post anchors require the same amount of preparation as sinking posts in concrete. Both require footings dug below the frost line. However, since only the metal fastener is sunk into the concrete, you can use shorter post lengths to reach a given height, making it the most economical choice for building a gazebo or pavilion.

A post anchor does not offer the same amount of lateral strength as sinking a post, so you wouldn't want to use anchors for a fence or a project such as the arbor with picnic table. But posts tied into a gazebo or other structure with

four or more sides don't have to handle a significant lateral load.

The hole diameter for a 4x4 post should be approximately 12 inches. In firm soil, concrete can be placed directly in the hole. Place a 6-inch layer of gravel in the base of the hole and fill it with concrete. When mixed to the proper consistency, the concrete will find its own level. Insert the post anchor before the concrete sets up. Work quickly if you are using fast-setting concrete. Use a torpedo level to make sure that the connector is plumb. This is a critical point in the project, so check your work several times and be sure anchors do not shift or sag.

Hint

Remember Post Dimensions

Keep in mind that for some projects the distance between foundation post locations does not equal the overall length or width of the project. But it's easier and more accurate to lay out the perimeter post locations and allow for slight overhang than it is to lay out the true perimeter and adjust inward. For all projects, check your plans carefully and measure along guide lines to determine all key dimensions.

For attached projects, the side of your home serves as the initial guide line.

In loose soil, you may have to dig a slightly larger hole and set a wood form over it so that 5 or 6 inches of concrete are located above ground.

Another alternative is to use a ready-made form available at most building supply stores. Simply cut the cylindrical cardboard form to length with a handsaw or saber saw and insert it into the hole. You can use the form to make the footing flush to the ground. Or, if you are placing posts in a wet area, you can leave the forms longer to create concrete piers a few inches above ground level. Any cardboard that protrudes from the ground can be trimmed away after the concrete hardens.

If you are building a small structure in a region with little or no frost-heaving problem, you may not need a footing. Check with your building inspector. It may be permissible to place your project on precast concrete pier blocks. Pier blocks are available with post connectors already set in place. They create a wider, firmer base than a post set directly on the ground, and prevent moisture problems by keeping the post out of the dirt.

Most water damage can be avoided simply by raising the posts off their anchors by less than $1/4$ inch. Cut a double-thick scrap of asphalt shingle to serve as a spacer.

CONCRETE DECKS

A concrete deck, or slab, is used for most attached projects and is also a great base for a gazebo or freestanding pavilion. A 4-inch-thick slab set $1^1/2$ to 2 inches above ground level is suitable for most outdoor projects. To provide drainage under the concrete,

Post Footings

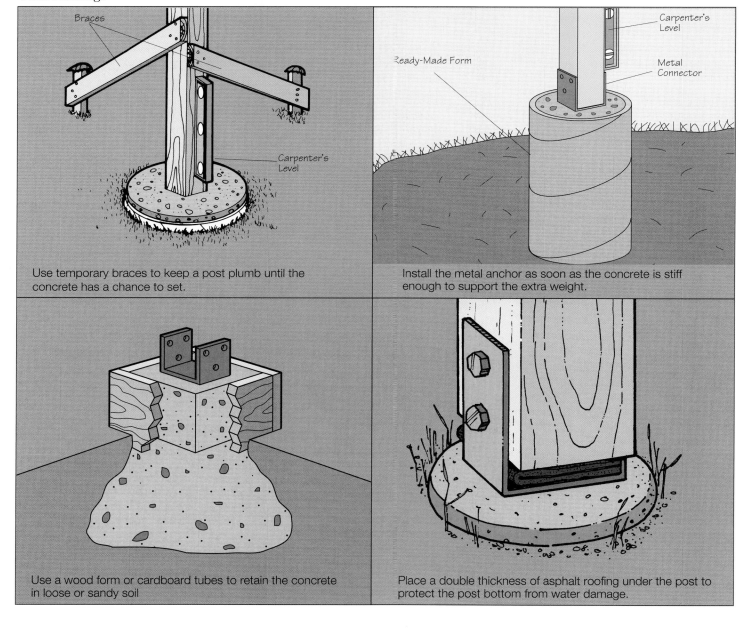

Use temporary braces to keep a post plumb until the concrete has a chance to set.

Install the metal anchor as soon as the concrete is stiff enough to support the extra weight.

Use a wood form or cardboard tubes to retain the concrete in loose or sandy soil

Place a double thickness of asphalt roofing under the post to protect the post bottom from water damage.

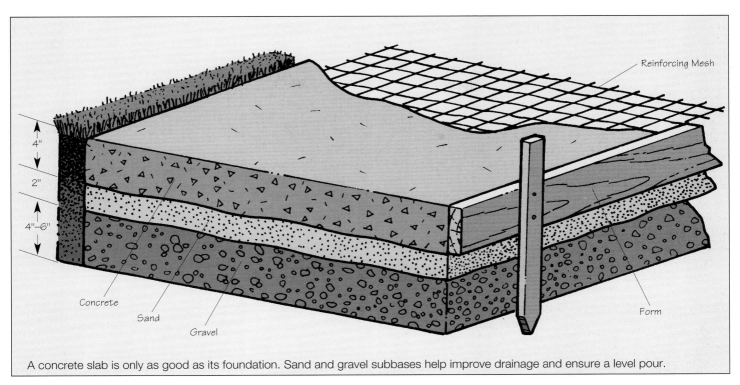

4"

2"

4"–6"

Reinforcing Mesh

Concrete

Sand

Gravel

Form

A concrete slab is only as good as its foundation. Sand and gravel subbases help improve drainage and ensure a level pour.

a 4- to 6-inch-thick subbase of 1-inch crushed stone is recommended in all but the driest of climates. Add 2 inches of sand or rock dust over the gravel to improve drainage and help level the subbase to ensure an even layer of concrete. Wire mesh reinforcement is recommended in climates subject to freeze-thaw cycles.

For outdoor slabs, plastic sheathing is not needed over the subgrade or subbase. The plastic would prevent excess water from leaving the fresh slab, bringing it to the surface as bleed water. On the surface, the bleed water will get in the way of finishing operations. It's better just to cast the slab on earth or on a porous subbase.

ESTIMATING AMOUNTS

The standard unit of measure in the concrete industry is the cubic yard. To estimate the amount of concrete needed, just multiply the thickness (in inches) of the slab by its width and length in feet and divide this number by 12. This gives you cubic feet. Divide the number of cubic feet

by 27 to find the number of cubic yards. The chart "Cubic Yards of Concrete Used in Slab Construction" on page 54, lists amounts needed for common slab areas.

FORM WORK

The wood form work for slabs must be strong and stable. Use simple butt joints at all corners, and stake and nail the forms firmly in place. Most form work for slabs is constructed of 2-by framing lumber set on edge. Because a 2×4 is only $3^{1}/_{2}$ inches wide, rake the sand or rock dust subbase along the perimeter to raise it $^{1}/_{2}$ inch off the subgrade and create a true 4-inch-deep form. Backfill the gap at the bottom of the form to prevent leakage.

After placing the gravel and sand or rock dust in place, lay down the wire mesh. Set the mesh on small stones or bits of brick and locate it in the center of the slab. Overlay individual pieces and keep the mesh at least 6 inches from the edge of the slab.

In areas subject to severe temperatures and frost heave, large slabs need an edge stiffener to prevent

chipping and breaking. The easiest way to do this is to build permanent wood forms instead of temporary ones. Use pressure-treated wood for this, so the frame won't rot away. Strips can also be installed in the body of the slab to serve as control joints. Mask the tops of the boards with tape during the pour to protect them from stains and abrasion from the concrete.

When pouring a large slab, you may choose to install some screed guides to help you level off the concrete. As with edge guides, you can choose to install temporary guides that can be removed as soon as that section has been screeded or permanent guides that can also serve as control joints for the slab. Screed guides are 2×4s supported on stakes. Permanent guides must be level with the tops of the forms and should be spaced evenly every 8 to 10 feet. For temporary screed guides, place one end of the 2×4 guide on top of the form, level it, and stake it into place. Work from the other side and repeat this process so that the guides meet in the center. With the screed guides in place, you will need a screed

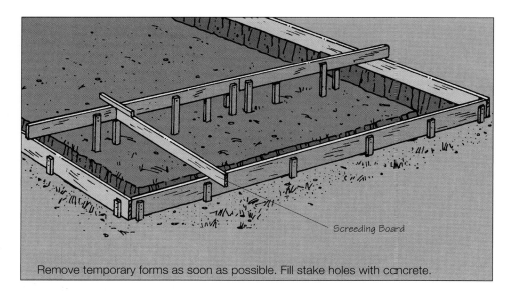
Remove temporary forms as soon as possible. Fill stake holes with concrete.

Screeding Board

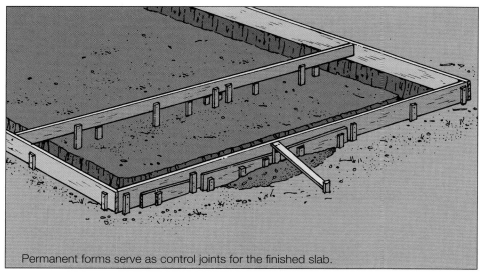
Permanent forms serve as control joints for the finished slab.

made from 2x4s. For the temporary guides, nail a 1x2 block to the top end of the screed, which will ride on the temporary guide. The other end of the screed rides on top of the form. For center screeds, use blocks on both ends of the screed. Remove the screed guides and fill in the stake holes after the concrete has been poured.

If you are pouring a slab against the house for an attached project, remember to pitch the slab away from the house at a slope of $1/8$ inch per running foot. Check for proper pitch after the forms and gravel base are in place. An expansion joint is needed where the slab abuts the structure. Control joints should be spaced 8 to 10 feet.

DELIVERY CONSIDERATIONS

One of the quickest and most economical ways to obtain several yards of uniformly mixed concrete is to work with a concrete supplier. But you should take a little time to consider exactly what this step of the job entails. You won't be able to handle a large volume of truck-delivered ready-mix concrete working alone. Assemble a crew of at least two helpers. Always have at least one helper with some experience in floating, final troweling, and edging. An experienced concrete finisher will keep the project moving and serve as

an adviser to less experienced crew members. Another idea is for you to do all the preparation—layout, form building, and sub-grade preparation—and then hire a professional to handle the actual concrete work.

If you plan to do the work yourself, discuss the project with someone at the ready-mix plant. He or she should know the local codes and the concrete specifications used in your area. Also be sure to check with the building inspector. You'll probably need a permit, and the inspector can let you know in advance if your plans follow code. Plan ahead for choice delivery times, such as Saturday mornings, and know the procedure for canceling delivery if the weather fails to cooperate. Be sure the truck will have access to your site. A delivery truck can tear up a lawn or sink into fresh fill.

Plan to work in good weather—late spring and early fall are ideal times for large concrete projects. At these times of the year there's usually no threat of freezing or drying out the concrete. Also, your workers won't have to contend with the hot summer sun.

CUBIC YARDS OF CONCRETE USED IN SLAB CONSTRUCTION			
Square Feet	Thickness of Slab (Inches)		
	4	5	6
25	0.31	0.39	0.46
50	0.62	0.77	0.93
75	0.93	1.16	1.39
100	1.25	1.55	1.86
200	2.50	3.10	3.72
300	3.75	4.65	5.58

MAKING THE POUR

1. *Fill the Form*

Plan the job before the truck arrives. Start pouring and spreading the concrete at the part of the form that is farthest from the truck.

Move the concrete with rakes and shovels. During the pour, fill all

1. Fill the Form

Pull wet concrete to the back of the form.

forms to their top edges. Pay special attention to corners, along the edges of forms, or at any turns or curves in the forms. Spade the concrete in these areas. A rake is easier than a shovel because you can easily pull the material in place and then lift the rake out. You will have to use a shovel in some instances to lift material and move it back into odd areas.

Pour concrete in only one section at a time. When that is done, move to the next area while your helpers screed off the first section.

2. *Screed*

Select a straight 2×4. Sight along the edge of the board to see if there is any noticeable "crown." If there is, place the concave side against the concrete. A slight crown on your pour will provide additional drainage. The convex side would dish out the surface.

Starting at one end of the pour, move the screed toward the front to strike off the excess concrete as you go. Move the screed back and forth sideways in a sawing motion as you progress to help slide it through the excess. This action not only removes the excess but also pushes the larger pieces of aggregate down just below the surface of the

pour. If you find low spots behind the screed in some areas, use the shovel to move some of the excess concrete to fill these areas, then screed again.

3. *Spade and Tamp Concrete*

Insert the shovel vertically into the concrete then pull the shovel up and down to remove the air pockets that may occur in the corners or along the sides of the forms. Be careful not to overdo this. Overworked concrete will separate—the water will break away from the cement paste and aggregate (sand and gravel) and float to the surface. Use the back of the shovel to press the concrete in place along the forms. Fill the forms to their top edges. Another way to eliminate air bubbles along the sides of the forms is to rap the forms sharply with your hammer, moving up and down the forms. This brings the cement paste out to the surface of the wall to cover the aggregate.

Tamping is similar to spading except that it is done over the entire pour. It removes most of the air bubbles and drives the large aggregate down in place so that they won't cause problems during the finishing process. Use a rake to jab

2. Screed

Move the screed in a sawing motion to strike off excess concrete and level the slab.

3. *Spade and Tamp Concrete*

Gently tamp the concrete to push down rocks and remove air bubbles.

aggregate down and work out any air bubbles. Be careful not to overwork the concrete at this step.

FINISHING

There are several different types of finishes for concrete, and each requires its own set of skills and tools. This section focuses on the two finishes most suitable for the projects in this book. Both are easy to learn. These finishes can be accomplished by floating or by brushing with a stiff-bristled brush.

1. Float the Surface

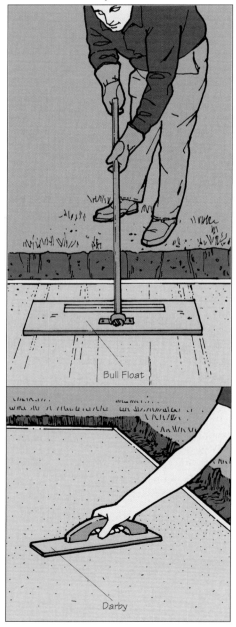

Bull Float

Darby

1. Float the Surface

The first step in finishing is floating the surface of the concrete. This can be done with either a bull float or a large hand float also called a darby. The bull float is used on large surfaces, such as patios and floor slabs. The float removes excess water from the surface and knocks down the small ridges left by the screeding operation. It leaves the pour smooth and level. The darby does the same thing, but can be used for smaller surfaces or finishing off a slab after working the bull float.

Push and pull the bull float over the concrete. At the end of each stroke, lift the float and move it to make another parallel stroke. When pushing it forward, tilt it so the front edge is raised; when pulling backward, tilt the back of the float so that it won't dig into the concrete.

2. Cut Edges and Joints

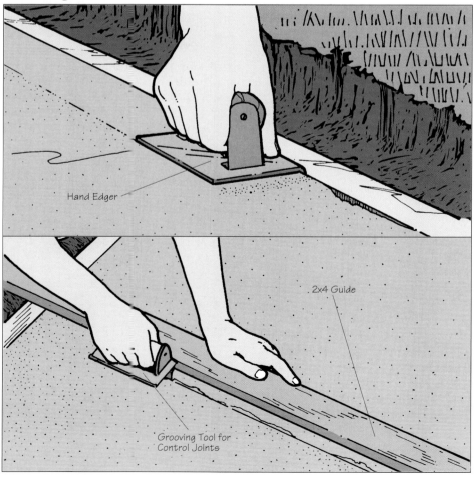

Hand Edger

Grooving Tool for Control Joints

2x4 Guide

After floating, cut the concrete away from the forms to a depth of 1 inch using a pointed mason's trowel.

2. Cut Edges & Joints

Your concrete slab should be edged to create round, smoothed edges. Round edges are safer to walk on and look more professional. A round edge will also tend to chip less than a sharp edge.

Run a hand edger back and forth along the edge of the pour, holding the tool flat on the surface and against the inside of the wood form. Again, try not to dig the edger into the wet concrete.

If you have not installed permanent wood forms for the slab, then it will be necessary to cut control joints every 8 to 10 feet. Cutting control joints is actually done in the same way but for different reasons. Besides providing a visual break in

3. Make a Textured "Broomed" Finish

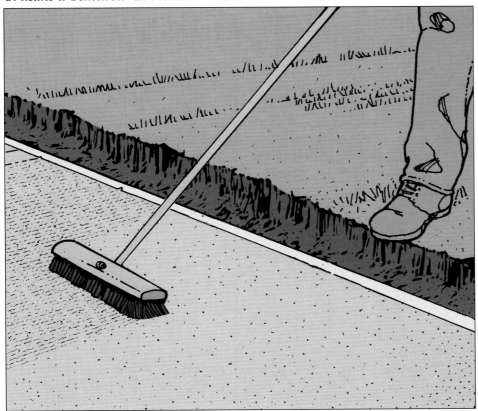

the expanse of a concrete slab, control joints provide a place for the slab to crack as it shifts and settles. Without control joints the cracks will be random and jagged.

Cut control joints with a grooving tool. Make the control joint one-quarter as deep as the thickness of the concrete slab. To provide a straight line, place the tool against a 2x4 guide strip tacked across the forms or a plank laid on the concrete. Work the hand groover along just like the edger. The V-shaped bottom will cut through the wet concrete to form the joint.

3. Make a Textured "Broomed" Finish

If you are pleased with the appearance at this point, you can choose to stop, or you may choose to try a "broomed" finish. A broomed finish is a bit rougher than a floated surface. The roughness provides more traction so the slab will be less slippery to walk on when it is wet.

Brooming can be done with almost any stiff-bristle broom. Put the bristles down on the slab and pull the broom toward you. Lift the broom after each stroke. Don't push the brush, because this may cause it to dig into the surface. For best results, broom the surface at right angles to the traffic pattern rather than in the same direction. You may have to touch up the edges and control joints with an edger after brooming the surface of the concrete.

CURING

Concrete continues to harden or cure for five to seven days after it is poured. Once you begin a concrete project, never allow the surface of the concrete to dry out completely. Mist the surface with water during the final finishing steps and begin curing immediately after final finishing.

The best and simplest method of keeping the slab moist is to hose it down at regular intervals or to set up sprinkling equipment. In all but the hottest climates, a good dousing at nightfall will keep the slab moist until the next morning.

The slab can also be sealed with plastic sheeting to keep in the moisture. Lay it flat and seal it completely at joints and along edges. Patch discoloration of the concrete can occur if the sheeting becomes wrinkled.

Form work can be removed a day after placing the concrete, but curing should continue for five to seven days.

ROOF FRAMING

Without a doubt, roof framing generates more anxiety than any other part of a construction project. And why not? One look at a rafter table with its measurements calculated to the second decimal point can be enough to make you give up. Often, it's the first time we are asked to leave the comfortable realm of right angles. And it's easy to confuse a hip jack with a valley jack or with a cripple jack. Considering all this, it's not surprising that so many people nowadays (professional carpenters included) turn to prefabricated truss systems instead of trying to tackle the roof on their own.

Trusses do save time, but they are expensive, and for highly customized projects such as your gazebo, they're just not an option.

Framing the roof on your gazebo is not as difficult as you might think. The layout is a bit more complex than other carpentry tasks, but the step-by-step instructions in this chapter will lead you through that. Once you understand the concepts, roof framing is just another bunch of straight cuts made with your circular saw.

THE BASICS

There are some basic terms that you need to know before you can start laying out your roof.

The *span* is the horizontal distance covered by a roof. This length is usually the width of the building measured from the outer faces of the frame. The *ridge* is the uppermost horizontal line of the roof. The *total rise* is the total vertical distance that the roof rises above the cap plate and the *total run* is the measure of the horizontal distance over which the rafter rises (usually half the span). The *line length* of a rafter is the hypotenuse of the right

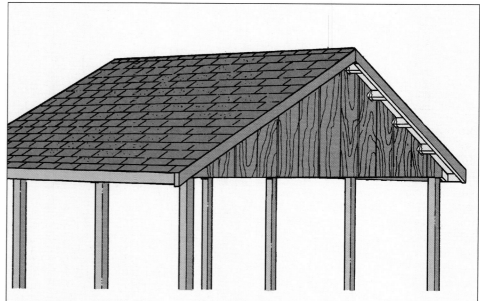

The simple gable roof s the most common roof form on houses in North America. It is also common on pavilions. Gable roofs use only common rafters. Although gazebos usually do nct have gable roofs, they do use common rafters.

triangle formed with its base as total run and its altitude as the total rise.

Rafter *slope* is expressed in the number of inches a roof rises per 12 inches of run. For example, a roof with a very shallow angle might be a "4 in 12"; a steeper roof might be a "9 in 12."

The most common type of roof, and the easiest to frame, is the gable roof. This is a roof with two slopes forming triangles on the gable ends. While gable roofs are very common on houses, they are not often used for gazebos. You will, however, often find gable roofs on pavilions such as the "Pavilion with Gable Roof" on page 134. On a gable roof, the span runs perpendicular to the ridge. The total run is equal to one-half the length of the span. And the total rise is the difference in height between the ridge and the cap plate. The line length is equal to the length of a board connecting the ridge to the cap plate plus half the thickness of the ridge board.

There are three types of rafters you need to know about to build the projects in this book. These are the common rafter, the hip rafter, and the hip jack. In gable roofs, common rafters run from the top plate to the ridge at right angles to both. They are the only rafters you need for a gable roof. Although most gazebos don't have gable roofs, they do use common rafters. For example, the six- and eight-sided gazebo projects in this book use common rafters that run at right angles to the top plates to meet at a key block at the peak. The key block is cut to meet the rafters at a right angle. Hip rafters run on a 45-degree angle from the top plate to the ridge, forming the line of intersection for the two surfaces of a hip roof. Hip jacks run parallel to the common rafters, from the hip to the top plate. The four-sided gazebo uses both hip and hip jack rafters.

Hip Roof Framing System

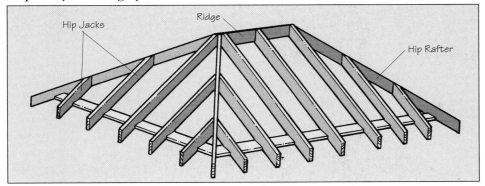

No matter what kind of rafter you are making, all of the cuts will be either plumb or level. A plumb cut is any cut on a rafter that is vertical when the rafter is in position. A level cut is any cut on the rafter that is horizontal when the rafter is in position. With the help of a framing square you can accurately lay out plumb and level cuts without lugging each board into position on the roof.

THE FRAMING SQUARE

For many people, the framing square is little more than a handy measuring device or a quick way to check if an angle is at 90 degrees.

But that same piece of metal is capable of doing much more. The lowly framing square not only can estimate a rafter's length, but will also precisely lay out the final cuts, without the help of any complicated rafter charts or conversion books. That's because the design of the square already calculates roof slope in inches of rise per 12 inches of run.

Framing Square

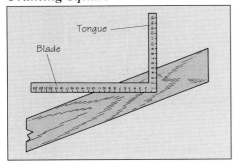

LAYING OUT AND CUTTING THE COMMON RAFTER

As mentioned, the common rafter meets the top plate and the ridge at a 90 degree angle. The common rafter meets the ridge board or key block with a plumb cut called the ridge cut. The bottom of the rafter fits over the top plate with a notch called a "bird's mouth." The bird's mouth consists of a level cut called the seat cut and a short plumb cut. The part of the rafter that overhangs the wall is called the rafter tail. In most designs, the rafter tail ends in a plumb cut. If there is no rafter tail, there's no bird's mouth either. Instead, the plumb cut is extended past the seat cut to make the end of the rafter flush with the wall.

Rafter Cuts

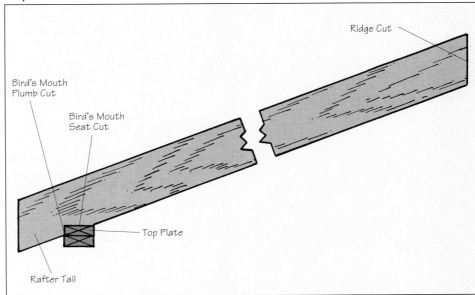

Calculating Rough Rafter Lengths

You'll need to know approximate rafter lengths when you order lumber. You can use your framing square to estimate this length. Let the blade of the square represent the total run and the tongue represent the total rise. Using a scale of 1 inch =1 foot, measure the distance from blade to tongue to find the length of the rafter. Don't forget to add in any overhang into your final calculation, if the rafter is supposed to hang past the plate. The overhang is traditionally measured in terms of a level measurement (how far it actually sticks out past the cap plate). Add that extra length to the blade before you do your calculations.

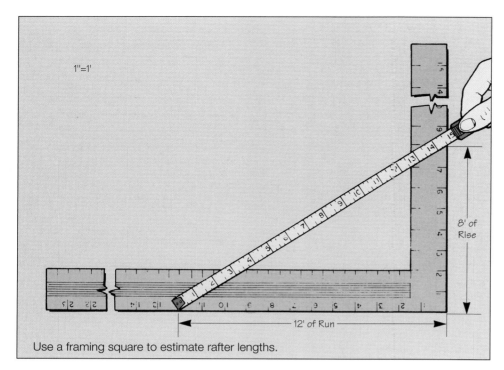

1"=1'

8' of Rise

12' of Run

Use a framing square to estimate rafter lengths.

Mark off the partial step first, and then proceed from that mark to step off full 12-inch units as described in Step 1.

Starting at the top of the rafter, hold the square in position and draw a ridge line along the edge of the tongue. Continue to hold the square in the same position as you measure and mark the length of the odd unit on the blade. Now shift the square to your right along the edge of the stock until the tongue is even with the 8-inch mark. Mark off a plumb line on the tongue of your square.

When you begin stepping off full units, remember to start not from the ridge cut but from that plumb line that you just marked to determine the odd unit.

What you are doing, essentially, is making and then measuring a scale model of your roof. If you wanted to, you could draft a scale drawing and then measure the rafter on your plan. Not only is the framing square just as accurate, but it will save you all those steps!

This estimate will be a little rough, it does not account for the vertical distance of the tail, but it should be adequate to determine which size stock you should be starting with. If your estimate is within less than a foot of a particular stock size, be sure to double-check your measurements. You might decide to purchase a few more board feet, just to be on the safe side.

This method works for hip rafters as well as common rafters. Keep in mind though, that since a hip runs diagonally, it has a longer run than a common rafter on the same roof. If you know the common run, you can get the hip run by using the following formula:

Run of Hip Rafter = Run of Common Rafter x 1.41

Cut a Common Rafter

1. Lay Out Ridge Cut

Lay out a straight piece of rafter stock across two sawhorses. Select the straightest piece possible, because this will be used as a pattern to mark the rest of the rafters. Position yourself so that you're on the crowned side of the rafter. It's easier to hold and work with the framing square from that position.

Let's say we are laying out a 8 in 12 roof. Lay the square down on the left end of the stock. Hold the tongue of the square with your left hand and the blade with your right. Move the square until the edge of the stock nearest you aligns with the unit rise mark (8 inches in this example) on the outside of the tongue and the 12-inch mark on the outside of the blade. Mark along the outside edge of the tongue for the plumb cut at the ridge.

2. Step Off Partial Step

If your line length is not an even number of 12-inch units, for example, 6 feet 8 inches, then you will have to include a "half-step" to accommodate this extra length.

1. Lay Out Ridge Cut

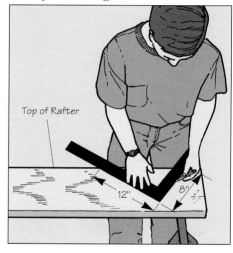

Top of Rafter

12"

8"

2. Step Off Partial Step

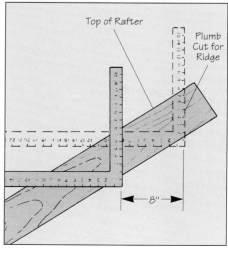

Top of Rafter

Plumb Cut for Ridge

8"

3. Step Off Run Units

Unless you're building a bird-house, your framing square won't be large enough to make a rafter layout in one setting. That leaves two options, either learning how to read and work with rafter tables or stepping off the units. In the latter method, the stock is "stepped off" in 12-inch units of run until the desired number of steps, or units, is reached. You'll discover that as long as your pencil is sharp and you measure carefully, the second technique is accurate and will eliminate the need to do any major calculations.

Let's work with that same 8 in 12 roof with a run of 6 feet 8 inches. Starting from the partial step mark, continue stepping off, to your right, by marking the stock on the outside of the blade and shifting the square until the outside of the tongue aligns with that mark. Repeat this step five more times.

On the last step, mark a plumb line along the outside of the tongue. This plumb line, called the building line, should be directly above the outside of the cap plate.

4. Cut Bird's Mouth

The bird's mouth of the rafter is a combination level cut and plumb cut. The level cut rests on the top plate of the wall and the plumb cut fits snugly against the outside edge of the cap plate.

Form the bird's mouth by measuring 1½ inches up the building line. Bring the seat cut over to intersect this point. That will drop the rafter over the cap plate but not the top plate below the cap. To mark the seat cut, you will still be using your square, but you will have to flip it over and work from the other side. Mark along the blade for the level cut. Use a handsaw to cut out the mouth.

3. Step Off Run Units

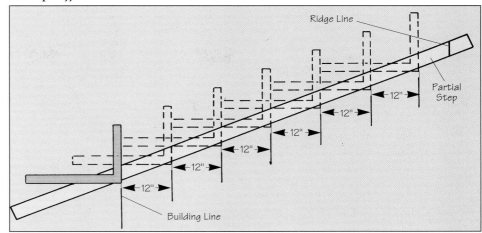

4. Cut Bird's Mouth

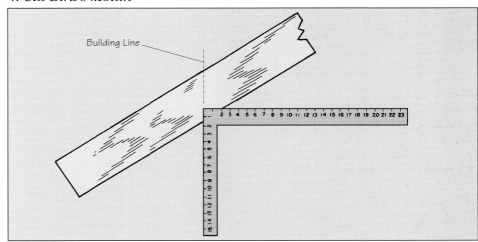

5. Measure the Tail

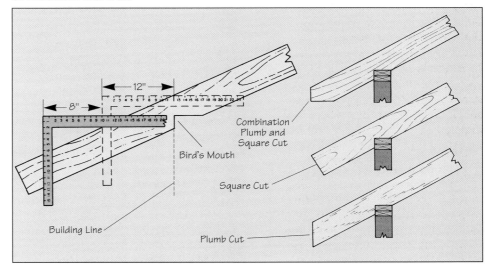

5. Measure the Tail

The rafter tail length is given in terms of a level measurement. To lay out the tail, simply add in the necessary amount of run (20 inches, in this example) measuring from the plumb line of the bird's mouth. The tail cut is at the end of the rafter overhang and may be a plumb cut, square cut, or a combination of cuts.

Framing Square Stops

It's important that you keep the square at exactly the correct angle throughout the step-off process. One way to ensure this is by purchasing special stops (sometimes called stair gauges) that clamp directly onto the blade and tongue.

Another way to do the same thing is to clamp a small straightedge across the tongue and blade of the square at the desired location to make sure that the square is kept in the same angle for every step.

Either way, make sure to measure and step carefully. Be sure your pencil is sharp. Any minute error will be multiplied with each step. A mistake of just $1/8$ inch will become 1 inch in eight "steps."

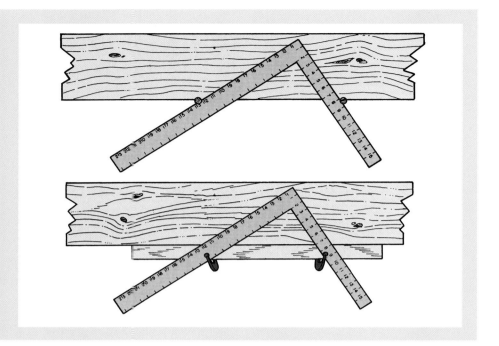

6. Shorten Common Rafter for Ridge

The length of the rafter has been calculated to the center of the ridge line. As a result, the rafter must be shortened to accommodate the ridge board. In the case of gazebos, where all the rafters come together at a key block, you need to shorten the rafters by one-half the width of the key block. To shorten a rafter, measure back at a right angle from the ridge cut a distance of one-half the thickness of the ridge board or key block. Lay out another plumb line at this point for the actual length of the rafter.

LAYING OUT AND CUTTING THE HIP RAFTER

Draw a square whose sides are 12 inches long. Measure diagonally across the square and you'll find that the diagonal line is 16.97 inches long. Now apply this fact to the geometry of a hip rafter, which runs diagonally to the corners of a building. It's easy to see that for every 12 inches a common rafter runs, the hip rafter must travel 16.97 inches, or for practical purposes, 17 inches.

6. Shorten Common Rafter for Ridge

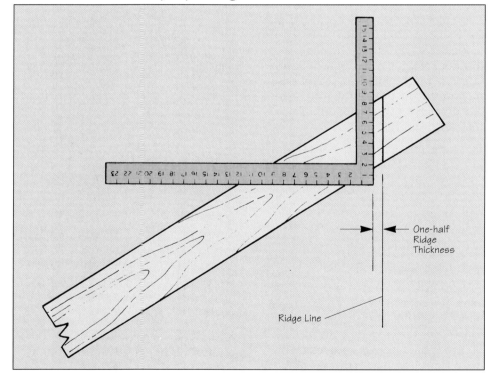

One-half Ridge Thickness

Ridge Line

So, if you are building a roof whose common rafters have a slope of 9 in 12, the hip rafters of the same slope will be laid out as 9 in 17. This means that hip rafters can be stepped off in the same way as common rafters. Just use the 17-inch mark on the blade instead of the 12-inch mark.

Cut the Hip Rafter

1. Lay Out Ridge Cut

Lay a straight piece of rafter stock across two sawhorses. Select the straightest piece possible, because this will be used as a pattern to mark the other hip rafters. Let's say

1. Lay Out Ridge Cut

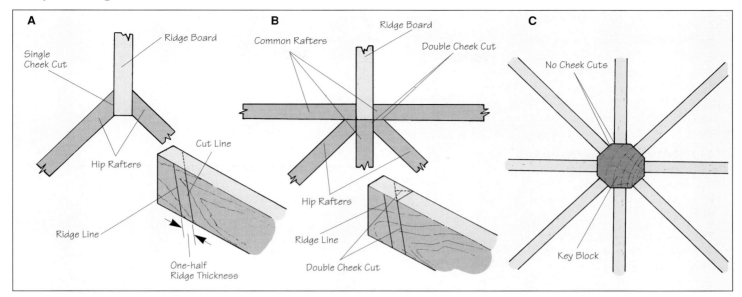

A Single Cheek Cut · Ridge Board · Hip Rafters · Ridge Line · Cut Line · One-half Ridge Thickness

B Common Rafters · Ridge Board · Double Cheek Cut · Hip Rafters · Ridge Line · Double Cheek Cut

C No Cheek Cuts · Key Block

2. Lay Out Hip Rafter Length

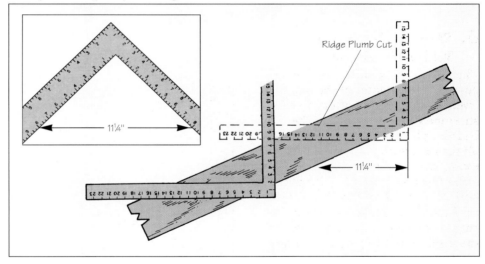

11¼" · Ridge Plumb Cut · 11¼"

you are laying out on 8 in 17 hip rafter. Lay the square down on the stock at its extreme left end. Hold the tongue of the square with your left hand and blade with your right. Move the square until the edge of the stock nearest you aligns with the unit rise mark (8 inches in this example) on the outside of the tongue and the 17-inch mark on the outside of the blade.

The major difference between a common and a hip rafter is at the ridge cut. The ridge cut of a hip rafter is a compound angle; that is, the cut is made at an angle through its thickness and also across its side. This kind of cut is also referred to as a cheek cut. Depending on the design of the roof, the hip rafters may need a cheek cut on one or both sides (see drawing). For a single cheek cut (A), mark along the outside edge of the tongue for the ridge plumb line. Measure back at right angles from the plumb line, one-half the thickness of the rafter stock, and lay out another plumb line. This is your cut line. For a double cheek cut (B), use your square to wrap the cut line around to the other side of the rafter. Set your circular saw to cut at 45 degrees and make the cheek cut.

Cheek cuts are necessary for hip roofs where hip rafters intersect the ridge board at 45 degrees. For projects such as the "Square Hip Roof Gazebo" on page 106, cheek cuts aren't needed. The octagonal key block takes care of the 45-degree angles for you (C).

Remember that hip rafters must be shortened just like commons to compensate for half the diagonal thickness of the ridge board or, in the case of a gazebo, half the width of the key block. When against common rafters, the hip is shortened by one-half the 45-degree thickness of the common rafter (key blocks are the same thickness from any angle). Avoid any unnecessary work by including all of these measurements

into the length of the rafter before making any cuts.

2. Lay Out Hip Rafter Length

The length of the hip rafter is laid out in a manner similar to that used for the common rafter. Remember to start any layout for length from the original plumb line before any shortening is done.

In the step-off method, the number of steps is the same for the hip rafter length as for the common rafter in the same roof. The same rise is used but the unit of run for the hip is 17. The odd unit must be adjusted for the 17-inch

Cutting the Perfect Roof

If you have decided to use a slat-style roof, it is possible to cut the slat boards so that they perfectly match up with the angle of the roof. Nail your slats onto the rafters and cut them in place so that each slat will match up with the next one right at the centerline of the rafter.

If you are cutting a slat that will butt up to a previously installed slat, you might find it easier to temporarily position it one slat-width above so that you can get the cutting angle and then install it in its correct location. Cut the other end once the cut end of the slat is fastened in place.

unit run. The length of the hip odd unit equals the diagonal of a square whose sides are the length of the common odd unit. If, for example the common odd unit is 8 inches, the hip odd unit is 11¼ inches.

3. *Back or Drop Hip*

Imagine a line drawn down the center of the top edge of a hip rafter. At this line, the roof planes on both sides of the roof meet to form the hip. But because rafter stock is not just a theoretical line but a piece of wood with thickness, the corners of the top edge of the stock will protrude above the roof planes. You need to adjust for this so your roof sheathing or slats sit flat at the hip. There are two ways to make this adjustment. One, called backing the hip, involves planing off the projecting corners. Dropping the hip involves deepening the bird's mouth so that the entire hip is lowered.

To back the hip, create a bevel on each of the top edges with either a block or jack plane. Do not plane the bevel down to a point with a

45-degree angle—all it takes is two or three strokes on each edge—too great an angle is almost as bad as no bevel at all. Try to work toward a 30 degree bevel. The angle does vary somewhat, depending on the roof's pitch, but don't worry if it is not exact, the most important step

in this operation is simply knocking off the corners.

A more accurate, and the most common, approach is to drop the hip. This involves adjusting the bird's-mouth to bring the top edges of the hip rafter into the same plane as the common rafters. First, use your framing square to lay out the unadjusted bird's mouth plumb cut in the same way as you did for common rafters, except that you are now using a unit run of 17 instead of 12. Next, align the outside of the square's blade perpendicular along the edge of the ridge's plumb cut, as shown in the illustration. Draw a line. The distance from that line to the peak is equal to twice the amount of drop. Measure this distance, divide the number in half, and add the required drop onto the seat cut of your bird's mouth.

Hip Rafter Tail

If you want to lay out the overhang of the hip rafter, use the same number of unit steps as used when laying out the overhang of the common rafter. Use 17 as the unit of run. The tail cut is usually a double cheek cut to accommodate fascia trim that must come together to meet at the corner.

3. Back or Drop Hip

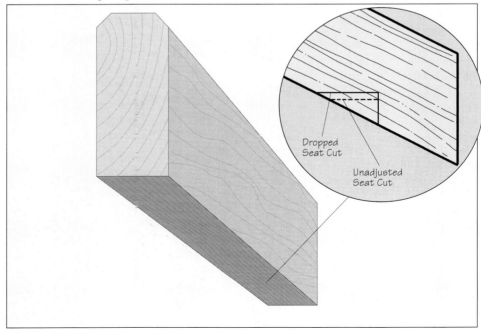

Dropped Seat Cut

Unadjusted Seat Cut

Hip Jack Rafters

Hip jack rafters are short rafters that run between the cap plate and a hip rafter. Jack rafters run parallel to commons and are laid out in the same "x in 12" manner with your framing square. They have an identical bird's mouth and tail cut (see "Laying Out and Cutting the Common Rafter" on p. 59). The two main differences between a jack and a common are that jack rafters require a single cheek where they meet the hip (commons are cut plumb), and as you travel down from the ridge line, jack rafters get shorter (commons are all equal in length because they all meet at the ridge or key block).

Jack rafters look a lot more difficult to lay out than they actually are. Assuming that you space the jacks equally along the hip rafter, the change in length from one rafter to the next will remain constant. This consistent change is called the common difference and is included on the rafter table printed on your framing square.

There's no trick to reading the rafter chart once you realize that it is already calculated to accommodate different roof pitches. The common difference for jacks on 16- or 24-inch centers can be determined on the third and fourth lines of the rafter table, respectively. Assuming you already know the pitch of your roof, look to that number on the outside edge of your square's blade. Simply read the numbers directly under the appropriate pitch.

For example, if you had a 6 in 12 roof, and wanted your jacks spaced 16 inches on center, you would look at the chart and learn that the common difference is 17$7/8$ inches. You would then cut the first jack 17$7/8$ inches shorter than the common rafter. Continue cutting each additional jack shorter by the same common difference.

To lay out jack rafters, lay out the bird's mouth and overhang from the common rafter pattern. Now lay out the line length of a common rafter. For the first jack rafter down from the ridge, subtract the common difference from the length. Finally, take off half of the 45-degree thickness of the hip. (This cheek cut is just like the one described under "1. Lay Out the Ridge Cut" on p. 62.)

Remember that every hip jack on one side of a hip rafter must be opposed by a jack of the same length on the other side. Opposing jacks will be identical except that their cheek cuts will be on different sides. Label each set of jacks to make sure that you are cutting the angles correctly. Continue running jack rafters down from the hip until the remaining distance is less than the common difference.

Hip Jack Rafters

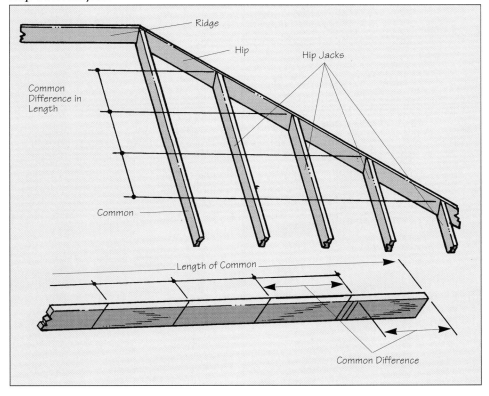

Rafter Scales

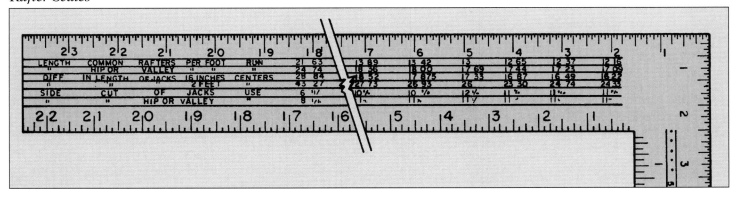

ROOFING

When designing and building a roof for your gazebo or arbor, your priorities may be different from those you would have if you were building a roof for your house. For one thing, your house roof must be waterproof. That's not necessarily the case for a garden structure roof. Perhaps you want to roof your gazebo with lattice just to defuse the heat of the sun while admitting dappled light.

Another difference is that most house roofs are visible only if you step a good distance away from the house. Small visual details are less important than function. In comparison, the roof of your gazebo or pavillion is much closer. And most gazebo roofs are steeply pitched, which adds to their visual impact. Your choice of materials will influence the style of your project; for example, standard square composite shingles provide a formal, practical structure; cedar shakes suggest a more natural feeling.

Perhaps cost would force you to roof your house with composite shingles, but when you consider the relatively small surface area of a gazebo roof, you'll discover that it won't cost that much more if you decide to spring for cedar shingles or shakes. Also, because the roof is small and easily accessible, you can take all the time you need to carefully craft roof details such as hips and peaks. A small project like this is a great opportunity to stretch your skills by trying new techniques and materials. This chapter will help you make the best possible choice by providing an overview of all your options and general installation instructions.

Different roof treatments help create entirely different effects with a basic eight-sided gazebo. The slat roof (top) creates the most open feeling. The shake roof (left) looks quite rugged but costs a bit more than the composite roof (right).

WOOD SHAKES AND SHINGLES

It's hard to beat the traditional elegance of a wood roof. Cedar shingles and shakes have been used for centuries, not just for appearance's sake but also because they have proven themselves as perfect roofing materials that can withstand many years of abuse. Cedar naturally resists decay much longer than other woods.

Although wood shakes and shingles have several things in common, don't confuse the two. They are made differently. There are four types of shakes: taper split, hand

Cedar shingles (left) are very different from cedar shakes (right).

ROOFING MATERIALS				
Type	*Cost*	*Durability (years)*	*Sheathing*	*Install*
Wood Shingles Wood Shakes	Moderate to Expensive	15–30 25–75	Slat Slat or Plywood	Moderate to Difficult
Composite	Inexpensive to Expensive	12–25	Plywood	Easy
Slat	Inexpensive	*	None	Easy
Lattice	Inexpensive	*	None	Easy

* These wood roof options should last about as long as the rest of the project. Durability depends on various factors, including the type of wood used; the type of finish or paint, if any; and the weather conditions the structure is exposed to.

Shingles and shakes are graded from 1 to 3 (with number 1 being the highest quality). Number 1 is used on most homes, because the shakes and shingles are cut from heartwood and are knot free. Lower-grade shingles (No. 2) are less expensive but are still more than adequate for use in a garden structure.

One obvious drawback of using a natural wood roof is that unless properly treated it's not fireproof. Shingles and shakes can be treated for fire resistance—some with a Class A rating—to fulfill most code requirements; however, this is an expensive option and may not be necessary. (This code may not apply for a garden structure; however, you still should check with your local building inspector just to make sure.)

split, resawn, and straight split. All but straight split are thick at the butt end and taper to a thin end. Straight split shakes are equally thick at both ends and are too bulky for most roofs. Tapered resawn shakes give a roof an even profile, because one face is smooth and flat. Shingles are sawn on both sides. They are smaller, thinner, and lighter than shakes and will create the most uniform appearance.

Wood shingles generally last 15 to 30 years, but shakes can last quite a bit longer, because they are split, rather than sawn from the wood. Wood's cellular structure consists of tiny pathways that carry water and minerals up the trunk to the leaves—similar to a bundle of straws. Splitting the wood along the grain leaves the straws intact so they remain open only at the ends of the face. Sawing slices into the straws creates lots of openings on the face that suck up moisture. Because of this, shakes are more resistant to damage from moisture changes than shingles.

Composite shingles are the most commonly used roofing material. They are inexpensive, easy to install and lend a traditional look to any project.

When designing and building a roof for your gazebo or arbor, your priorities may be different from those you would have if you were building a roof for your house. For one thing, your house roof must be waterproof. That's not necessarily the case for a garden structure roof. Perhaps you want to roof your gazebo with lattice just to defuse the heat of the sun while admitting dappled light.

Another difference is that most house roofs are visible only if you step a good distance away from the house. Small visual details are less important than function. In comparison, the roof of your gazebo or pavillion is much closer. And most gazebo roofs are steeply pitched, which adds to their visual impact. Your choice of materials will influence the style of your project; for example, standard square composite shingles provide a formal, practical structure; cedar shakes suggest a more natural feeling.

Perhaps cost would force you to roof your house with composite shingles, but when you consider the relatively small surface area of a gazebo roof, you'll discover that it won't cost that much more if you decide to spring for cedar shingles or shakes. Also, because the roof is small and easily accessible, you can take all the time you need to carefully craft roof details such as hips and peaks. A small project like this is a great opportunity to stretch your skills by trying new techniques and materials. This chapter will help you make the best possible choice by providing an overview of all your options and general instal-

Stack unused shingles out of direct sunlight. Excessive heat will cause them to stick together or bend out of shape.

Composite shingles are now available in hundreds of different colors. Some types are textured to mimic shake or cedar shingle roofs.

LATTICE- AND SLAT-STYLE ROOFING

Lattice- and slat-style roofs cannot offer the same degree of protection as the other types, but their overall effect is hard to beat. These open-air roofs allow all of the summer breezes in while filtering out just the right amount of sunlight. They can also serve as a support for plants or flowering vines to grow on, so that your project can completely blend in to the rest of your garden.

Although lattice and slat roofs are a more custom option, they can be easier and less expensive to construct than roofing your project with shakes or shingles. For example, you would essentially have to install a slat-style roof before you could start nailing on wooden shingles. By stopping at this step, you would save yourself the money that you would have spent on the additional material.

Estimating Roofing Materials

Roofing material is sold by the square; 1 square is equal to 100 square feet. To estimate the amount of shingles you'll need, you must determine the number of squares in the roof's surface. The simplest way to do this is to climb up onto the roof and measure the area (length x width) of each surface, add those figures together, and divide the result by 100. Add 10 percent to allow for waste. Round up to the next highest figure. (At this point, it's better to overestimate what you will need. Unopened bundles can be returned, and since different pallets of the same shingle may have slightly different colors, you should order more than you need to finish the job on your first try.)

You will also have to include in your estimate certain specialty shingles. To approximate the number of hip and ridge shingles that you will need, measure the lengths of the hips and ridges, and divide the total by the exposure recommended for the shingles. For example, the Eight-Sided Gazebo (page 124) has eight hips, each about 7$\frac{1}{2}$ feet long. The hips have a combined length of almost 60 feet, or 720 inches. Assuming that you want a 5-inch exposure, you would need 144 (720/5 = 144) hip shingles, or 48 regular shingles cut in threes. Don't forget to measure the total length of eaves and rakes for drip-edge flashing.

With wood shingles, 1 square will cover about 240 lineal feet of double course; 1 square of shakes will cover about 120 lineal feet. One bundle of factory-produced ridge units will cover 16$\frac{2}{3}$ lineal feet for both wood shingles and shakes. On shake roofs you must also figure about one and a half rolls of 30-lb felt 18 inches wide, for each square of shakes at a 10-inch exposure.

For roofing nails, use 1$\frac{1}{2}$ lb per square of composite shingles and 2 lb per square of wood shingles or shakes. You'll also need about 3 lb of nails for the starter course and the hip and ridge shingles.

Sheathing with Plywood

Plywood sheathing is a perfect base for composite shingles or for shakes. Use $\frac{3}{4}$-inch exterior plywood, B-grade or better. Install the good side down, since you will be able to see it from inside your gazebo.

Run the panels perpendicular to the rafters. Use 8d hot-dipped galvanized nails every 6 inches along the ends and every 12 inches on the inside of each sheet. Leave $\frac{1}{8}$-inch gaps at the edges to allow for expansion.

Texture 1-11 (T1-11) is a form of plywood made to resemble slat-style

A slat-style roof is perfect for filtering out the worst of the summer sun. For additional shade, consider climbing vines or flowers.

T1-11 used under a shake or composite roof can create a finished slat appearance, unlike ordinary plywood sheathing.

figure out. Start with the second sheathing board—this is where the first row of shingles must be nailed. For example, if the roof exposure is to be 5 inches, set the second board right next to the first board. Next measure from the second sheathing board and set the third board on a 5-inch center from the second board. Now measure the space between the two boards and make a wooden gauge to space the rest of the sheathing. Solid-slat sheathing for the first 12 to 24 inches makes installing the first few courses much easier.

Many people prefer the open-air feeling of a slat-style roof. If you are concerned with letting in the sun more than keeping out the rain, you can stop right at this step. Obviously, you will not plan your slat width or slat spacing on shingle layout, but on the amount of light that you want inside your structure.

Felt Underlayment

Standard rolls of felt underlayment are 36 inches wide and 144 feet long. When used under asphalt or fiberglass shingles, plan on four standard rolls of 15-pound asphalt-

paneling. Typically, it is used for exterior siding, but in this case, it can also be used effectively for roof work. Install the T1-11 so that the slat pattern is facing down into the gazebo. Make sure that the sheets are positioned so that the slats are oriented in the same direction.

Sheathing and Roofing with Spaced Slats

Spaced slats are simply 1x4s or 1x6s, nailed directly to the rafters. They are used primarily with wood shingles and shakes, because these materials need air to circulate on both sides to prevent moisture from rotting or cupping the wood.

The measurement for spaced sheathing depends on the exposure of the shingles and is easy to

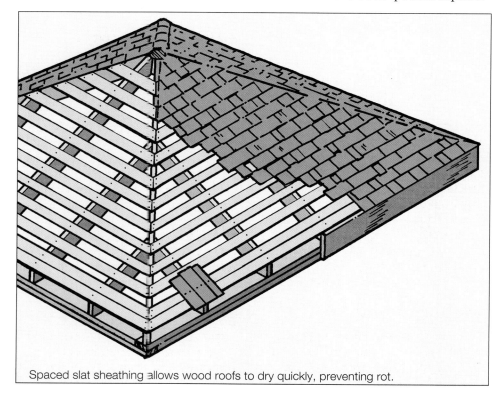

Spaced slat sheathing allows wood roofs to dry quickly, preventing rot.

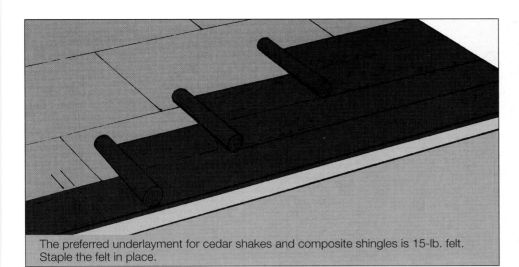

The preferred underlayment for cedar shakes and composite shingles is 15-lb. felt. Staple the felt in place.

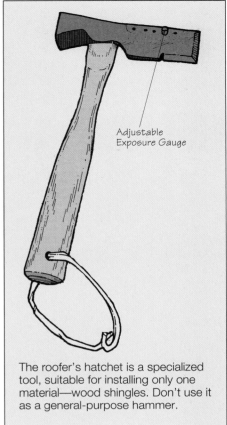

Adjustable Exposure Gauge

The roofer's hatchet is a specialized tool, suitable for installing only one material—wood shingles. Don't use it as a general-purpose hammer.

saturated felt for every square of shingles. For a composite roof, lay each course of felt over the lower by at least 2 inches. Overlap each end by 4 inches. Lap the felt at least 6 inches over all hips and ridges.

Underlayment is used a little differently with cedar shakes. Shakes require 18-inch rolls instead of 36-inch rolls. The half-size rolls are "woven" between each course to ensure a watertight roof. Plan on using approximately one and a half rolls of felt for shakes at 10-inch exposure. If 18-inch rolls are not available, you can cut pieces from a 36-inch roll in half with a utility knife.

INSTALLING WOOD SHINGLES AND SHAKES

Wood shingles and shakes can be applied by anybody reasonably skilled with a few simple tools. This section will provide you with all the necessary fundamentals, but don't expect to be able to work at the rate of an accomplished wood shingler. Realistically, doing a job like this for the first time will demand some patience, but you will surprise yourself with professional-looking results.

Tools and Equipment

One tool that you will need is the roofer's hatchet. The hatchet has a nonskid head that prevents it from slipping off the rough galvanized nails and a blade for cutting and splitting shingles; the better hatchets also have a shingle gauge. The gauge is important for spacing wood shingles. A peg fits into the gauge holes and is used to set shingles quickly to the correct exposure. If you use a hatchet with a sliding gauge, be careful—if it slips slightly you'll wind up with misaligned shingles. You will also need a saw for cutting shingles across the grain and a block plane for beveling the edges so that you can ease in the shingles and clean up cuts.

Material Selection and Exposure

Proper application starts with selecting the right shingles for the job. A good wood shingle roof is never less than three layers thick. Consequently, the exposure of any given shingle must be slightly less than one-third its total length. The amount of shingle or shake exposed to the weather varies with the shingle's length and the roof's slope. Thinner wood shingles should be installed in a straight line like composite shingles. Thicker wood shakes, on the other hand, look great when installed in a more random pattern.

See the table "Recommended Exposures," but again, it's a good idea to check with your local building department.

Recommended Exposures

Shingle Size	3 in 12 Roof	4 in 12 and Steeper Roofs
16 inch	3¾ inches	5 inches
18 inch	4½ inches	5½ inches
24 inch	5¾ inches	7½ inches

The nails are the next most important part of a wood shingle or shake roof. Use only rust-resistant nails, either zinc coated or aluminum. Figure a little over 2 pound per square for both shingles and shakes. Use 3d nails for 16- and 18-inch wood shingles and 4d for 24-inch wood shingles. Handsplit shakes require a 6d roofing nails. A rule of thumb is to make sure that the nail penetrates at least ½ inch into the sheathing.

Installing Wood Shingles

Do not use a felt underlayment with wood shingles. Nail them directly over spaced sheathing. Take a little extra time getting started—the rest of the roof will be gauged from your beginning course.

1. Lay Out First Course

Begin by nailing a shingle at each end of the eaves so that they over-hang the eaves by 1 inch and the rake by $1/4$ to $3/8$ inch. Drive a nail into the butt of each shingle and stretch a line between them to help align the rest of the starter course.

Right handers normally start in the left corner and apply enough shin-gles so that they are able to sit down on the job. If you're a lefty, start on the right corner.

2. Run the Course

Leave a $1/8$- to $1/4$-inch gap between shingles. Double the first course of shingles, staggering gaps by at least $1^1/2$ inches.

3. Start Second Course

Start the second course of shingles at the recommended exposure. Proper positioning of the nails is very impor-tant. Two nails are required per shin-gle, regardless of width, to prevent the shingle from cupping. Always nail within $3/4$ inch (1 inch for shakes) of the side edge of the shingle. Nail high enough so that the nails will be cov-ered by the next course. On wood shingles with a 5-inch exposure, nail about 7 inches from the bottom edge of the shingle. On shingles with a 10-inch exposure, nail about 12 inch-es from the bottom edge. If you nail too high or too far in from the edge, the shingles will be able to curl up.

To locate the correct placement for each nail, measure up from the butt of the shingle you are nailing a distance equal to the exposure plus 1 or 2 inches. For a quick guide, mark the handle of your hammer with tape or a notch. Nail carefully; pounding too hard can break the wood fibers. If a shingle is crooked, pull it out and replace it.

Stagger gaps between shingles at least $1^1/2$ inches between courses. Gaps should not line up over gaps two courses below.

If the shingle splits while you are nailing it and the crack offsets the joint in the shingle below by at least $1^1/2$ inches, place a nail on each side

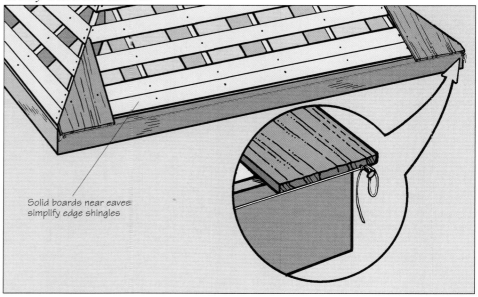

1. Lay Out First Course

Solid boards near eaves simplify edge shingles

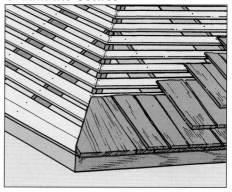

2. Run the Course

of the split. You can treat the split shingle as two shingles. If the crack does not offset the joint in the shingle below, remove the split shingle and apply another.

3. Start Second Course

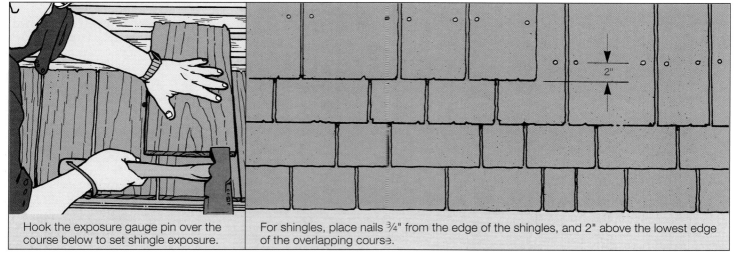

Hook the exposure gauge pin over the course below to set shingle exposure.

For shingles, place nails $3/4$" from the edge of the shingles, and 2" above the lowest edge of the overlapping course.

2"

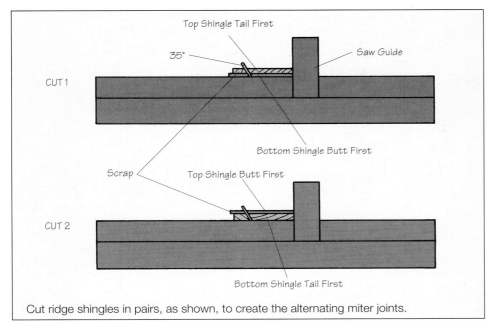

Cut ridge shingles in pairs, as shown, to create the alternating miter joints.

Splitting Shingles

Because of their pronounced grain, shingles are surprisingly easy to split accurately along the grain. To split a shingle to width, embed the blade of a roofer's hatchet into the tapered end of the shingle then strike down. To fine-tune a cut, shave the shingle with a utility knife.

Shingling the Ridge

You will not have to deal with valleys with any of the projects in this book, but you will have to know how to roof a ridge. The gazebos in this book all have hips, which are treated just like ridges. The appearance of your project (and its ability to shed water) depends on the neatness of the ridge. Factory ridge units are available and will make the job easier, because the two pieces are already fastened together and offset mitered joints are stacked alternately to speed installation. However, it's not too difficult to cut the ridges yourself.

Cutting Your Own Ridge and Hip Shingles

Set your table saw's blade to a 35-degree angle and the fence to 4 inches (this measurement may vary according to the roof pitch). Cut two shingles at a time—one butt first, the other tail first. The top piece of ridge will come out about $1/4$ to $3/8$ inch wider than the bottom piece. The next piece will be reversed, giving you the same alternating mitered joints as the factory-made ridge pieces. For the next set, flip the pair (if the first pair was cut with top shingle tail first, make the second ridge unit with the top shingle butt first).

Each ridge unit must have two nails on each side, placed 6 to 7 inches above the butt edge. Make sure that you offset ridge joints so that water will not seep through the joints as the roof ages. Give each ridge the same exposure as the roof shingles. For additional protection, it wouldn't hurt to lay a narrow strip of 30-pound felt over the ridge before installing the shingles. And always use a chalkline to make sure that the lines remain straight.

When starting a ridge run, start with a double course, as you did with the regular shingle courses. At those spots where the ridge meets the peak, you may have to trim the shingles to make a tight fit. Make the ridge in the middle and build a saddle by reversing two units on top of each other. Trim back the tail ends and leave about 8 inches of the butt portion. Use longer nails to apply the ridge to ensure that the nails penetrate the sheathing.

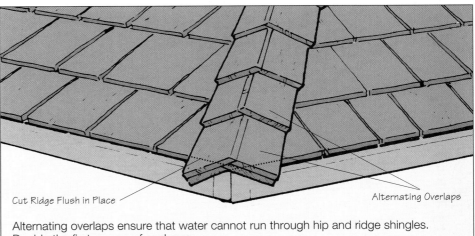

Alternating overlaps ensure that water cannot run through hip and ridge shingles. Double the first course of each run.

APPLYING ROOF SHAKES

Shakes work best on roofs with at least a 6 in 12 slope, particularly in wet, humid climates. Shakes measuring 18 inches are overlapped $10^1/2$ inches, leaving an exposure of $7^1/2$ inches. Shakes measuring 24 inches are overlapped 14 inches, exposing 10 inches. This amount of overlapping provides standard two-ply coverage. You can get even better coverage by using a three-ply roof; in this case you need a $12^1/2$-inch and $16^1/2$-inch overlap, respectively. Nail shakes with 6d box nails in the same way as you would for wood shingles, allowing $1/2$ inch of space between shakes.

Preparing the Roof for Shakes

Shakes are usually installed over spaced sheathing, either 1x4s or 1x6s. However, because shakes are irregularly shaped, enough air can still circulate under them, even when using a solid plywood sheathing so that neither rotting nor cupping is a problem. If you decide to use plywood sheathing, you should

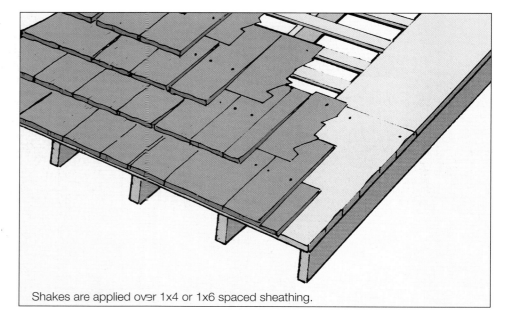

Shakes are applied over 1x4 or 1x6 spaced sheathing.

not use any felt underlayment. The extra layer of underlayment will create a condensation problem; moisture under the shakes will affect your roof's life expectancy.

Except for a few minor considerations, shakes are installed exactly like shingles. When used to roof homes, wood shingles require 18-inch-wide strips of 30-pound roofing felt interwoven between the courses of shakes. This underlayment ensures that any water that

penetrates under the shakes will quickly be carried back out to the roof surface. If you want a completely watertight roof and cannot locate 18-inch-wide felt in your area, cut a 36-inch-wide roll in half with a utility knife. Either apply the felt as you install each course of shakes or felt only the area you plan to install in a single day.

There is a disadvantage to using felt in this particular application: Those black felt strips will be visible from the underside of your gazebo. You can choose to omit the felt entirely, but you may have to put up with a few leaks.

Applying Hip and Ridge Shakes

Cut and fit shakes at hip lines so that they end at the center of the hip. Shakes for covering hips and ridges are made with mitered edges. They require 8d nails or longer. Position shakes at the bottom and top of the hip and snap a chalk line between them along one edge to serve as a guide. Apply a double hip shake at the eaves, cutting the first one so that its top edge butts against the next course of shakes. Proceed up the hip, alternating the overlaps of the mitered corners.

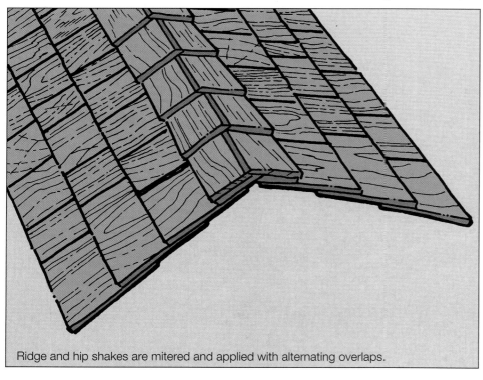

Ridge and hip shakes are mitered and applied with alternating overlaps.

1. Install Starter Course

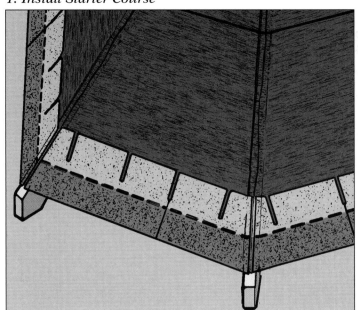

2. Start Installing Rows

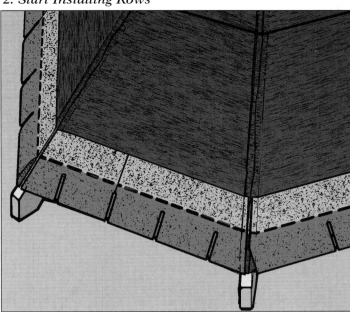

APPLYING SHINGLES

3. Maintain Consistent Spacing

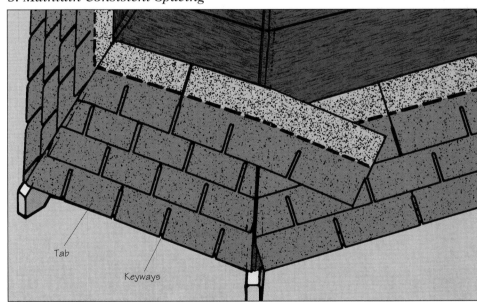

1. Install Starter Course

After installing the felt underlayment and metal drip edge, begin with a row of solid roofing along an eaves, using either starter-strip material or three-tab shingles turned upside down. Snap a chalk line to keep the top edges straight. Overlap the starter course 3/8 inch beyond the edge of the roof.

2. Start Installing Rows

Next apply the first row directly on top of the starter strip. Make sure the ends do not line up over the gaps below. Work from one end toward the other as far as you can reach, then begin the next course without changing your position. Start as many courses as you can reach before moving.

3. Maintain Consistent Spacing

The weather exposure for composition shingles is 5 inches. Keep the courses from drifting out of line by measuring up from the eaves at several points along the course being applied. Stop and check your progress from the ground to make sure your lines remain straight.

Nail each three-tab shingle using four nails, each about 3/4-inch above the top of the keyways.

When working on a six- or eight-sided gazebo, concentrate on installing the shingles in rows parallel to the bottoms of each panel. On the ridges that separate the panels, overlap the shingles. Cut them away in place. The ridge caps will cover up this unsightly overlap.

How to Cut Shingles

You'll save a lot of wear and tear on your knife by cutting asphalt and fiberglass shingles from the back. Use your knife to mark the top and bottom edges of the shingle, from the front. Flip the shingle over and cut through the marks. Save the larger pieces for use on the opposite rake.

4. Install Ridge Shingles

Apply Roofing Compound on Exposed Seams and Nail Heads

4. *Install Ridge Shingles*

Install the ridge shingles with the same amount of exposure. Fasten these shingles to the roof with two nails, one on each side of the ridge. Where the shingles meet the key block, fill the seam and cover the remaining exposed nail heads with roofing compound.

Applying Hip and Ridge Composite Shingles

Although hip and ridge shingles can be bought, it is easy to cut the required 12-inch squares from standard shingles, using a sharp utility knife. To shingle a hip, begin with a double layer of shingles at the bottom and work up to the peak. Leave a 5-inch exposure. Nail 1 inch in from the edge just below the self-sealing strip.

When shingling a ridge, begin at the end opposite from the prevailing wind. Apply roofing in the same way as hip shingles, caulking the exposed nail heads of the last shingle.

LATTICE ROOF INSTALLATION

Installing a lattice roof is more akin to installing trim than to any of the other roofing options. The lattice roof offers little in the way of structural strength; subsequently, special care should be taken during installation . . . you just can't climb on top to set the last screw.

1. *Install Bottom Cleats*

Rip 1-inch strips off a piece of 1-by stock and fasten them on both sides of the opening that you plan to install lattice in. Nail or screw the cleat 1³/₄ inches down from the top of the rafter.

It's not necessary to surround the lattice completely on all four sides. The lattice will not have any load resting on it, nor are the spans in the projects in this book that great to justify the extra support. On the Six- and Eight-Sided Gazebos, for example, there's no need to worry about cleating around the point. Leaving the base open emphasizes the stepped pattern of the lattice.

1. Install Bottom Cleats

Bottom Cleat

12"   12"   12"

Three shingles for use on a hip or ridge can easily be cut from one three-tab shingle.

2. *Measure & Cut Lattice*

Measure each opening individually, just in case they differ. Mark the measurements on each piece of lattice. Use a chalk line to ensure straight cut lines.

When cutting the lattice, rest the entire panel on a scrap of plywood. Make a straight edge jig by screwing a narrow board to a wider board. Trim the wider board by running the base of your saw against the narrow board. Clamp the jig along the chalk line. Adjust the depth of your saw's blade so that it cuts through the lattice and just barely scores the plywood underneath.

Install each cut panel on top of the backing cleats, and tack them in with a few brads.

3. *Install Top Cleat*

Cut the top cleat out of 1-by stock just as you did for the bottom cleat. Nail this cleat in to secure the panel.

FINISHING AND MAINTENANCE

Red cedar does not need any finishing or preservatives under ordinary weather conditions. It will weather naturally to a silver-gray color. Over a long period, it will become almost black. In year-round warm, humid areas such as the U.S. Southeast, or in any site below overhanging trees, you should use a fungicide to control mildew and fungus growth. Some shingles may come pretreated; you can also apply a wood preservative and water repellent after installation. Wood shingles and shakes may also be colored. Use a penetrating wood stain—not paint—for this job. (Paint will seal the shingles or shakes so moisture can't escape.) Composite shingles require no special attention.

Clean wood roofs periodically to remove accumulated debris and to prevent moisture buildup. Use a stiff broom or brush to keep the joints clear between the shingles.

2. Measure and Cut Lattice

3. Install Top Cleat

STAINS AND PAINTS

Your choice of stain or paint will do more than affect the way your outdoor structure looks, it will affect the life of your project. Stain and paint have different appearances, chemical properties, and coverage characteristics and should be chosen carefully. This chapter discusses and compares the available paints and stains that are most suitable for exterior application.

Stain has excellent hiding power and good color retention. Overall, it provides a more mellow look to a surface, since it allows the natural texture of the wood to show through a translucent color. Stains differ from paints in the way they adhere to wood. A stain penetrates into the surface of the wood, while paint creates a waterproof shell on the surface. In stained wood, moisture moves freely in and out so stain does not blister or peel off. There is no surface buildup with stain, thus no cracking or any of the other problems typically associated with multiple coats of paint. One possible disadvantage is that once you have chosen a stain color, you might be able to darken it with another stain, but you can't use another stain to lighten it. You can, however, cover over a dark stain with a light paint.

Paint is the choice for achieving an historically reminiscent appearance and the most effective way to protect wood from the elements. Paint creates a protective film that seals your project against moisture, insects, and the abrasion of everyday use. Because paint contains a higher proportion of pigment, painting is the most effective way to protect your project from the effects of UV radiation and to cover over knots or other imperfections in the wood.

STAINS

Stains come in a variety of colors, from the lighter shades of gray to the darker wood colors. How well a particular stain performs, depends not only on the stain itself but also on the type of wood it is covering and the climate of your area. Because they are not as durable as paint, stains require more frequent periodic refinishing.

Stains are available in both water- and solvent-based formulas. Water-based stains have less odor and are easier to clean up, but they tend to sit on the surface of the wood and may not last as long. Solvent-based stains sink deeper into the wood's pores to provide a longer-lasting finish.

If you wish to create a special color, tint bases are available in three grades of solid stains (light, medium, and dark) and two of semitransparent stains (light and dark).

Semitransparent Stains

Semitransparent stains are classified as pigmented penetrating finishes. The resin or oil in semitransparent stains soaks into the pores of the wood, acting as a sealer. Enough pigment remains on the wood's surface to affect the color without covering the grain pattern or creating a surface film. The pigment particles in a semitransparent stain act as UV absorbers or UV blockers, with the oils acting as the penetrating sealers. If you want the stain to resist water and rot, choose one that contains a water repellent and a preservative.

Because they are relatively thick and contain pigment, semitransparent stains should be mixed frequently to ensure color consistency. Be sure to order more than enough stain

to finish the job. Manufacturers sometimes discontinue or alter their selection of tints, so that one may not exactly match others made in a different batch.

Solid-Color Stains

Solid-color stains are sort of a hybrid between paints and stains. They are highly pigmented, and in this regard are actually more like thinned paint. But they do still show some wood texture like a stain. Because they are so heavily laden with pigment, solid-color stains will provide better UV protection than semitransparent stains. However, the disadvantage to this is that they do not sink in as deeply as the lighter-bodied stains and are less durable than semitransparents.

Solid-color stains are designed primarily for use on exterior siding and aren't recommended for horizontal surfaces, such as decks, where they would be worn down quickly by foot traffic. Latex solid-color stains do not penetrate as deeply as the oil-based variety and are even less weather resistant. When applying solid-color stains, it is best to pretreat the lumber with a paintable wood preservative to ensure a more even coat. Make sure that the product you use can accept a topcoat of stain.

Deck Stains

Deck stains are specially formulated to withstand not only the weather but also the abrasion that a deck receives from everyday foot traffic. They are typically alkyd oil based and contain water repellants to provide protection from moisture. Since they are available in shades that resemble cedar and redwood, deck stains are a way to change the look of your pressure-treated deck, while providing additional protection.

Deck stains are formulated for immediate application to new pressure-treated wood as well as periodic application to older decks. Deck stains can be applied by a variety of methods—spray, roller, pad, or dip. Your deck should be dry enough for use 24 hours after application.

SELECTING THE PROPER PAINT

Considering recent paint industry technology, there are several reasons why latex paints are preferred over oil-based paints. First, latex paint dries quicker, retains its color better, and stays on a project longer than oil-based paint. Latex paints dry to a rubbery film, which takes the flexing that results from changes in temperature and humidity. Since it is also more porous than oil-based paints, moisture can pass through it (this is called "breathing"), which helps prevent peeling.

Second, by using latex paint, you avoid the entire problem concerning volatile organic compounds (VOCs), the gases formed by the solvents that evaporate from oil-based paints. Several VOCs are known health and environmental threats; others are strongly suspected to be unhealthy. Some states and municipalities have made it virtually impossible to obtain and apply oil-based paint.

The third reason is cost. Latex paint costs less than oil-based paint. And with latex, you do not have to buy expensive solvents for cleanup—soap and water is sufficient.

There are not many applications that still require the use of oil-based paints instead of latex. When painting redwood or cedar, you may decide to use oil paints to block the resins that would bleed from the wood and stain the paint job. However, today there are also latex paints specially designed to prevent bleeding.

Watching the Weather

Proper painting procedure requires a dry and clean surface. The weather can seriously undermine the integrity of a paint job. Heat and cold must be considered. Remember that water is the solvent for latex, and rain can wash latex paint away if it's not fully dry.

Painting in Hot Weather

The hotter the weather, the quicker latex paint dries. When paint dries too fast it causes the following problems: brushes and rollers gum up, paint fails to bond properly with the surface underneath it, and uneven drying times cause a patchy appearance.

The ideal painting temperature is around 70°F, although you can do a perfectly good job when the temperature is in the 90s. If the temperature is between 55 and 70°, plan your work so that you are in the sun. If the weather is warmer, stay out of direct sunlight. During hot weather, do not paint on windy days, because wind speeds up drying.

Painting in Cold Weather

Latex paint does not cure at temperatures below about 45°F. That is why manufacturers' specifications always call for latex paint to be applied at temperatures no lower than 50°. It is best to plan paint

Hint

Checking for Moisture

It is okay to apply latex paint to a surface that is slightly damp (cool to the touch) but not wet. Let wet surfaces dry out before painting. If rain or dew gets on latex paint before it is dry, there may be no effect, but the paint may also mottle and blister or wash off entirely. If the paint bubbles it has to be scraped or sanded off before the surface can be repainted.

Cedar   Driftwood   Redwood

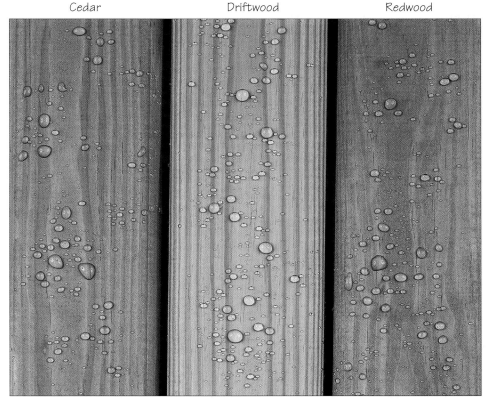

Natural-looking toners can transform CCA-treated southern pine into a host of attractive alternatives.

jobs for spring, summer, or early fall. Do not paint when the mercury falls below 50°. There are few things more discouraging than watching paint slide off the walls in sheets.

Porch and Floor Paint

If you choose to paint the decking of your project, use porch and floor paint. This is an oil-based, heavy-duty paint that is formulated to resist peeling and withstand the abuse of foot traffic and furniture scraping. Porch and floor paint usually comes in dark colors (black, battleship gray, dark green) to hide scrapes and markings. Prime new lumber with oil-based primer. When the primer is dry, sweep the deck clean and then roll on the porch and floor paint. This paint is extremely thick and does not need to be brushed in. You'll probably want to throw away the roller cover, as porch and floor paint is very difficult to clean off. Porch and floor paint dries to a hard, glossy finish and should last for several years.

PRIMERS

Priming is not so much the first coat of paint, as it is the last step of preparation. Primer allows the finish paint to stick—and stay stuck—to the surface. Primer provides resistance to moisture, fills in cracks, and smooths the surface; it also keeps stains, such as turpentine that weeps out of knots in wood, from bleeding through the finish coats.

Oil-Based Primer

An oil-based primer is considered best for general exterior use. Oil-based primers dry slower than latex primers and are absorbed deeper into the wood's pores. Latex primers that depend on a good surface bond may not adhere as well. Oil also has a moderate advantage in its ability to hold out stains for example, from knots. Once it has dried, you can use either a latex or an oil-based paint as a top coat. Be sure the surface is very dry, or the oil primer

will not adhere. If water gets between the wood and the primer, the primer can lose its bond, causing the paint to peel down to the bare wood.

Latex Primer

There are two disadvantages to using latex primers: latex-primed surfaces sometimes require an extra topcoat and latex primer sometimes allows rust stains from nailheads to show through the finish paint. (Even if you use hot-dipped galvanized nails, the rust-resistant coating takes a beating from hammers and nail guns.) If rust stains show through, your only alternative is to spot-prime the nailheads with an oil- or shellac-based primer.

Working with Primer

When applying a primer, cover everything that you intend to paint. With fascia and other trim pieces, it's a good idea to "backprime," which means covering all the surfaces, including the sawn edges that don't show. Backpriming will help restrict moisture movement and will extend the life of these decorative elements. Try priming the wood before installation. Although it seems like an extra step, priming first will save you time and money later on.

If you cannot adequately seal the more resinous knots try a shellac-based primer. These primers dry very quickly; most are ready for a top coat in less than 1 hour. The downside to these primers is that they cost quite a bit more than latex- or oil-based primers, and because they dry so fast they are not intended for large surfaces. For that reason, you might want to purchase just a small can to spot-prime the most difficult spots. When the patch has

dried, you can finish up with the regular primer.

As a general rule, the faster the primer dries, the sooner you should start painting. If the primer is allowed to weather beyond a critical point, it will fail or will cure so hard that the topcoat cannot stick to it. Read the manufacturer's specifications for the optimum time between priming and applying the topcoat. With some primers, you should recoat in a matter of hours. With others, you can wait a few weeks. Whatever you do, do not prime in the spring and plan to finish painting in the fall. You will end up redoing the entire job.

WHEN AND HOW TO PAINT

Ideally, you should paint or stain your project before it's even brought outside, but this is impractical. Painting blocks the UV radiation that breaks down the lignin in the exterior cells of boards exposed to sunlight. This breakdown affects the adhesion strength of any top coat. In fact, painting tests have observed a difference in bonding strengths when painting wood that received as little as four weeks of exposure.

Realistically, you should aim at finishing your project as soon as possible to avoid any damage to the wood. Of course, if your lumber is visibly wet, you will have to let it "weather," but only for a few weeks at most. The old rule of "waiting a year" is no longer considered the right way to do the job. By that time, the wood will already have been damaged enough to prevent you from applying a finish that will adhere well.

Chemical Compatibility

It's important to look for chemical compatibility when choosing a water-repellent primer and top coat. Buying materials from the same manufacturer helps ensure compatibility; however check all the labels just to be sure.

THE USE OF COLOR

Perhaps you will choose simply to paint your gazebo white. If you do, the result will look very elegant and tradition-al. If however, you choose to add color to your scheme, you'll also have plenty of historical precedent.

Before the era of premixed paints, white was a prevalent choice, main-ly because it was easy for painters to produce a reliable match. But even a century ago, some people began to think that white was used in excess. According to Samuel Sloan, one of America's most influential Victorian architects,

> *"The only color which meets the eye is white. Everything is white; the houses, the fences, the stables, the dog kennels, and sometimes even the trees cannot escape, but get a coat of white wash. . . . Is this taste?"*

Apparently, he thought not.

Houses built during the Victorian period were characteristically or-nate. At that time, those who began experimenting with color quickly recognized that a good color scheme could accentuate the architectural beauty of their home. Unfortunately, many others were still puzzled about what colors to use. To avoid confu-sion, they continued to rely on good old white. Today, many of us contin-ue to rely on white (or something near white) for all of our painting needs. But if you have made the effort to customize your project with elaborate cornice pieces or specialty-cut balusters, you really should con-sider a bolder use of color.

You may be thinking to yourself, "Now if the Victorians didn't know what colors to use, how am I sup-posed to?" Don't worry, chances are that if you are concerned with color, you already have a good eye for it. Predetermined color combinations

White is a simple, elegant color choice that has stood the test of time.

A carefully selected color scheme will make your gazebo a striking addition to your yard.

Whether you choose to use a combination of colors or paint your gazebo white, your goal should be to unify architectural elements.

and modern computer imaging will free you from much of the guess-work. And this chapter will provide you with the additional information you'll need to make the initial deci-sions on your own. Also included is information detailing the proper steps for achieving a historically accurate color scheme, one piece at a time.

EFFECT OF COLOR

Used properly, color can increase the feeling of space; act as a link to your house and the rest of your property; draw the eye; or act as a softening influence, letting your gazebo hide in a shady corner of the yard. Your overall goal should be, however, to create a unity of the architectural elements, where no single element dominates and the features of the house appear balanced.

In general, the same rules that apply to interior design also work outside. For instance, light colors will make your project feel larger; darker colors will make your pro-ject feel more intimate. Depending on your project's surroundings, both light and dark colors can be used to make your building stand out, as long as the color contrasts

with the background. Traditionally, when painting Victorian homes, architects would choose a darker paint for houses that were exposed and a very light shade for houses that were concealed within a knoll of trees or shrubs.

It's possible to enhance the effect of shadows by using light colors on projecting elements and dark colors on the insets. But be care-ful when applying accents. Subtle changes in color and small detailed highlights will do more for your project than you might think—whatever you think you like, try cutting it in half.

A high-contrast scheme holds the eye at each detail and will make your project appear smaller. To make you project seem larger, opt for a low-contrast scheme. Light colors reflect more light, heat, and UV rays so they tend to last a little longer; however, they also show more flaws in the prep work.

Color Considerations

There's more to consider than choosing your favorite colors. You should also think about how your project will fit in with the colors of your house and yard.

First consider the givens—colors that you cannot or will not change. These may include the colors of the roofing material, the nearby landscape, your house or perhaps your neighbors' houses. For example, using the same color as your house is a great way to tie your project in with the rest of your property, using a contrasting color will give the gazebo its own identity. Likewise, you will want to avoid clashing with the colors over which you have no control. It's also important to realize that if other elements are close enough, their reflected light can actually affect the way you perceive your chosen color.

Of course, you can overdo your con-cern with the givens. For instance, during the Victorian period, some people tried to "blend" their homes in with the surroundings by copying the harmonious colors of nature, such as soil, rocks, and wood. According to Henry Hudson Holly, another archi-tect of the period, too often the result was a dirty yellow house that seemed to spring up out of the mud.

USING A COLOR WHEEL

The purpose of a color wheel is not merely to demonstrate the relation-ships between colors but also to iden-tify particular associations between colors. Whether a color complements or contrasts with another color is not a matter of individual taste; even clashing can be predetermined by using a precise system. For example, colors that lie next to one another on the wheel share a common base color and are considered harmonious. Contrasting colors are located on opposite sides of the wheel. Following are some examples of various types of color pairs:

• Similar colors are nearby neigh-bors on the color wheel. Using colors that are too similar can create an awkward look. If the colors come from adjacent wedges of the wheel, or even the same wedge, vary them by pairing pastel, muted, or shaded versions. This is a great way to add

Understanding the Color Wheel

It is said that the human eye can distinguish more than 10 million different colors. But every one of them is based on red, blue, and yellow, plus black and white.

The color wheel shows how these basic colors relate to one another and how they combine to make all the other colors.

Primary Colors
The three key colors are pure red, pure yellow, and pure blue. These colors are considered primaries because you cannot mix them from other colors. All other colors are mixed from the primaries, white and black.

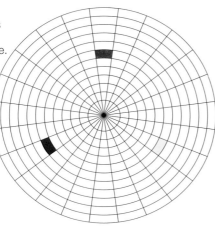

Pastel Colors
A pastel is simply a color mixed with white. Any pastel color will coordinate with any other pastel, even those opposite on the color wheel, because they all contain a lot of white. Pastels blend effortlessly with the lighter range of muted colors and with modern and traditional styles. Pastels can be used to create a light, airy feel.

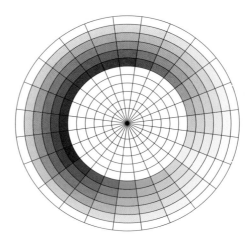

Secondary Colors
Orange, green, and violet are mixed from equal amounts of two primaries.

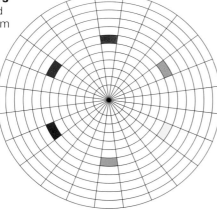

Shaded Colors
Pure colors that are darkened with black are known as shaded colors.

Muted Colors
Muted colors are pure colors mixed with varying amounts of black and white. The most neutral color of all is gray, which is simply a mixture of black and white. The gray scale on the drawing shows various mixtures of black and white. The boxes running along the top and right side of the drawing represent a wedge from the color wheel. All the other boxes show muted colors of a single hue.

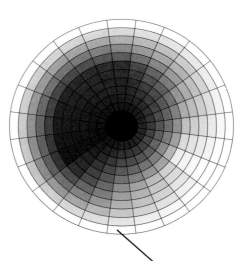

All Other Colors
In between the secondary colors comes an infinite array of intermediate colors. This chart slices the color continuum into 24 segments.

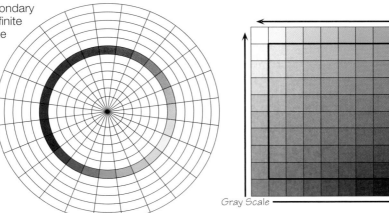

Gray Scale ➡

Borrowing the colors of nature will make your project blend into its surroundings.

visual interest to your scheme.

• Complementary colors are any two colors opposite each other on the wheel. They create a familiar contrast and are generally considered harmonious. When complementary colors are placed close together, they intensify each other, and the result is particularly vibrant. Contrasting colors used in equal amounts tend to compete with each other and can create an uneasy effect, so make sure that one dominates (is used more frequently) in the overall scheme. A good rule of thumb is to use the dominating color on at least two-thirds of the overall project. Use one as the base color and the other to accentuate special architectural elements.

• Triad harmony uses three colors that are equidistant on the wheel to create an exciting trio. As with complementary colors, it's important to have one dominating color so that the scheme does not feel too busy.

• Split complementaries consist of one color combined with the hues on either side of its contrasting color.

White, Black, and Gray

White, black, and gray are unique because they can be used to enhance the appearance of any color placed next to them. White will make colors appear deeper, black will make colors look lighter, and gray will make colors look richer.

Similar Colors

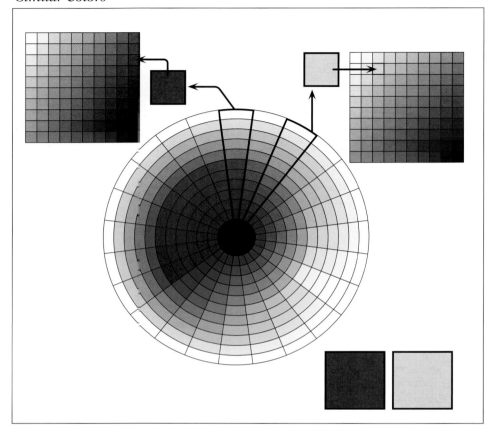

Complementary Colors

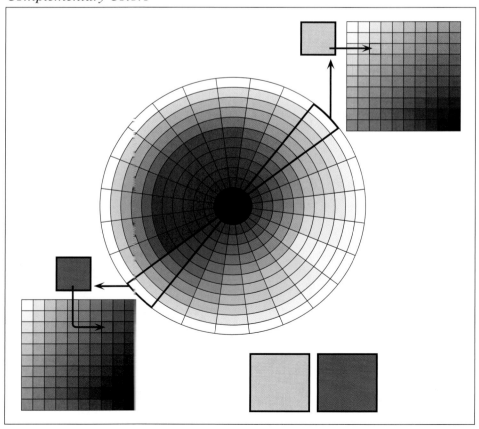

Triad Harmony

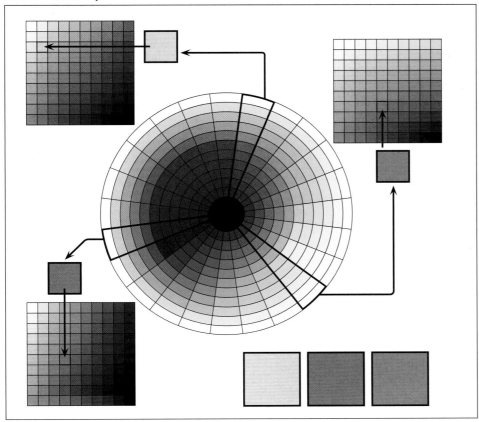

Split Complementary Colors

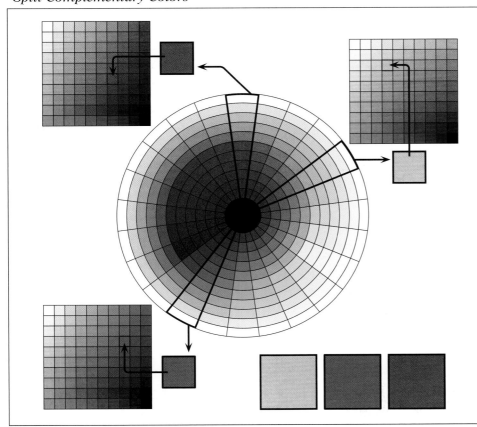

SELECTING A COLOR SCHEME

Even when you are equipped with an understanding of the effects of color and how colors interact, selecting a scheme for your particular project can still seem like a daunting task. Here are some specific procedures you can follow to help you zero in on the perfect color combination for your garden structure.

Determine the Color Values

You can start deciding on color placement without actually using color. Trace or sketch a line drawing of your project and then make several photocopies so you can try different schemes. Now, using a pencil, try shading different features to experiment with highlighting possibilities. Decide which features you would like to emphasize and which ones you would like to hide. The different degrees of shading will later correspond to appropriate values of color. (Value refers to the lightness or darkness of a color.) The goal here is to create a well-balanced whole in which no element seems to dominate.

Color In the Sketch

You can experiment with various color possibilities by coloring a sketch of your project. By "prepainting" in this manner, you not only will avoid any disappointment but will also be encouraged to try some distinctive schemes before you pick up the paintbrush.

Some paint stores feature computers that will "paint" your house for you right on the screen; these systems can also allow you to get some sense of how to paint your gazebo. The better systems are equipped to scan a high-contrast photo of your project; others have preprogrammed home styles. Even if you are unable to get an exact reproduction of your project, these programs will give you a sense of what sorts of combinations are pleasing and demonstrate some ideas of how you might distribute color on your project.

Testing Color

Everyone knows what white looks like, but if you decide to use something a little different, you should invest some time in testing that choice to make sure that it's the color that you think it is. Remember that perceived color is affected by several factors:

• Colors look different in different types of light. What you thought was a wonderful pink under the fluorescent lights of the paint store, may appear too pale or even garish in sunlight. The best place to compare colors is outside, preferably on a shady, or overcast day. That way you'll be able to study the color under the full spectrum of light, but without worrying about glare.

• Color is affected by the colors next to it. Pink might make a wonderful contrast to a blue trim, but it could also clash horribly with the pine trees in the yard.

• How much there is of a color affects how you see it. It is possible to have too much of a good thing. What looks fine on a can lid may not look as becoming covering your entire project. Colors seem to intensify with size.

The first thing you should do before selecting any color from a chip is to isolate it from the other colors on that card. Cut out a small frame of white paper to expose just one color value at a time. When you are starting to select color scheme combinations, try framing them against a white background, and then against a black background to help bring out the undertones in the colors.

Most professional color designers will not pick colors from chips. Chips are too small to show adequately the impact that the color will have on a large project. And since chips are printed from printer's inks and not pigment, you cannot be sure that the chip color will match the actual paint. You can avoid later disappointment by purchasing quart-size cans of paint and testing the colors on a scrap board or piece of plywood (this is called swatching). Paint large swatches and be sure that the colors that will be used together are located next to each other on your test. Try to swatch roughly the same percentage of area that each paint will cover on the project. Position the test board next to your project and note the colors at different times of the day since different levels of sunlight, will also affect how a color "reads." Remember also that the colors will seem to darken as the paint dries. It's also a good idea to look at your project from a distance so that you can get some idea of how the color scheme will work in with the rest of the yard.

PAINTING: WHAT GOES WHERE

Now that you have selected a color palette for your gazebo, it's time to decide which colors should be assigned to specific architectural elements. You can just go ahead and paint your project however you like, but chances are you won't be 100 percent delighted. Whether you have consciously thought of it or not, you have already chosen the "look" of your gazebo. And just as the colors have been determined through a set formula, the treatment of each piece of your project also must fit within certain guidelines to look "right." These guidelines do have a certain design basis, but they also represent an evolution in the use of color. People have been experimenting with color for centuries. When something looked good, others were more likely to copy it when it didn't, chances are it would wind up under another coat of paint

Each major architectural element of your structure will be discussed, along with suggested color specifications. Since these suggestions must be adapted to your own color scheme, actual colors are not mentioned as much as they are referred to in relation to the other colors and architectural elements in your project. An accurate Victorian color scheme warrants special attention, because it is probably the most color-specific. If you prefer a slightly different effect—for example, something suggesting a country or even an Asian decor—then these suggestions can be used as a general outline. Use the drawing on page 87 to help you identify various elements of a gazebo.

Roof

"A roof should not be painted in a light color, but some dark color that will strongly contrast with the main paint on the building." This advice from a Sherwin-Williams promotional book is as true today as was in 1884, the year it was published.

In the Victorian scheme, a dark roofs helps define the structure's boundaries and creates a feeling that the gazebo is firmly rooted to the ground. Typical Victorian colors include staining or painting roof shingles dark red, dark reddish brown, or dark olive green. Even if you are using composite shingles, various colors are available to assist your color scheme. These colors will also help the structure blend in to a natural setting.

Hint

Prefab Color Schemes

Deciding on the specific colors in a multicolor scheme is a little tricky. It's for that reason that almost all of the major paint companies have created "combo cards" to help you to pick base and trim colors in one step. These colors are available in historic shades designed to match the most prevalent color schemes of a particular period. One nice feature of these cards is that the trim and accent color chips often overlap the body color, which more realistically shows how the colors will look together.

Frieze

An historically appropriate treatment for the frieze is to use both the trim and body colors. Be careful not to introduce too many colors, though, you could end up with an effect that is too busy.

Corner Brackets

These are probably the most popular and most often incorrectly painted elements on Victorian structures. Brackets need to be perceived as part of the overall structure and should be painted so they do not appear to be "floating free" of the structure. Use the principal trim color. Avoid using too much color. Some painters add a leading edge of scarlet to their cornices; this may look nice, but it's a misunderstanding of the Victorian exterior decoration.

Posts

If you have simple rectangular wood posts you probably don't want to emphasize them with their own color. Paint them to match either the overall trim or body paint of your project. However, if your posts have special millwork, such as a chamfer on a square post or a ring on a turned post, it is perfectly acceptable to highlight these decorations with a flourish.

Rails

The rails are essentially extensions of the posts. Therefore, they are usually painted in the same color as the posts.

Balusters

Try painting the balusters a lighter color than the rails. If the posts and rails have been treated in the main body color, try using the trim colors to make them stand out. Even if you have elaborately worked balusters, don't use too many colors to demonstrate your handiwork. Besides the amount of time that would be involved in detailing each baluster, the effect will look busy.

Floors and Ceiling

Because a Victorian-style gazebo is a sort of detached porch, your gazebo will look traditional if you base your floor and ceiling color scheme on traditional porch colors. Victorian porches were painted certain colors, not only for decoration but for matters of practicality. Back then, porches needed to reflect light to keep them from being too dark. Painting porch ceilings blue is a technique that has been used for centuries to suggest the sky overhead. The gray floor is even more practical; it is less likely to show dust and tracks than lighter or darker colors. These color choices would be just as useful today for the same reasons that they were used a century ago. However, the trim or body color can also be used if it is neither too light nor too dark.

If the undersides of your gazebo ceiling rafters are exposed, you might paint them by using a combination of the body and trim colors.

Steps and Risers

The risers of wood steps are normally painted the trim color, while the treads carry the deck to the ground and should be painted in the same color as the deck.

The handrails and balusters on the steps follow the same rules applied on the gazebo itself; top and bottom rails in the trim color and the balusters in the body color.

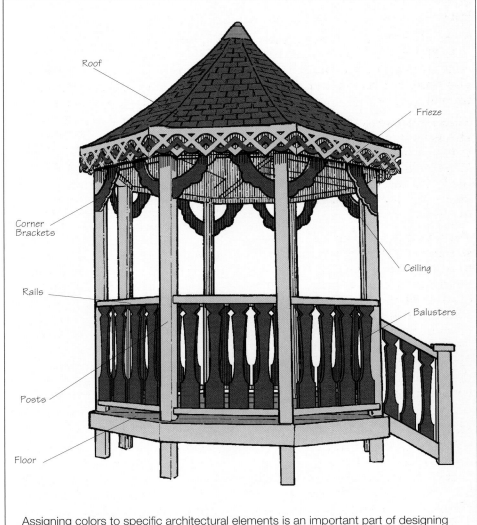

Assigning colors to specific architectural elements is an important part of designing a color scheme for your gazebo or other outdoor project.

CUSTOMIZING OPTIONS

Whether it is a railing of your own design or custom brackets, it's surprising how just a few simple design changes can make the difference between a "nice" gazebo and a project that perfectly complements your property.

Some of the options discussed in this chapter can be purchased premade at your lumberyard or home center (take your plans along so that you'll have dimensions handy and will know whether or not an accessory will fit in with your project). Other options will require

you to spend a little ime in the workshop. Making these accessories from scratch not only will save you money but will also allow you a chance to showcase your sense of style and woodworking skill. Either way, the final projec will be something that money can't buy.

This chapter introduces you to the various options, element by element. Some of these ideas can be used without any alteration to your project and can be attached to just about any structure. Others require a little more consideration and must be worked into your design before

construction. Read this chapter carefully and be sure that you understand just how a particular element will work in to your project before you start building.

POSTS

With the introduction of steam-powered woodworking machinery in the 1850s, elaborately turned posts were being produced by hundreds of small mills. Since most of these mills have closed down in the last century, people seem to think that they have no alternative but to use ordinary square-cut posts. This is not the case. Today, you can still purchase turned posts through a variety of specialty millwork catalogs and even in some lumberyards that carry special materials for restoration work.

Deciding to use turned posts instead of typical square-cut 4×4s can be one of the most dramatic enhancements to the appearance of your project. Although they may look spindly, especially when compared with square-cut posts, they have about the same compression strength as the thicker members and can be worked into any project in this book without any structural changes. Pressure-treated pine, redwood, and cedar spindles are all available to match any project. If you are planning to seal and paint them anyway, you can save money by using turned posts of poplar. Just be sure that your posts are designed to be load bearing and built specifically for outside use.

Another nice feature about using turned posts is that most manufacturers also make matching turned balusters. Using turned posts and balusters is a quick way to turn your project into a very elegant addition to your property. These turned elements do cost more than

Small details such as custom-cut slat railings and corner brackets can transform a plain gazebo into something special.

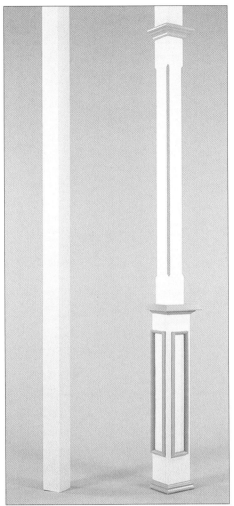

A few simple moldings and router cuts transform a plain 4x4 post into an architectural column.

Embellishing Square Posts

Even if you decide not to use turned posts, don't think that you have to settle for plain square-cut 4x4s. It's easy to build up your posts to resemble formal columns that would have cost hundreds of dollars if you had ordered them.

Baseboard and crown moldings can both be used to jazz up nondescript square posts. Build up the bottom with a combination of molding treatments to create a solid-looking pedestal.

Carefully miter the small sections of molding using either a miter box or a power saw. Fasten the pieces onto the posts using finishing nails. You will want to fill the nail holes with putty and paint the entire post to achieve a more elegant effect.

Another approach, which can be used alone or in conjunction with molding, is to rout decorative edges. By equipping your router with a few decorative bits, it's possible to do your own custom millwork. You can rout the posts themselves or you can rout pieces of 1-by and apply them to the posts.

RAILINGS AND BALUSTERS

Of all the decorative accessories mentioned in this chapter, the railing deserves special attention, be-

A little extra sawing and sanding finishes a rail with a hand-crafted look.

cause of its structural significance. People depend on the rail for support and protection; invariably they will be leaning against it or even sitting on it. It will have to withstand a great deal of use and abuse.

It's for these reasons that building codes have placed special requirements on the construction of railings. Whether or not your project is required to adhere to code (if you received a building permit, it will), it's common sense to follow their specifications to ensure a safely built project. Most building codes specify that railings must be 36 to 42 inches high. Whenever a deck is above a certain height (typically 18 inches), balusters should be placed no more than 4 inches apart. And, above all, make sure that your railing is securely fastened to the posts.

The simplest railing option is to use a 2x4 horizontally between each set of 4x4 posts. Cut the lengths to fit snugly. The rails can be secured either by toe-nailing them to the post or by using metal connectors, angle irons, or simple wood cleats. Additional 2x4 railings or 2x2 balusters can be installed to provide even more support.

If you are reading this chapter, you're interested not just in function, but also in form. There are several ways of beautifully integrating the railing in with the rest of your project.

the typical square-cut variety, but considering the relatively small size of your project and all the years that you will enjoy your outdoor haven, the difference in price is negligible.

Attach rails to posts with metal connectors or angle irons for strong construction. Horizontal rails may be supported on a wood cleat and toe-nailed to the post and cleat.

Balusters

There's no reason why you have to settle for the square-cut 2×2 baluster when turned spindles cost only a fraction more. These spindles are also available in pressure-treated wood as well as redwood and cedar. Spindles, like turned posts, are a nice option, because they offer just as much strength and security as square-cut stock, but they look lighter and less confining. What is especially handy about these turned balusters is the fact that they are formed from standard 2×2 CCA stock and, therefore, will fit into pressure-treated railings. Most suppliers offer matching posts and spindles, which create a very elegant effect.

Premade rails and channels make assembly easy and solid.

Premade Rails and Channels

Premade rail and channel molding pieces can speed up assembly while giving you a professional-looking result. Essentially, these are 2×4s or 2×2s that have a double groove routed on one face to receive either 2×2 balusters or lattice panels. The grooves ensure that the balusters or panels are properly seated and reduce the amount of toe-nailing required.

Turned balusters are a beautiful alternative that costs only a bit more than square-cut balusters.

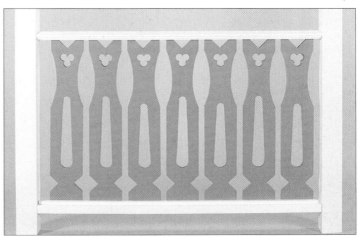

The top 2×4 rail pieces are milled to resemble and feel like a traditional curved rail. To fasten the balusters to the rail, nail through the top of the 2×4 directly into the ends of each baluster. Lattice may require using additional strips of lath on the edges to provide a larger nailing surface and to help wedge the lattice into the groove.

Premade mortised rails are one of the easiest ways to add an elegant detail to any rail unit. These rails are also designed to work with standard 2×2 rails, so you can "mix and match" various stock pieces to create your own unique railing.

Custom Building a Slat Railing

Factory-cut slats are available through many custom millwork companies, but the cost of these pieces might be a little intimidating. You can save a lot of money by

Railing slats can be made in an endless variety of styles.

doing the cutting yourself. Following are instructions for cutting 1-by slats that can be used instead of typical 2×2 balusters. Use these instructions as a guide; you may decide to use one of the patterns presented here, or you can create

your own. The patterns shown have been drawn on a grid in which 1 box equals 1 inch.

Using a design element from your house is a great way to integrate your project with the rest of your

1. Cut Slats to Size

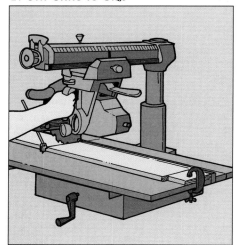

property. Just remember that you will have to do a lot of cutting, so it's advisable to keep the design simple. When cutting custom slats, it is also a good idea to try to make sure that your slat width will fit evenly between the posts. The best way to ensure against having to cut a strip off one or more slats is to position all of the the slats in place before you fasten them to the rail. That way, any large gap on one side can be evenly worked in to the spaces between each slat.

When cutting balusters, or any of the other custom accessories in this chapter, it helps to first use a drill or drill press equipped with a circle cutter to cut out the circles. A Forstner bit, a hole saw, or even a sharp spade bit will cut the curves quickly and more uniformly than a saw blade. A drilled hole also allows a blade more room to negotiate sharp turns.

Hint

Water has a bad habit of collecting in the routed grooves of bottom rail sections and channel moldings. Eventually, this will lead to some sort of water damage, unless you take the proper precautions. When using these pieces, drill 3/8-inch-diameter "weep holes." Space the holes about every 8 inches.

2. Create the Template

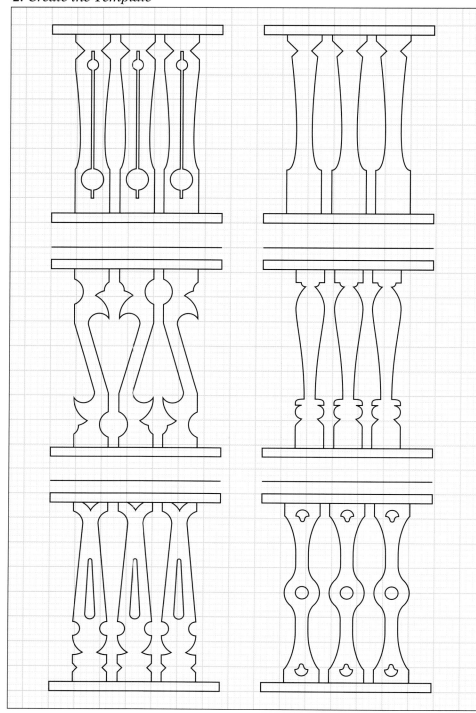

1. Cut Slats to Size

Using $5/4$x6-inch decking boards, 1x6 stock, or a good quality plywood (at least $5/8$ inch thick), rip and cut the desired number of slats. All of the slats in the patterns are 29 inches long, which will create a rail that is 36 inches tall. You can adjust the length if you want a lower rail.

2. Create the Template

Enlarge one of our designs or draw your own slat pattern on a scrap of hardboard. Cut the hardboard with a band saw or a saber saw to make a template. Use this template to mark the pattern on all the slats. (**Note:** If you can stack and cut the slats, you'll only have to mark every other or every third board.)

3. Cut the Slats

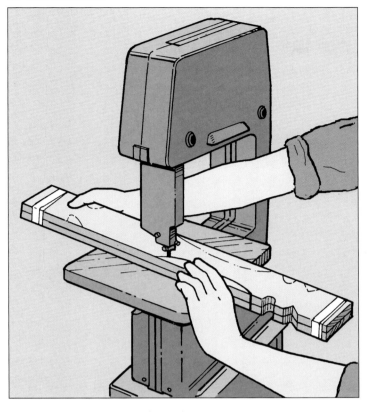

4. Install Rails & Ledgers

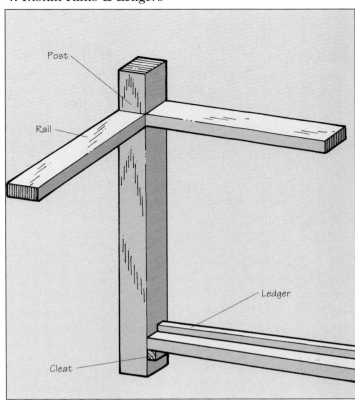

5. Install Slats & Inside Ledger

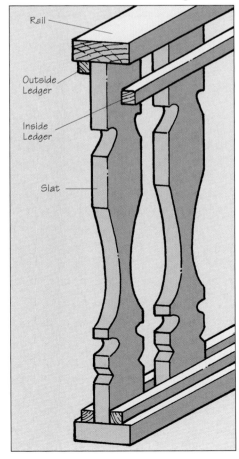

3. Cut the Slats

If you have a band saw, stack and tape two or three slats together, with a marked slat on top. Cut the pattern. If you are using a saber saw, you might still be able to stack and tape two slats at a time. Cut slowly to prevent the blade from drifting off the pattern line.

4. Install Rails & Ledgers

Rip ³/4x1-inch ledgers from 1x4 stock. Cut the two outside ledgers to fit between the posts, underneath the top rail and on top of the bottom rail. Nail the outside ledgers in with 6d common nails or use 1½-inch bugle-head screws.

5. Install Slats & Inside Ledger

Place the slats between the top and bottom rails and against the outside ledgers, spaced ¹/2 to ³/4 inch apart. Adjust the positions of the slats until they appear to be spaced evenly. Use 6d common nails to toe-nail the slats in place into the top and bottom rails.

Cut the inside ledgers to fit between the posts. Nail these ledgers in with 6d commons.

CORNER BRACKETS

The corner bracket is commonly referred to as Victorian gingerbread, because it resembles the fancy sugar frosting trim common on a gingerbread houses. These trimmings, also called carpenter's lace, bric-a-brac, and carpenter Gothic, have been integral to American architecture since the middle of the 19th century. A striking result of the advent of steam-powered woodworking machinery, these brackets add a sense of weight and solidity to the

Hint

It is difficult to prime and paint the slats once you've installed them. The job will go a lot quicker and look more professional if you paint the slats before you put them in.

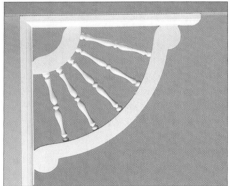

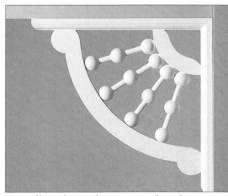

Whether you cut your own or order them from a millwork catalog, corner brackets are an excellent way to integrate the roof with the rest of the project.

homes of the period. Corner bracket treatments are an excellent way of integrating the roof with the posts and the rest of the structure.

These elements are available in just about any home center or millwork catalog, but because they are particularly labor intensive, they can be fairly expensive. There's no reason why you can't make these brackets on your own. All you need is a saber saw (or band saw) and a little patience. Make sure that you use a water-resistant glue.

Note: Because of the short span between the posts on most of the projects in this book, corner brackets may not work well with other pieces of top trim, like a frieze board. For this reason you should decide which particular element you would rather incorporate into your project before you start building.

Mahogany, cedar, redwood, and oak will all work well for corner brackets. Fir, pine, and poplar are also good choices, especially if the brackets will be painted. It is important to use tight-grained, knot-free wood on larger, more elaborate pieces, but you'll discover that

No. 2 pine can be used effectively on smaller jobs. When laying out your pattern, run the longest dimension parallel with the grain of the wood.

Brackets can be secured with finishing nails, but since you have

spent the extra time building them, you may want to screw them on through predrilled holes, minimizing the chance of splitting or dinging the bracket with a misaimed hammer stroke. For the templates shown, 1 square equals 1 inch.

Corner Bracket Templates

FRIEZES

A frieze is another classic element that you may choose to customize your project. Essentially, a frieze is a band, or line, near the roofline that adds a decorative flair to your project. The frieze is built similarly to a railing, but the stock dimensions are smaller.

Building a Frieze

You may choose to copy one of the classical patterns shown on page 97. These patterns are shown against a grid in which 1 box equals 1 inch. Most older houses, and some newer ones, have a particular pattern right under the roofline. Copying this frieze pattern off your home would be a one way of integrating your project with the rest of your property.

1. Create & Cut Out the Pattern

Trace your frieze pattern on a scrap of hardboard. Cut the hardboard with a band saw or

saber saw to make a template. You will use this template to mark the pattern on all the slats. If you have decided on a repeating pattern, it is not necessary to create

A frieze is a decorative element below the roof. It can take many forms.

a pattern that will reach the full length of the frieze. Instead make a template of one or two repeat units that you can move down the board.

Using 1-by stock that is wide enough to fit your entire pattern, cut each board to length to fit exactly between each pair of posts. Remember that on some projects, the edges will have to be mitered to fit flush. Label each board to ensure that they are installed between the posts that they were cut to fit.

2. Lay Out & Cut the Frieze
Mark the center of each frieze board. Starting from the center, transfer the template pattern onto each of the boards. Starting at the center and working out is the best way to ensure that the pattern ends evenly on both sides of each board.

3. Attach Finished Frieze
Rip 1 1/2-inch strips from a piece of 1-by stock and cut them to the same lengths as the prepared frieze boards. You will have to miter the ends of the cleats to match the mitered frieze boards against the posts, or you can simply cut the cleats 1 inch shorter on each end so that they can clear the posts. Attach the frieze board to the cleats using either 6d finishing nails or 1 1/2-inch screws. Use 1 1/2-inch screws to fasten the cleats to the 2x4 cap plates. Drill these screw holes to prevent splitting.

1. Create & Cut Out the Pattern

2. Lay Out & Cut the Frieze

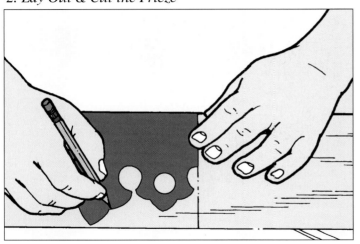

3. Attach Finished Frieze

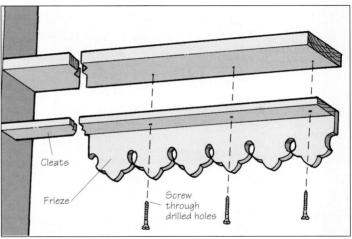

Cleats

Frieze

Screw through drilled holes

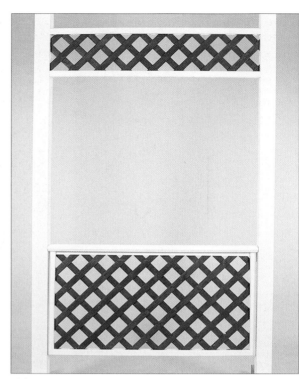

Full-length lattice walls (left) offer privacy without blocking breezes. A railing and frieze made of lattice (right) tie a project together.

LATTICES

Lattice can be effectively used for a variety of different applications for your project. It can provide shade, privacy, protection, or simply a place for climbing flowers to grow. It's easy to use lattice as a railing treatment, in a frieze panel, or even as a wall-size panel.

Lattice panels are available in pressure-treated wood, redwood, and even plastic. A panel is composed of two layers of strips oriented to overlap each other at a 90-degree angle and form a grid that is stapled or nailed together. Vinyl lattice panels are fused together with a solvent during production. Several different grid densities are available. Stiffer, heavier lattice panels are made from ³/8-inch-thick lattice strips and would be a good investment if you expect the panels to receive a lot of abuse.

Building with Lattice

Because the panels are relatively delicate, lattice must be handled and installed carefully. Store lattice panels flat until you're ready to use

them. Left standing on their edge, these panels will bow or even come apart. Lattice panels should be installed in a frame to hide and protect their edges. Channel molding is very helpful when using lattice; that way, the panel's entire edge can rest in the groove.

The following instructions describe how to use lattice panels to build an enclosed railing. Since the installation steps for including lattice in any of these applications is nearly identical, simply substitute your specific measurements and use these steps as a general outline.

Lattice Panel Installation

1. Install Channel Molding or Backing Cleats

For a post-and-rail framework, first fasten the backing cleats to the posts and rails, using either galvanized finishing nails or screws. If you use screws, drill holes to avoid splitting the wood.

If you opt to use channel molding, install bottom and side pieces with galvanized 4d finishing nails, but

leave the top molding off until the lattice panel can be slid into the side and bottom channels. Be sure to drill ³/8-inch-diameter drainage holes through the bottom channel molding about about every 8 inches.

2. Cut & Install Lattice

Place the panel on a flat surface (such as a sheet of plywood). Mark the cutting lines by snapping a chalk line or using a pencil and straightedge. Use a straightedge jig as described on page 77. Adjust your saw's depth of cut to match the thickness of the panel before making the cut. Most lattice panels are stapled together at each intersection. Don't worry, it's okay to cut through these staples, but it's all the more reason to invest the extra money in a carbide-tipped blade. And, as always, make sure that you are wearing safety glasses or goggles.

Find some one to help hold the panel against the backing cleats until the front cleats are installed. You can also try tacking the panel to the backing cleats with several brads.

Install the front cleats, holding each one firmly against the panel.

1. Install Channel Molding or Backing Cleats

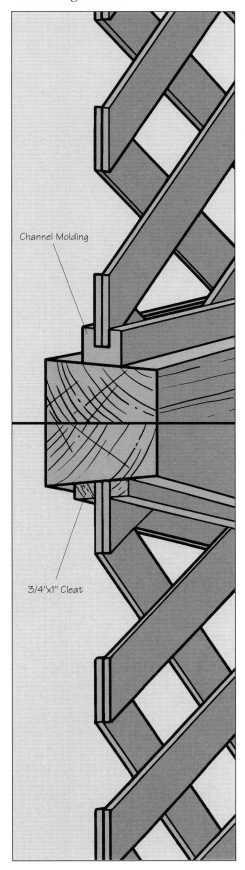

Channel Molding

3/4"x1" Cleat

2. Cut & Install Lattice

If you're using molding, fasten the top piece to the underside of the top rail, then install the top rail.

TONGUE-AND-GROOVE FLOORING

If you were to examine the floorboards of a older porch floor, you would notice that it was not made of the typical 5/4-inch biased-edged decking boards that is so prevalent today. Porches typically have floors made of tongue-and-groove boards. Each board is milled with a tongue on one edge and a groove on the other edge. The tongue of one board fits into the groove of the next to make a tight, strong floor.

Besides providing a neater overall appearance, tongue-and-groove floorboards have some structural advantages over regular decking material. Since the boards interlock, tongue-and-groove floors distribute loads better than regular decking; the floor acts more like a

single unit than individual boards. Tongue-and-groove floors are also much less likely to develop wide cracks like planking does when wet wood starts to shrink as it dries out. Tongue-and-groove floors aren't a good idea for projects that don't have rain-shedding roofs. the boards don't allow water to run through the way 5/4-inch decking does. The water will puddle on the surface and will eventually damage the wood. When working with roofed or enclosed projects, like the gazebo projects in this book, tongue-and-groove flooring is a viable (and historically accurate) option.

Traditionally, tongue and groove boards were also used to conceal the rafters in the porch ceiling. These boards are installed just like the flooring boards, except that everything has to be done overhead. Renting a pneumatic nailer will make this awkward job much easier.

Installing Tongue-and-Groove Flooring

1. Lay Starter Board

Snap a work line that is 1/2-inch less than the thickness of the board. This will start the first board with the overhang that you want for the deck. Lay out the first line of boards so that the tongues are positioned to receive the next course. Drill holes into the back edges of the boards and over the joists and face nail this starter course to the joists.

2. Nail Through the Tongue

Drill holes through the tongue of the first course of boards into the joists. Use casing nails and set them with a nail set.

3. Laying the Field

Lay out several courses of board in the way that they are to be installed. Try to stagger the joints so that no adjoining joint is on the same joist. Fit the boards so that each row runs over the edge of the deck by at least 1/2 inch (the excess will be cut off later).

4. Fitting & Nailing

As you lay each row, use a scrap tongue-and-groove board as a tapping block. Do not hit the block too hard or you may damage the tongue. To keep from marring the board with the hammer when you nail, do not hammer nails flush into the tongue. Instead leave the nail head exposed, and hammer it home with a nail set.

1. Lay Starter Board

2. Nailing Through the Tongue

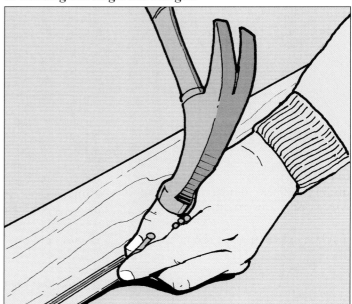

3. Laying the Field

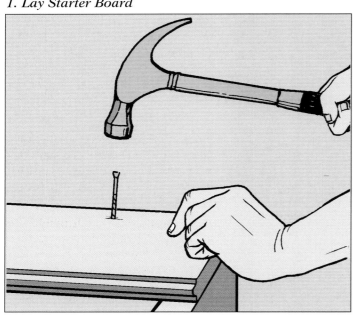

4. Fitting & Nailing

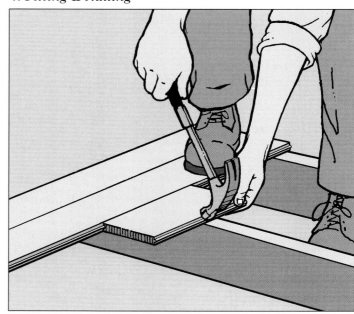

MAINTENANCE

Your project will begin its battle with the forces of nature the moment you set the first post. Sunlight will erode it. Moisture changes will crack it. Insects and fungus will eat it.

The most effective defense is a judiciously maintained paint job. But if you have invested in the natural beauty of redwood, cedar, or even teak, painting is not an option and staining may not be your first choice. There are other defense strategies. You can use water repellents, wood preservatives, clear penetrating finishes, or any combination of the three to add years to a structure's useful life and keep it looking good.

Before deciding what preservatives to use on your project, it helps to understand the natural forces that will work to destroy it.

INSECTS AND FUNGUS

Like all living organisms, wood-eating insects and rot-causing fungus have four basic needs: food, water, air, and warmth. Remove any one of these elements and a well-built structure will last indefinitely. Of course, it's not possible to keep air or warmth away from an outdoor structure, so that leaves you the choices of removing the water and removing the food.

Remove the Food

Wood preservatives work by poisoning the food. Some woods, including redwood and cedar, have natural rot- and insect-repelling toxins. But no natural toxin is as effective as pressure treating with chromated copper arsenic (CCA).

Wood that has been pressure treated does not rot because organisms will not eat it. For this reason, pressure-

Regular application of preservative can keep your project looking new like the decking boards at the left.

treated wood is an excellent choice for wood that will be in contact with the ground, a situation that makes it nearly impossible to eliminate moisture. (There is one exception to this rule. CCA-treated wood does not hold up as well in a marine environment. Apparently, there are some sea critters that consider chromated copper arsenic rather tasty!)

An advantage of pressure treatment is that the poison cannot leach out to harm animals, plants, or the environment. Of course, you release these dangerous chemicals whenever you saw the wood. Also you should never sand or burn pressure-treated wood, because these practices will release large amounts of toxic chemicals.

There are other chemicals that you can apply to wood on your own. These chemicals are safer than the older types of preservatives, but they still cannot provide the ground-contact protection of pressure-treated wood. This difference is due to the methods of application. These chemicals are applied only on the surface and not injected into the wood. Both will keep fungus and

termites at bay reasonably well as long as the wood is not constantly wet. In areas of prolonged exposure, pressure-treated wood is still your best choice.

Copper napthenate is a fungicide that has been used safely for many years. This heavy-duty green preservative is designed to protect any wood that will be in contact with soil or water. It can be applied by brushing, dipping, or spraying. Because it is nontoxic to plants and animals, it is especially ideal for treating garden structures. This preservative can also be used to treat

Hint

Toxic Compounds

Although they were once highly regarded as effective chemical preservatives, the EPA has labeled several compounds highly toxic to humans: creosote, inorganic arsenic compounds, and pentachlorophenols. These chemicals have been proven to be poisonous to you and your garden. And improper disposal of these products will create still more problems. Simply stated, don't use these chemicals at all.

the ends of freshly sawn pressure-treated boards to ensure uniform weather resistance.

Zinc napthenate is another type of preservative that also has been used safely for many years. It is designed to protect wood above ground from rot and mildew while allowing the surface to weather naturally. This preservative is traditionally used on fences, outdoor furniture and wood house siding. It can be applied by brushing, dipping, or spraying.

Both copper and zinc napthenates typically include water repellents (such as paraffin) in their formulations to help prevent wood warping and cracking. It should also be noted that although the EPA considers these chemicals "safe," proper precautions should be taken, since both are toxic in the concentrations used during application.

REMOVING THE MOISTURE

Fortunately, removing the moisture doesn't mean the wood can never become wet. It just means the wood must be able to dry out before mildew and mold get a chance to do any damage. That's why wood siding and roof shingles don't rot even though they get wet with every rain. A deck in direct sunlight is probably safe from rot, especially if you have thwarted termites by building the under-structure out of pressure-treated wood. But decking under shade trees is particularly susceptible to rot. Not only is there no sun to dry out the wood but leaves and other bits of tree debris that accumulate on your deck retain additional moisture.

Although mold and mildew limit their activities to the wood's surface, they can attract other micro-organisms and insects that feed on the cellulose cell structure of the wood. Wood-eating insects such as termites, carpenter ants, and bees will bore through the wood, leaving a riddled shell with little structural strength.

One surprisingly effective way to thwart rot is simply to keep your outdoor structure clean. A regular thorough sweeping will keep moisture-retaining debris from collecting in the cracks.

EFFECTS OF RAIN

Moisture can attack outdoor wood in a way that has nothing to do with rot. Wood swells when it's wet, and shrinks when it's dry; this natural tendency is exacerbated by freeze-thaw cycles. Cycling through these conditions will really take a toll on boards, especially at all the points where boards are fastened. Following a good rain, the underside of a decking board will retain moisture while the sun-drenched surface will quickly dry. The difference in moisture will create stresses that can eventually lead to cupping, cracking, and splitting. Boards may even begin to pop free from their fasteners. These cracks and other nail holes will serve as new spots for water to seep into, creating even more water damage down the line.

Pressure treatment and other chemical preservatives are not designed to provide defense against this kind of moisture damage. Moisture will move in and out of a treated board just as readily as if the board had not been treated. Either way, the board will have the same tendency to crack, split, and warp.

In general, heavier woods (for example, southern pine, the most common pressure-treated wood) will suffer more from moisture movement than will lighter woods. Heavier woods are denser, and so have more internal tension. Lighter woods, such as redwood and cedar, are more spongelike; moisture can pass through them with much less effect.

The only defense against water movement is to reduce it by using a water repellent. An excellent water repellent is a good coat of paint. The alternative is a clear repellent often marketed as a sealer. The most common clear repellents on the market are little more than paraffin wax dissolved in mineral spirits. When you apply the repellent, the solvent evaporates, leaving the wax in the pores of the wood. The wax impedes the flow of water vapor in and out of the wood and this decreases the rate of expansion and contraction. As a result, the wood is less likely to cup. You can buy water repellents that also contain fungicides. Exterior stains often contain paraffin and fungicide.

Some clear penetrating finishes are formulated with linseed oil, tung oil, or alkyds, like many paints or varnishes; but instead of acting as a film-forming agent, the resin will act as a sealer. A limited amount of resin can help seal the wood and will accent the grain pattern. But some care should be taken with these finishes, since multiple coats could create a build up.

EFFECTS OF THE SUN

Sunlight, or more specifically ultraviolet (UV) light, is the single most pervasive weathering factor on any exterior structure. Fortunately, the effect is cosmetic, not structural. UV radiation breaks down the lignin (the binding agent that holds the cells together) in exterior wood cells, but only penetrates to a depth of about $1/100$ inch. The damaged cells will block out any further degradation, unless the loose fibers are washed away by either wind or rain. Don't worry too much—the combined effects of these two weathering agents is, on average, about $1/4$ inch per century.

Absorbers, Blockers, and Inhibitors

If you want to prevent the weathering effect of the sun, look for a finish that contains either UV absorbers or UV blockers. Absorbers and blockers are particles that either absorb or reflect UV light to minimize its effect on the wood. There are also more expensive finishes that contain UV inhibitors. These compounds are designed actually to disrupt the normal chemical action caused by UV light. Sealers containing UV inhibitors are more expensive than sealers containing either absorbers or blockers, but are not that much more effective in the long run. UV inhibitors disrupt the chemical reaction caused by UV light, but it breaks down in the process and becomes less effective. In comparison, the particles in the other two compounds do not degrade under UV radiation and provide more consistent protection.

All of these finishes will need to be reapplied typically every other year.

FILM-FORMING FINISHES

You might think that by using a clear polyurethane or other similar film-forming finish (such as clear varnish), you would be able to achieve a more durable finish while still preserving the appearance of the wood. Clear film-forming finishes such as these are not generally recommended for extended outside wear.

Polyurethane is generally not suitable for sealing decks or other outdoor structures because it is hard and inflexible. It tends to crack and flake, rather than moving with the wood through natural changes in temperature or moisture.

The other problem with a clear polyurethane finish is that it still allows UV rays through to the wood. The UV light destroys the lignin in the cells as if the wood were unfinished. When the surface cells have been broken down, the polyurethane has nothing left to adhere to and will start flaking off in sheets.

Reapplying a new coat on top of a cracked one is extremely difficult, since the first coat has to be completely stripped. Stick with penetrating finishes or paint for outdoor structures.

Polyurethane can be used effectively on portable projects such as outdoor furniture that you want to protect yet still show off the wood. Make sure you use polyurethane formulated for exterior use. You can extend the life of the finish (and the project) by bringing it inside for the winter.

For those who insist on using polyurethane, there are mixes available that contain powdered iron oxides. These formulas are not perfectly clear. They will add a tint of orange or red to the overall color, but these particulates make the project completely opaque in the UV spectrum. They can extend the useful life of the finish from 1 to 3 years.

APPLICATION

The thing to remember when applying a penetrating finish is that you want the wood to absorb as much as it can. By its very nature, you will not be able to notice brush marks, and any finish that isn't absorbed can be wiped off. The most common mistake when applying finish is not using enough to saturate the wood fibers. Remember that the end grain of a dried piece (such as the ends of posts or railings) will absorb sealer almost as quickly as you can brush it on. Check these spots during application and reapply as necessary.

Avoid breathing vapors or spray mists. Work outside. Wear rubber gloves and long-sleeved garments during application to reduce exposure and minimize the chance of skin irritation. Always wear goggles or safety glasses to protect yourself from any backspray or drips.

1. Prepare the Wood
Sanding cedar, redwood, or cypress will increase the sealant's penetration and give you a cleaner-looking surface. Do not sand pressure-treated wood. Sanding will release the toxins

1. Prepare the Wood

2. Apply the Finish

3. Remove Excess Finish

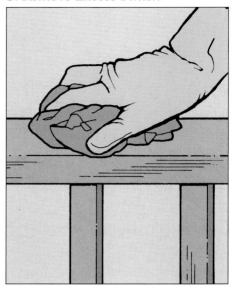

bonded to the wood's cells and could make you sick. The best way to clean the wood before finishing without exposing yourself to any toxins is to use a power washer.

The timing of your application is not that critical. Two dry, windy days should be an adequate amount of time for your project to dry sufficiently to accept a finish.

2. Apply the Finish

Horizontal decking boards can be coated with a roller or spray equipment. (Small pump-pressured sprayers can be purchased inexpensively at most hardware stores.) Follow the sprayer with a brush to spread out the finish. Apply the sealer to the underside of decking and to joists, beams, and posts. For posts, railings, and stair stringers, brush application is best. Remember that visible end grain will absorb more sealer than the flat surfaces.

3. Remove Excess Finish

With a clean rag, wipe off excess finish that isn't absorbed after a half hour. Be sure to dispose of all rags properly. The heat generated from the evaporating finish can cause rags to burst into flame. Allow used rags to dry completely

outside before disposing. If the rags will be reused, store them in an airtight container.

DIPPING

Short of pressure treating, dipping is the most thorough way of applying sealant after a piece has been cut to size. In this kind of treatment, the wood is immersed in a bath of sealant for several minutes, and then allowed to air dry. This maximizes coverage and penetration.

There are some drawbacks to this method, however. Logically, the dip treatment can be done with lumber only before it is nailed in place. And it is time consuming, because you must allow each piece to soak. The size of the trough also limits the size of the members that you will be able to dip.

While it may not be practical to dip decking boards, you might consider the dip treatment for balusters or shorter parts of the project that can benefit from complete coverage. For instance, if you are using more expensive, turned balusters, you might want to give them extra protection to prevent them from cracking or splitting.

One way to make a dip treatment trough is to place a seamless plastic sheet in a wooden frame. The frame should rest on a flat surface. Use a heavy-duty sheet (6 mil) and make sure that its edges are well away from the edges of the frame. Including a drying rack to your trough will enable your pieces to dry while funneling back excess sealant.

Any excess sealant can be reused. Filter out the wood and debris through a piece of cheesecloth, and store the remaining sealant in a tightly sealed container.

Make a temporary trough to completely seal small parts.

Part 2

Gazebos:
- SQUARE HIP ROOF
- SIX-SIDED
- EIGHT-SIDED

Pavilions:
- WITH GABLE ROOF
- FREESTANDING

Arbors:
- OPEN AIR
- WITH DECK
- PICNIC TABLE

Gazebo

SQUARE HIP ROOF

CUTTING & MATERIALS LIST

Name	Quantity	Size
Gazebo Deck Framing		
Posts (Roof Support)	7	4"x4"x8'
Posts (Rail)	2	4"x4"x54"
Beams	6	2"x8"x8'
Stringer and Intermediate Joists	4	2"x6"x93"
Header Joists	2	2"x6"x8'
Center Joist	1	2"x6"x89½"
Decking Cleats	8	2"x6"x5"
Decking Cleats (Middle)	2	2"x6"x6½"
Stair Stringers	3	2"x10"x30"
Stair Treads	4	⁵⁄₄"x 6"x33"
Decking	18	⁵⁄₄"x 6"x10'
Roof Framing		
Top and Cap Plates	8	2"x4"x89½"
Key Block	1	5½"x5½"x 8"
Common Rafters	4	2"x6"x59"
Hip Rafters	4	2"x6"x74¼"
Long Hip Jacks	8	2"x6"x39¾"
Short Hip Jacks	8	2"x6"x20½"
Rafter Fascia	4	1"x8"x94½"
A/C Exterior Grade Plywood Sheathing	4	¾"x4'x8'
15-lb. Roofing Felt		100 sq. ft.
Metal Drip Edge	4	8' lengths

Name	Quantity	Size
Composite Shingles		100 sq. ft.
Composite Hip and Ridge Shingles		Needed to cover approximately 26'
Railing		
Rails	12	2"x4"x41¼"
Front Rails	4	2"x4"x20½"
Rail Cap Piece	2	1½"x5½"x5½"
	2	1½"x3½"x3½"
Balusters	48	2"x2"x30"
Nails & Fasteners		
Carriage Bolts	18	³⁄₈"x8"
Nails		
16d Common		
12d Common		
10d Common		
8d Common		
10d Finishing		
Roofing		
Post Anchors	9	
Stair Angles	4	
Framing Angles		2 for stair stringers
Premixed Concrete		As required to set post & step footings below frost line

This basic gazebo plan offers many advantages. First of all, it is square, so the need for the many special-angle cuts that you would find with six- or eight-sided gazebos is eliminated. The 8-foot-square design is modular, so standard-length lumber can be used with a minimum of cutting.

The roof in this roof-over-deck design is supported by 4x4 posts. The deck size is 8 feet across with a deck-to-roof distance of 78 inches. These proportions create an intimate, cozy structure. (Read this entire chapter as well as "Roofing" and "Customizing Options" before finalizing your design.)

Overall View

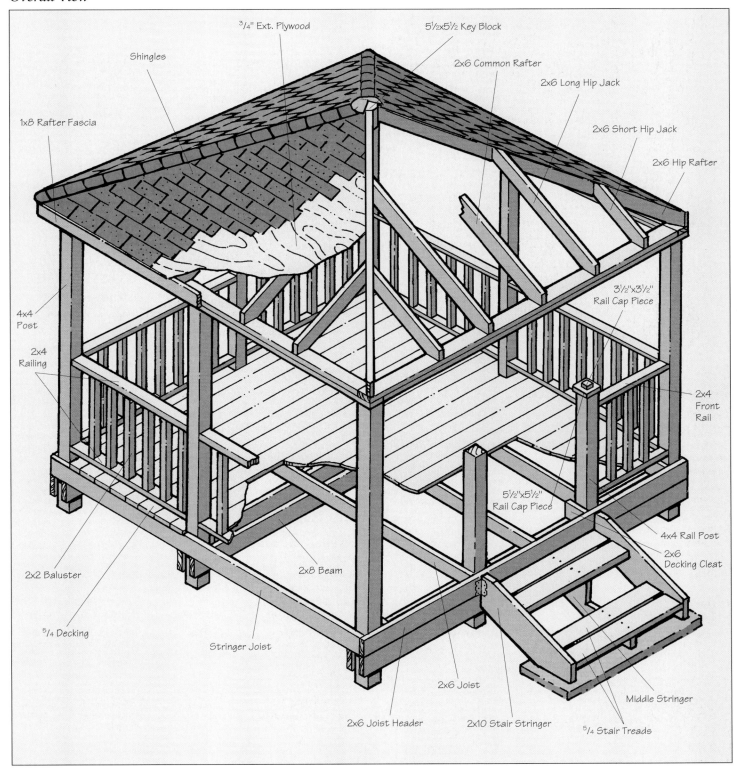

- ³/₄" Ext. Plywood
- 5½x5½ Key Block
- Shingles
- 2x6 Common Rafter
- 2x6 Long Hip Jack
- 1x8 Rafter Fascia
- 2x6 Short Hip Jack
- 2x6 Hip Rafter
- 4x4 Post
- 3½"x3½" Rail Cap Piece
- 2x4 Railing
- 2x4 Front Rail
- 2x2 Baluster
- 5½"x5½" Rail Cap Piece
- 4x4 Rail Post
- 2x6 Decking Cleat
- ⁵/₄ Decking
- 2x8 Beam
- Stringer Joist
- Middle Stringer
- 2x6 Joist
- 2x6 Joist Header
- 2x10 Stair Stringer
- ⁵/₄ Stair Treads

Measure and cut stock as you work. Take the extra time and give yourself the opportunity to correct slight errors before they become big ones.

The basic structural components of the gazebo deck are 4x4 posts that support the deck beams and roof headers; 2x8 beams that bolt to the posts and support the floor joists; and 2x6 joists, stringer joists, and joist headers that fasten to the beams and support the 1-inch-thick decking. (Decking of this dimension is commonly known as $^5/_4$-inch stock.) The gazebo must be square, level, and built to exact dimensions. Study the floor framing layout. All sides of the deck should measure 8 feet. The corner posts are located $1^1/_2$ inches inside the outside cor-ners of the layout so that standard 8-foot lengths of lumber can be used for beams, joists, and decking. Note that accurate post placement is critical.

To lay out the gazebo accurately, construct batter boards at each corner location and use the 3-4-5 layout method to locate each post (see "Laying Out the Site," page 50).

Framing Plan

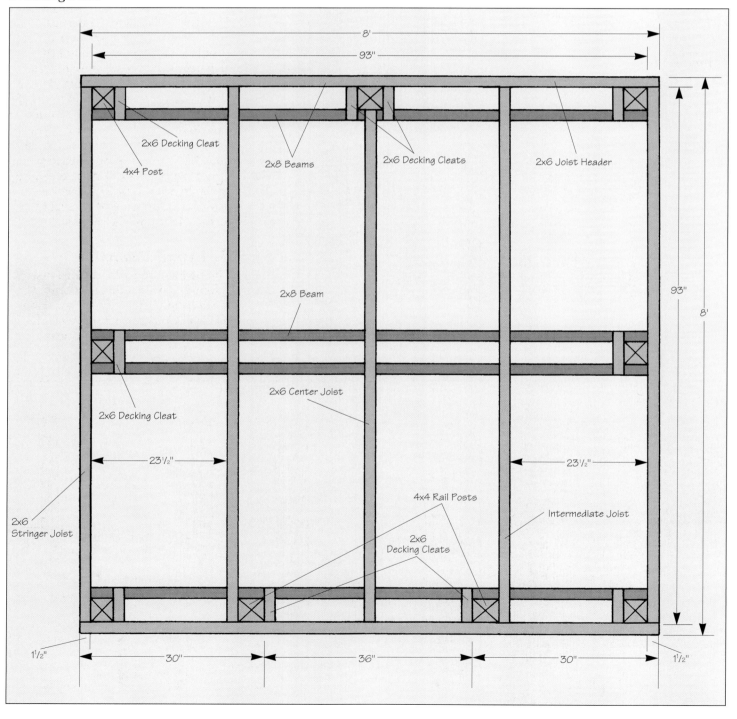

1. Install Posts

The seven posts that support the roof are 8 feet long. The two posts that terminate at railing height at the front of the gazebo are 54 inches long. These are not final dimensions. Final post sizing will be done when you finalize deck and roof heights later in the construction process.

Set all posts on concrete footings so that they rest on undisturbed soil beneath the frost line. The posts must be in their proper locations and exactly plumb for the floor and roof components to fit properly.

Place the nine concrete footings and metal post anchors, according to the instructions outlined in "Groundwork" on page 49. Remember, the distance between the outside edges of the corner posts must be no more than 93 inches. Use an 8-foot length of lumber to double-check for the required 1 1/2-inch over-length at each corner as shown in the "Framing Plan."

1. Install Posts

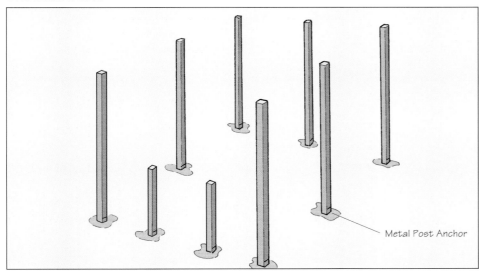

Metal Post Anchor

2. Place Step Footing

Build a support for the bottom end of the step stringers by placing a 4-inch-thick concrete slab at the base of the step location. The slab measures 18×40 inches, with the front edge of the slab 26 inches out from the edge of the deck. Make the surface of the slab flush with the ground.

3. Establish Deck Height

The finished deck is 16 inches above grade. This allows for a simple two-riser step design. It also keeps the framing members about 2 inches off the ground. Mark this 16-inch height on one of the posts, and transfer this dimension to all other posts using a line level or carpenter's level. Once the deck height is marked, measure down 1 1/4 inches to find the height of the top of all joists. Measure down an additional 5 1/2 inches to locate the top of the beams.

4. Install Beams

The beams are formed from two 8-foot 2×8 pieces through bolted to the posts using two 8-inch-long 3/8-inch-diameter machine or carriage bolts at each post location.

2. Place Step Footing

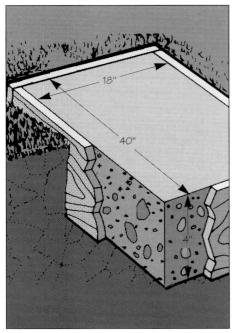

18"

40"

4"

3. Establish Deck Height

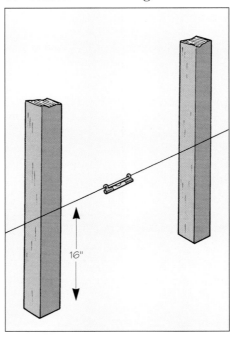

16"

4. Install Beams

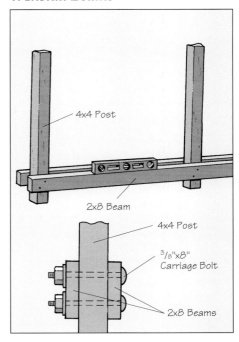

4x4 Post

2x8 Beam

4x4 Post

3/8"x8" Carriage Bolt

2x8 Beams

Temporarily tack-nail the beams to each post at the correct height, and check for level with a carpenter's level. Attach the remainder of the beams in the same manner, leveling them with the first beam. Then lay a straight 2x4, diagonally across the beams with a level on top, to check for level.

When all beams are tack-nailed in place and level, drill ³/₈-inch-diameter holes through the beams and posts and install and tighten the bolts, washers, and nuts.

5. Install Joists

Rest the two stringer joists across the beams, against the outside of the posts. Fasten each of them to the posts with two 16d nails.

As shown in the "Framing Plan," one joist is centered across the deck, running from the front header joist to the back center post. Toe-nail each side of this joist to the back center post and to the beams with 8d nails.

Face-nail the two remaining joists to the front posts and toe-nail them to the beams.

Decking boards will have to be supported whenever they end at a post. Use ten 2x6 decking cleats to provide this support. Eight of these cleats are 5 inches long and rest on inside beams, ending flush to the outside of the posts. The two middle decking cleats are 6¹/₂ inches long and span the two middle beams. Attach the cleats to the posts with 16d nails. Predrill the cleats so they won't split.

6. Install Joist Headers

Use 16d nails to face-nail 8-foot 2x6 joist headers to the exposed ends of the joist at the front and rear of the gazebo. Nail the headers to the ends of the cleats and to the posts.

7. Lay Out End Stringers

The gazebo uses a two-step "housed stringer" stair design. The 1-inch-thick stair treads are fastened between two 2x10 stringers. The

5. Install Joists

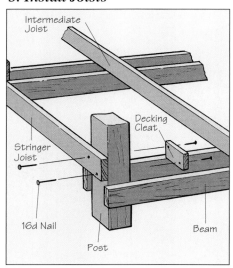

6. Install Joist Headers

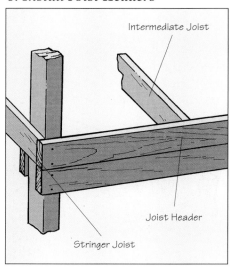

7. Lay Out End Stringers

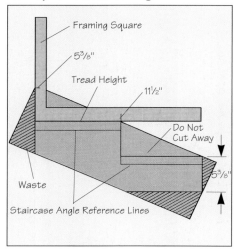

8. Lay Out Middle Stringer

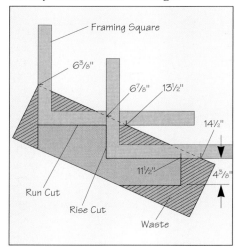

connections between treads and stringers are made with a piece of hardware called a stair angle.

The stair has a rise of 5³/₈ inches and a run of 11¹/₂ inches. To make the end stringers, start with two pieces of 2x10, each about 30 inches long. Place a framing square on a stringer as illustrated so that the 5³/₈-inch mark on the outside of the square's tongue and the 11¹/₂-inch measurement on the outside of the square's blade both align with the top edge of the stringer.

Mark out the rise and the run. Extend the rise line to the bottom of the stringer. You'll cut along this line to make the upper end of the stringer. Now move the square down to lay out the second step as shown in the

drawing. Use the square to lay out the cuts for the front and bottom of the stringer. Measure down 1 inch from the top of the treads and draw layout lines for the stair angles. Lay out the other end stringer. Make cuts at the back, front, and bottom of the stringer.

8. Lay Out Middle Stringer

You will have to include a middle stringer to support the 33-inch-wide tread. The middle stringer is designed so that its risers will be recessed 1 inch behind the front end of the treads. As you did for the end stringers, use the framing square to lay out the rise and run cuts and the bottom cut. Note that to mark out the top step, the tongue

9. Assemble Stairs

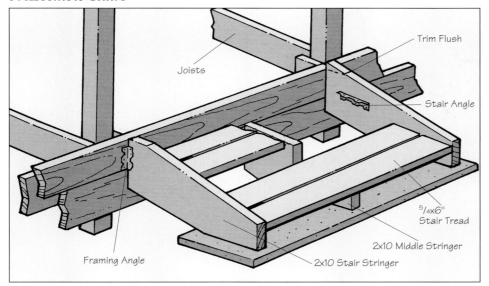

Joists

Trim Flush

Stair Angle

⁵/₄x6"
Stair Tread

2x10 Middle Stringer

2x10 Stair Stringer

Framing Angle

10. Install Decking

of the square is at 6⅜ inches while the blade is at 13½ inches. For the second step the tongue is at 6⅞ inches while the blade is at 14½ inches. To lay out the bottom rise, start from the 11½-inch mark on the blade and draw a 4⅜-inch-long perpendicular line as shown in the illustration for this step. You can do most of the cutting for the middle stringer with a circular saw. Finish with a handsaw.

9. Assemble Stairs

Nail the stair angles to the stringers with the nails recommended or provided by the manufacturer.

Use framing anchors to install the stringers to the joist header, spacing them 33 inches apart, equidistant

from the rail posts. Nail the middle stringer to the front beam, centering it between the two outer stringers. When the bottom of the stringers sit flat on the concrete slab, the top points of the stringers should extend about 1 inch higher than the header joist. This is because the calculation for the rise and run of the stair included the 1-inch-thick decking. However, the decking will overhang the header slightly. To allow for this, use a handsaw to cut the top of the stringer flush with the header after the stringers are installed.

Each tread is made of two pieces of ⁵/₄x6-inch decking. Cut the treads 33 inches long. Attach the front tread pieces flush to the front

of the stringers. Leave ½ inch of space between the front and back treads. This will improve drainage on the steps.

10. Install Decking

Install the decking boards perpendicular to the floor joists, starting at the front of the gazebo and working toward the rear. Let the boards overhang the stringer joists. You'll cut them all off even later. For better appearance, align the first board so it overhangs the header by ½ inch. Several deck boards must be notched to fit around the posts. When cutting these notches, leave about ⅛ inch of clearance around the post. Both ends of each piece of decking must be supported, either by the joist headers, stringers, joists, or decking cleats.

Nail the decking to each joist with two 8d nails driven at a slight angle. You can use deck fastening clips instead of nails. Use a 10d nail as a gauge to space the deck boards.

After every three or four boards, measure to make sure the boards are running parallel to the back joist header. As you near the opposite end of the deck, note the remaining distance to the edge of the back joist header. It may be necessary to rip the last board to fit or to alter the spacing of the last few boards so you don't come up short at the end. Plan ahead by laying the last few deck boards in place before nailing them. Remember, you want the last board to overhang the back header by about ½ inch.

Snap chalk lines across the ends of the deck boards ½ inch from the outside faces of the stringer joists. If you have a steady hand and eye you can use a circular saw to cut freehand along the lines. Otherwise, tack a board to the deck as a guide for the saw. The posts will get in the way of the circular saw, so you'll have to cut a few boards off with a handsaw.

FRAME THE ROOF

This square hip roof has four types of rafters, all made of 2x6 stock. As shown in the "Roof Framing Plan," there are four common rafters, four hip rafters, eight short hip jacks and eight long hip jacks. The rafters don't have bird's mouth cuts or tails that overhang the cap plate. Instead, they have a seat cut and a tail plumb cut that ends flush with the outside of the plates. If you are not an experienced roof builder, refer to "Roof Framing" on page 58 to learn how to lay out common rafters. The method for laying out hip rafters is only slightly different and is also explained in "Roof Framing."

Roof Framing Plan

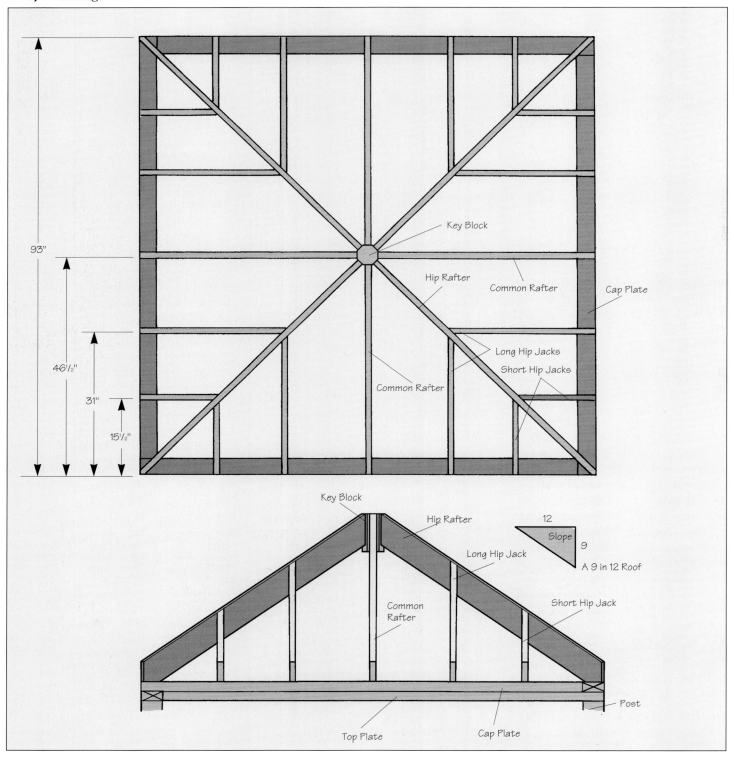

1. Measure & Cut Posts

Measure up 78 inches from the deck floor along one of the posts. Use a line level or a water level to transfer this height to the other posts. Mark and cut off the roof support posts at this height.

2. Install Top Plates

Cut the top plates and cap plates to form lap joints at the corners as shown. Nail cap plates to top plates with 8d nails. Nail one of these assemblies atop the front posts and another atop the back posts with 12d nails. Install the remaining two assemblies.

3. Make the Key Block

The key block will be at the peak of the gazebo roof. It has eight sides to meet the four common rafters and the four hip rafters.

Make the block on the table saw from an 8-inch piece of 6x6 stock. Set the table saw rip fence 3⅞ inches from the blade. Set the blade at 45 degrees and raise it to 2¾ inches. Now rip off the four corners to form the octagonal key block.

4. Cut Common Rafters

The common rafters and the hip jack rafters have a rise of 9 inches per 12 inches of run. If the perimeter measures 93 inches by 93 inches as planned, make your rafters to the lengths given in the materials list. If you built a gazebo of a different size, calculate your rafter lengths as described in "Roof Framing" on page 58. Use a framing square to lay out the tail plumb cut, the seat cut, and the peak cut as shown. To lay out the tail plumb cut, align the top edge of the rafter to the 9-inch mark on the inside of the framing square tongue. Align the 12-inch mark on the inside of the square's blade to the top edge of the rafter. Flip the square over as shown to lay out the peak plumb cut. Align the 9-inch mark on the outside of the tongue and the 12-inch mark on the outside of the blade with the top of the rafter.

1. Measure and Cut Posts
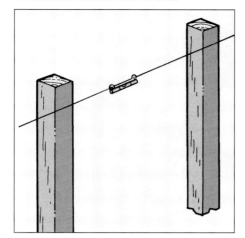

2. Install Top Plates
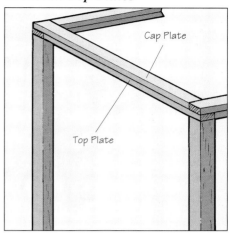

3. Make the Key Block
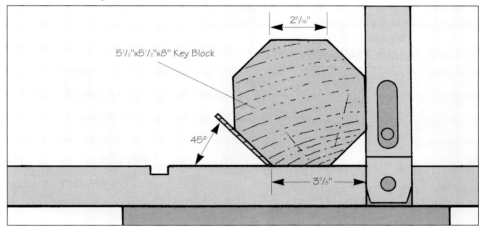

4. Cut Common Rafters
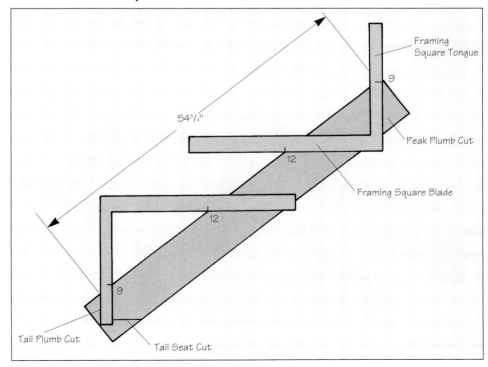

Gazebo

SIX-SIDED

CUTTING & MATERIALS LIST

Name	Quantity	Size
Posts	6	4"x4"x8'
Center Post	1	4"x4"x48"
Inner Rim Joists	6	2"x8"x52½"
Outer Rim Joists	6	2"x8"x54¼"
Diagonal Girder Support	2	2"x8"x cut to fit
Girders	2	2"x8"x8'8½"
Center Beams	2	2"x8"x46¹⁵⁄₁₆"
Inner Diagonals	4	2"x8"x11"
Outer Diagonals	4	2"x6"x12⁵⁄₁₆"
Long Joists	4	2"x6"x47⁵⁄₁₆"
Short Joists	4	2"x6"x34½"
Skirt Boards	5	1"x10"x59¹⁄₁₆"
Stair Stringers	3	2"x10"x30"
Stair Treads	4	⁵⁄₄"x6"x 47½"
Center Hex	1	⁵⁄₄"x6"x6"
Decking	24	⁵⁄₄"x6"x10'

Roof Framing

Name	Quantity	Size
Headers	6	2"x4"x54¼"
Cap Plates	6	2"x4"x52¾"
Key Block	1	6"x6"x8"
Rafters	6	2"x6"x81¾"
A/C Exterior Grade Plywood Sheathing	8	³⁄₄"x4'x8'
15-lb. Roofing Felt		100 sq. ft.
Composite Shingles		100 sq. ft.
Metal Drip Edge	3	10' lengths
Composite Hip and Ridge Shingles		Needed to cover approximately 40'

Name	Quantity	Size
Railing		
Railing	10	2"x4"x54¼"
Balusters	40	2"x2"x30"
Nails & Fasteners		
Nails		
20d Common		
16d Common		
10d Common		
8d Common		
Roofing		
Post Anchors	7	
Joist Hangers	4	Single 8" (for beams)
	16	Single 6" (for joists)
	2	Double 8" (for girder)
Roof-Peak Gazebo Ties	1 set	
Plate-Rafter Gazebo Ties	6	
Stair Angles	4	
Framing Angles	3	For stringers
Premixed Concrete		As required to set post & step footings below frost line

A six-sided gazebo is the classic design. It requires careful planning and accurate angle cutting, but for those with patience and skill, the results are well worth it. The deck of this gazebo measures 9 feet 6½ inches across, and the roof is constructed with a moderate overhang that extends beyond the sheltered area.

With six identical rafters, the roof of this gazebo is simpler to build than the roof on the Square Hip Roof Gazebo. You can make the roof framing even easier by using hardware specifically designed for attaching rafters on a six-sided gazebo.

You also can substitute a concrete deck for a raised wood deck foundation or add permanent benches or seating to your gazebo. We recommend that you measure and cut stock as you work. The angles involved in most gazebo construction make precutting lumber risky, so take the extra time, and give yourself the opportunity to correct slight errors before they become big ones.

Overall View

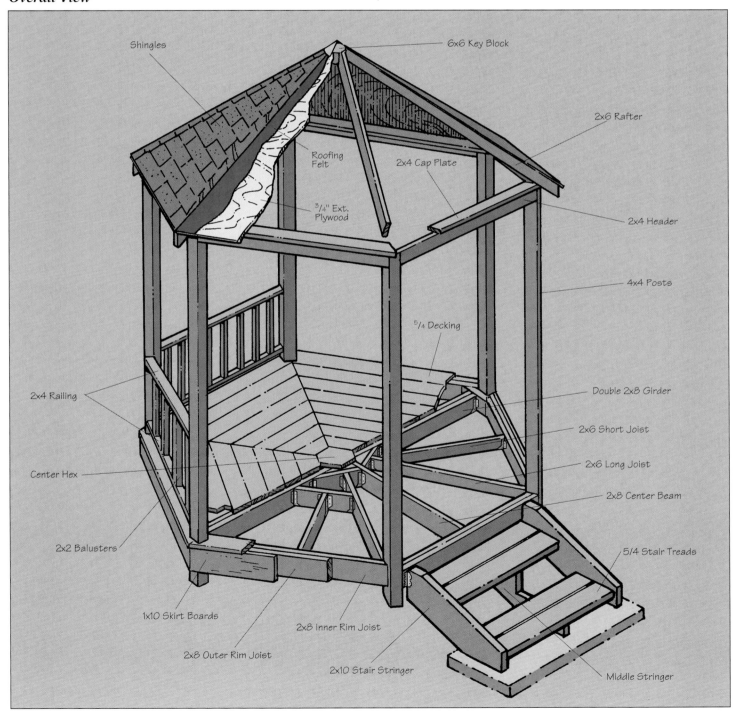

Shingles
6x6 Key Block
2x6 Rafter
Roofing Felt
2x4 Cap Plate
³/₄" Ext. Plywood
2x4 Header
4x4 Posts
⁵/₄ Decking
2x4 Railing
Double 2x8 Girder
2x6 Short Joist
Center Hex
2x6 Long Joist
2x8 Center Beam
2x2 Balusters
5/4 Stair Treads
1x10 Skirt Boards
2x8 Inner Rim Joist
2x8 Outer Rim Joist
2x10 Stair Stringer
Middle Stringer

CONSTRUCT THE DECK

Study the "Overall View" and the "Framing Plan" before beginning construction. The main support member or girder is made of two 2×8 pieces nailed together. Double 2×8 rim joists are used along with a network of 2×8 and 2×6 interior joists. Short diagonal pieces are installed between interior joists to create the 90-degree nailing angles needed to install joist hangers.

Framing Plan

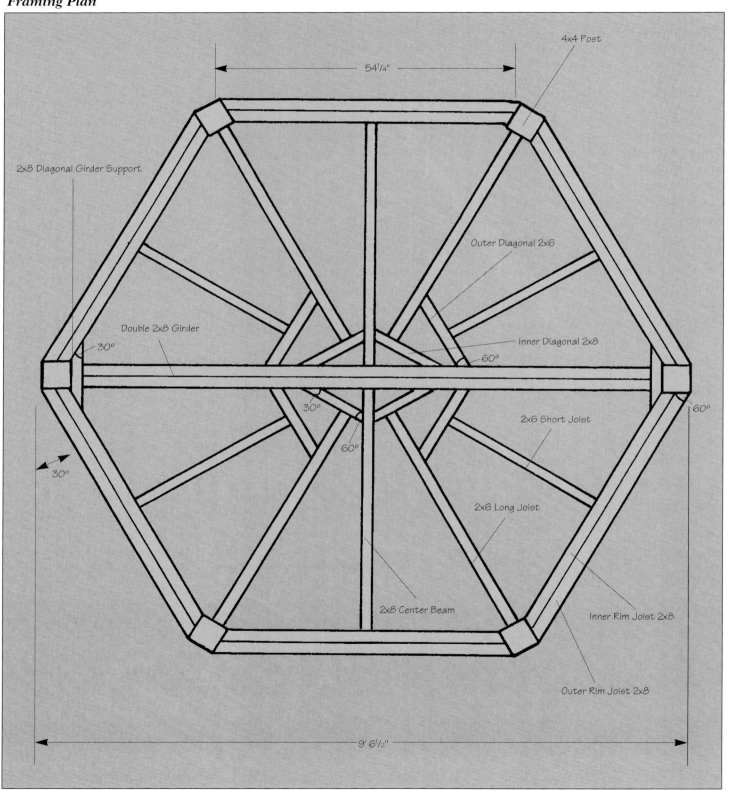

1. Lay Out Post Locations

Six posts support the roof at the perimeter of the gazebo. A single short post at the center of the deck helps support the main girder.

Before laying out the post locations, make certain the site is level. Select the center of the gazebo and drive a stake into the ground at this point. Drive a nail into the top of the stake letting the head protrude an inch or so. Cut a piece of straight lumber about 5 feet long and drill two holes $55\frac{1}{2}$ inches on center. Fit one of the holes over the nail in the stake and then scribe a circle on the ground by rotating this measuring stick. You may wish to sprinkle sand along the scribe line to clearly mark the circle's circumference.

Now use the same measuring stick to lay out six equidistant points along the circle. Each point will be $55\frac{1}{2}$ inches from its neighbors. These points locate the center of the posts. A second measuring stick is helpful in marking out anchor bolt locations.

2. Set Posts

All the posts are fastened to post anchors set in concrete footings. Use adjustable post anchors and fast-setting concrete to make this job easier. Dig holes for the footings at the center and six perimeter locations. Pour the concrete footing in the center post hole and position the bolt for the adjustable post anchor.

Pour the footing for the first perimeter post. To position the anchor bolt accurately, slip the measuring stick over the center bolt and mark the $55\frac{1}{2}$-inch distance on the concrete.

Continue placing the five remaining footings and anchor bolts around the circumference of the circle. Each anchor bolt will be $55\frac{1}{2}$ inches from both the center anchor bolt and the adjacent anchor bolt. Remember, the posts must be in their proper locations and exactly plumb for the floor and roof components to fit properly.

After the concrete sets, slip the post base anchor over the bolt and install the washer and nut. The slot in the anchor makes it possible to adjust anchor location slightly and rotate the anchor to set the required 30-degree angle between posts. When the concrete has cured and you are certain a post base is properly positioned, install the post on the base using the recommended size galvanized nails.

3. Place Step Footing

The steps can be located at any of the gazebo's six sides. Build a support for the bottom end of the stair stringers by placing a 4-inch-thick concrete slab at the base of the step location. Make the slab $18\times54\frac{1}{2}$ inches, with the front edge of the slab 26 inches out from the edge of the deck. This way, the slab will extend 2 inches farther than the sides and front of the steps. Make the surface of the slab flush with the ground.

4. Establish Deck Height

The finished deck will be 16 inches above grade. This allows for a simple two-riser step design. It also keeps framing members from contacting the ground. The deck boards are 1 inch thick, so the top of the joists will be 15 inches from the ground. Mark this height on one of the posts and transfer this dimension to all other posts, using a line level.

5. Install Rim Joists

The inner and outer rim joists are made of 2x8 stock with 60-degree angles cut on each end to meet the posts. If your posts are located properly and are exactly $3\frac{1}{2}$ inches square, the inner rim joists should be $52\frac{1}{2}$ inches long. The outer rim joists should be $54\frac{1}{4}$ inches long. But measure between posts before you cut the joists. Measure down $7\frac{1}{4}$ inches (the actual width of a 2x8) from the $14\frac{3}{4}$-inch marks on the posts, and mark the height of the bottom of the rim joists. Nail a temporary 2x4 cleat to each of the

1. Lay Out Post Locations

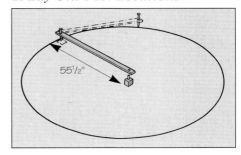

2. Set Posts

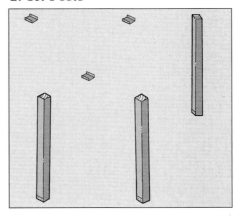

3. Place Step Footing

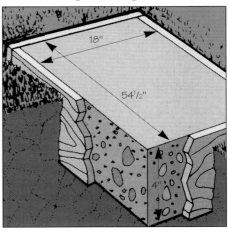

4. Establish Deck Height

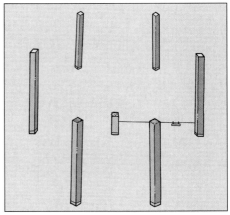

perimeter posts so the top of the cleats are on this layout line. Set the inner rim joists between the posts and rest them on the cleats. Rotate the post anchor to set the 30-degree angle and then tighten the anchor. Check the joists for level and tack them in position with a single 16d nail in each post. When all inner rim joists are in place, check for level, and fasten each joist to the post using three 16d nails.

Once the inner rim joists are installed, size and angle cut the

5. Install Rim Joists

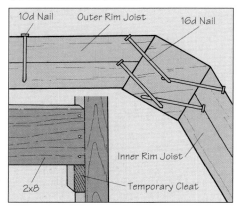

6. Trim Center Post

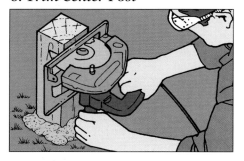

outer rim joists. Spike the inner and outer joists together with 10d nails every 12 inches.

6. Trim Center Post

Cut the center 4x4 post to final height using a portable circular saw. The top of the post is at the same height as the bottom of the rim joists and main girder beam.

7. Install Floor Framing

Because the main girder and the beams and joists that join it on an angle serve as a guide and nailing base for the decking, they must be positioned correctly. Measure as you go and use the dimensions given as a guide only. Center the joists and girder either on posts or on the exact center of rim joists as indicated.

Begin by installing the two diagonal girder support pieces that hold the hangers for the main girder. Cut 30-degree miters on each end of these pieces to meet the inner rim joists. Nail the diagonals to the posts and rim joists using 20d nails. Install the double hangers and then the girder. Spike the two 2x8 girder pieces together with 10d nails. Toe-nail the main girder to the center post. Locate the midpoint on the main girder and attach joist hangers for the two 2x8x46^{15}/$_{16}$-inch beams centered on this mark. Locate the center of the two inner rim joists that run parallel to the girder. Center joist hangers at these points for the other ends of the beams and install.

As shown in the "Framing Plan," the ends of all 2x6 joists are fixed on short joists by hangers attached to diagonals. Install the four inner 2x8 diagonals between the girder and the beams. Make these diagonals 11 inches long with a 30-degree miter on one end to meet the girder and a 60-degree miter on the other end to meet the beam. Install 2x6 joist hangers on the post across from these 2x8 diagonals. Set one end of a 2x6 approximately 60 inches long in the hanger on the post, then move the other end until it centers on the midpoint of the main girder. Mark where the center of long joists fall on the diagonal and install hangers at these points. Cut these joists to length and install them into their hangers.

Cut and install the outer diagonals between the long joists and the girder. Make these diagonals 12^{15}/$_{16}$ inches long with 30-degree miters on both ends. Install hangers onto the centers of these diagonals and on the corresponding inner rim joist. Cut the short joists to fit and nail in place.

8. Install Skirt Boards

Measure and cut 1x10 skirt boards to fit over the outer rim joists. Cut the ends at 60-degree angles (using a circular saw or table saw) to meet at the middle of the outside face of the posts. Cut a small scrap of 2x4 to fit between the skirt and post to serve as a nailer block. Don't use a skirt board between posts where the stairs will be installed.

7. Install Floor Framing

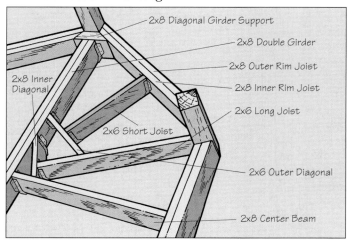

8. Install Skirt Boards

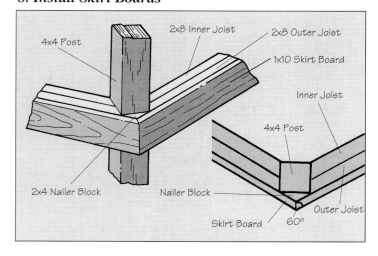

9. *Lay Out End Stringers*

The gazebo uses a two-step "housed stringer" stair design. The 1-inch-thick stair treads are fastened between two 2x10 stringers. The connection between treads and stringers is made with a piece of hardware called a stair angle.

The stair has a rise of $5^3/_8$ inches and a run of $11^1/_2$ inches. To make the stringers, start with two pieces of 2x10, each about 30 inches long. Place a framing square on a stringer, as illustrated, so that the $5^3/_8$-inch mark on the outside of the square's tongue and the $11^1/_2$-inch measurement on the outside of the square's blade both align with the top edge of the stringer.

Mark out the rise and the run. Extend the rise line to the bottom of the stringer. You'll cut along this line to make the upper end of the stringer. Now move the square down to lay out the second step, as shown. Use the square to lay out the cuts for the front and bottom of the stringer. Measure down 1 inch from the top of the treads and draw layout lines for the stair angles. Lay out the other end stringer.

10. *Lay Out Middle Stringer*

You will have to include a middle stringer to support the $47^1/_2$-inch-long tread. The middle stringer is designed so that its risers will be recessed 1 inch behind the front of the treads. As you did for the end stringers, use the framing square to lay out the rise and run cuts and the bottom cut. Note that to mark out the top step, the tongue of the square is at $6^3/_8$ inches while the blade is at $13^1/_2$ inches. For the second step the tongue is at $6^7/_8$ inches while the blade is at $14^1/_2$ inches. To lay out the bottom rise, start from the $11^1/_2$-inch mark on the blade and draw a $4^3/_8$-inch-long perpendicular line as shown in the illustration for this step. You can do most of the cutting for the middle stringer with a circular saw. But you'll have to use a handsaw to finish the cuts where rises meet runs so they aren't overcut.

11. *Assemble Stairs*

Nail the stair angles to the stringers with the nails recommended or provided by the manufacturer. Use framing anchors to install the stringers, spacing them $47^1/_2$ inches apart and equidistant from the ends of the outer rim joist. Nail the middle stringer to the front beam, centering it between the front 4x4 posts. Use two 16d nails driven through the inside face of the beam.

When the bottoms of the stringers sit flat on the concrete slab, the top point of the stringers should extend about 1 inch higher than the header joist. This is because the calculation for the rise and run of the stair included the 1-inch-thick decking. However, the decking will overhang the header slightly. To allow for this, use a handsaw to cut the top of the stringer flush with the header after you install the stringers.

Each tread is made of two pieces of $5/_4$ x 6-inch decking. Cut the treads to $47^1/_2$ inches long. Attach the front tread pieces flush to the front of the stringers. Leave a $1/_2$-inch space between the front and back treads. This improves drainage on the steps.

12. *Install Decking*

Once the floor framing components are in place, the 1-inch-thick (commonly called $5/_4$-inch stock) decking can be laid. Nail the decking to the joists with two 8d nails driven in at each joist location. Use a 10d nail as a gauge for spacing the deck boards.

9. *Lay Out End Stringers*

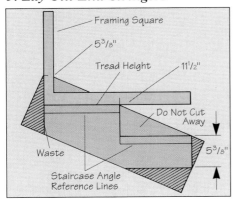

Framing Square
$5^3/_8$"
Tread Height
$11^1/_2$"
Do Not Cut Away
Waste
$5^3/_8$"
Staircase Angle Reference Lines

10. *Lay Out Middle Stringer*

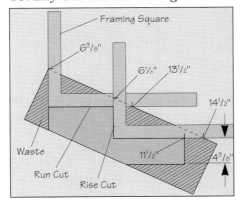

Framing Square
$6^3/_8$"
$6^7/_8$" $13^1/_2$"
$14^1/_2$"
Waste
$11^1/_2$" $4^3/_8$"
Run Cut
Rise Cut

11. *Assemble Stairs*

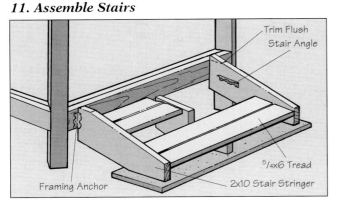

Trim Flush
Stair Angle
$5/_4$x6 Tread
Framing Anchor
2x10 Stair Stringer

12. *Install Decking*

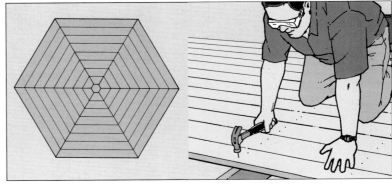

Start by cutting a center hex piece from a 6x6-inch scrap of clear deck board. Add blocking to each side of the double girder at the center beam intersection. Strike chalk lines centered along the length of each joist that runs to a post. Make a mark on each line 2³/4 inches from where they intersect. Align the center hex with these marks.

Nail the center hex piece in place and use it as a guide to measure and cut the first row of decking. The first row then serves as a guide to cutting the second row and so on. End joints should fall along the chalk lines that run at angles from the center hex. A power miter set to cut the 60-degree cut will speed up this work. Consider renting one if you don't own one.

Trim the last row of decking so it extends ³/4 inch or so beyond the skirt board. Since these are rip cuts, they'll be easiest to accomplish before the last boards are installed. You'll have to notch the last row of deck boards to fit around the posts.

FRAME THE ROOF

The six-sided gazebo looks like it has hip rafters, but it really has six identical common rafters. This is because the rafters meet the posts at 90-degree angles. The rafters have a rise of 9 inches per 12 inches of run. If you are not an experienced roof builder, read "Roof Framing" on page 58 to learn about laying out rafters and cutting plumb and bird's mouth cuts. This is especially important if your gazebo is not exactly the same size as the one described in this project.

As mentioned, you can avoid bird's mouth and peak plumb cuts by using special peak and plate ties designed for roofs on six-sided gazebos. The instructions below explain how to frame the roof with and without this hardware.

1. Cut Posts

Mark one of the posts 78 inches from the deck floor. Use a line level

or carpenter's level to transfer this height to the other five posts. Mark and cut the posts at this height.

2. Install Roof Headers

Cut the 2x4 headers to the same length as you cut the outer rim joists, with the same 60-degree angle on each end. Nail the headers to the posts with 10d nails. Make sure the tops of the headers are level with the post tops. If you will be using peak and plate ties, cut the cap plates now so that they meet each other over the posts with 60-degree miters on each end. Make sure the sides of the plates are flush with the faces of the headers. Nail the plates to the headers with 10d nails. The mitered corners of the plates will overlap the posts a little. You'll need to cut the ends flush with the posts to allow for the plate ties. If you will not be using plate and peak ties, do not cut or install the top plates yet. You will install the top plates after the rafters are in place.

3. Make the Key Block

The six-sided key block is used only if you are not using peak ties. Make the block on the table saw from an 8-inch-long piece of 6x6. Set the fence 4¹/8 inches from the blade. Tilt the blade to 60 degrees. Cut the block as shown.

4. Cut Rafters

If you use peak and plate ties, the roof will be a few inches higher than if you don't, but the rafter length and tail plumb cuts will be the same either way. To lay out the tail plumb cuts, align the top edge of the rafter to the 9-inch mark on the inside of the framing square tongue. Align the 12-inch mark on the inside of the square's blade to the top edge of the rafter. That's all the layout you have to do if you are using ties.

If you are not using ties, slide the square up 12 inches to lay out the bird's mouth plumb cut. Now align out a 3¹/2-inch seat cut per-

1. Cut Posts

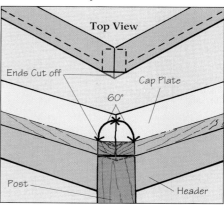

2. Install Roof Headers

Top View

Ends Cut off

Cap Plate

60°

Post

Header

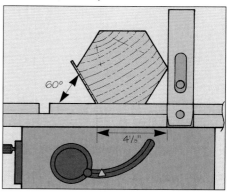

3. Make the Key Block

60°

4¹/8"

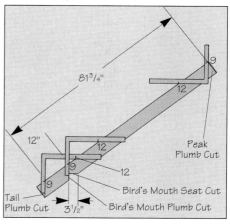

4. Cut Rafters

81³/4"

9
12

12"

12
9
12

12"
9

Peak Plumb Cut

Bird's Mouth Seat Cut

Tail Plumb Cut

3¹/2"

Bird's Mouth Plumb Cut

5. Install Rafters

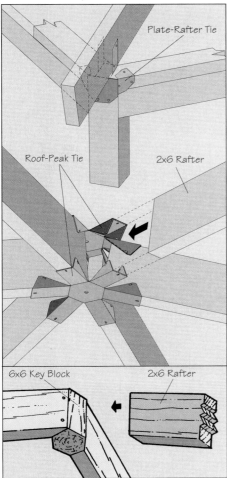

Plate-Rafter Tie

Roof-Peak Tie

2x6 Rafter

6x6 Key Block

2x6 Rafter

6. Install Cap Plates

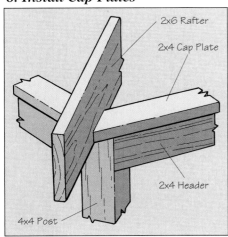

2x6 Rafter

2x4 Cap Plate

2x4 Header

4x4 Post

pendicular to the plumb cut as shown. Flip the square over as shown to lay out the peak plumb cut. Align the 9-inch mark on the outside of the tongue with the top of the rafter. Align the 12-inch mark on the outside of the blade and the 9-inch mark on the outside

of the tongue with the top of the rafter. Cut the rafters to size.

5. *Install Rafters*

The plate ties are made to accommodate the gazebo's 120-degree angles. If you are using plate ties, simply nail them to the cap plates and posts as shown, using the nails provided or recommended by the manufacturer. The peak ties consist of a top plate and a bottom plate that hold the rafters as shown. Bend the legs of the plates down to accommodate the roof pitch.

If you are not using ties, nail two opposing rafters to the key block. Then, with a helper or two, lift the assembly onto the header with the bird's mouths seated on top of opposing posts. Toe-nail the rafters to the posts with 8d nails. Assemble the remaining rafters.

6. *Install Cap Plates*

If you are not using ties, you will now install the cap plates. Measure and cut them with 30-degree angles at each end to fit snugly between rafters. Nail the cap plates to the headers with 10d nails. Use 8d nails to toe-nail the cap plates to the rafters.

INSTALL THE ROOF COVERING

The plans shown here call for a ³/₄-inch exterior-grade plywood roof covered with composite shingles. Cut the plywood triangles to size and install them over the rafters using 8d common nails spaced 12 inches apart. Complete the shingling. Instructions for installing wood shingles and shakes, composite shingles, and other roofing alternatives are given in "Roofing" on page 66.

INSTALL THE RAILING

You can build and install your own railing using 2x4 top and bottom rails with equally spaced 2x2 balusters.

Lay out the top rail height 33 inches above the deck. Measure and cut each top and bottom rail section separately to ensure a snug fit between the posts. Cut the balusters to 27 inches long and spaced 5 inches on center. Miter the ends of the rails at 30 degrees using a circular saw or table saw.

Attach the balusters (eight per section) to the rails. Nail through the bottom rail into the balusters, but carefully toe-nail the top of the balusters to the top rail from the underside so there are no exposed nailheads on the top rail. Attach the assembled section to the posts, using railing brackets, 2x4 cleats, or by toe-nailing with 10d nails.

Install Roof Covering

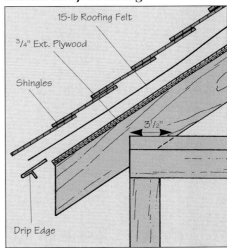

15-lb Roofing Felt

³/₄" Ext. Plywood

Shingles

3 ¹/₂"

Drip Edge

Install Railing

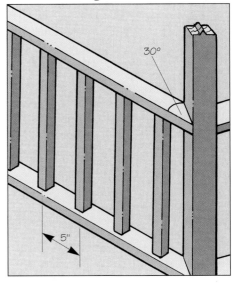

30°

5"

Gazebo

Eight-Sided

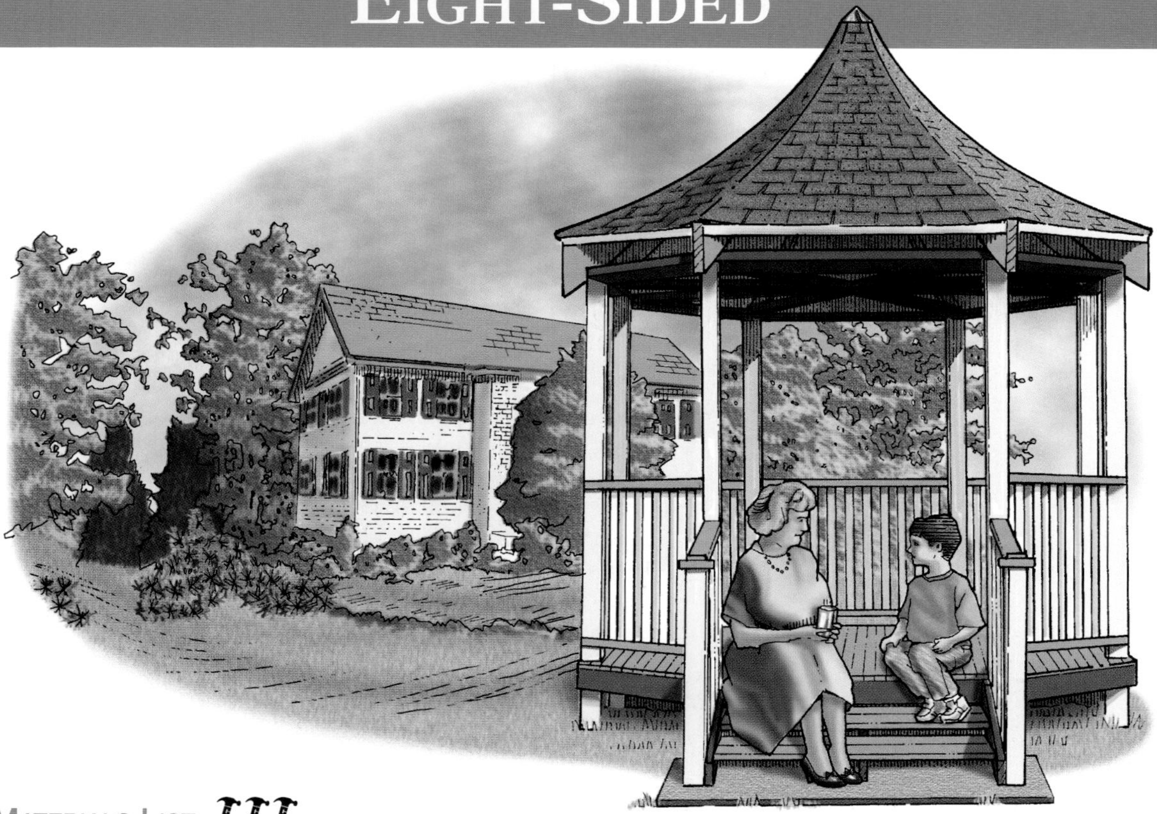

Cutting & Materials List

Name	Quantity	Size
Gazebo Deck Framing		
Roof Posts	8	4"x4"x12'
Long Beams	4	2"x8"x93"
Short Beams	2	2"x8"x45¾"
Square-End Rim Joists	4	2"x6"x42¾"
Decking Cleats	4	2"x6"x5"
Decking Cleats	4	2"x6"x4⅜"
Mitered Rim Joists	4	2"x6"x37 11/16"
Long Joists	3	2"x6"x93"
Short Joists	2	2"x6"x51½"
Mid-Length Joists	2	2"x6"x78⅛"
Stair Stringers	3	2"x10"x30"
Stair Treads	4	5/4"x6"x32¾"
Newel Posts	2	4"x4"x41¼"
Stair Rails	4	2"x4"x24¾"
Large Newel Block	2	1½"x5½"x5½"
Small Newel Block	2	1½"x3½"x3½"
Stair Balusters	8	2"x2"x27⅝"
Decking	14	5/4"x6"x10'
Roof Framing		
Top Plates	4	2"x6"x39¾"
Top Plates	4	2"x6"x37 11/16"
Ceiling Joists	2	2"x4"x8'5⅛"
Ceiling Joists	2	2"x4"x49 13/16"
Ceiling Joists	2	2"x4"x49½"
Cap Plates	4	2"x6"x39¾"
Cap Plates	4	2"x6"x37 11/16"
Key Block	1	5½"x5½"x12"

Name	Quantity	Size
Rafters	8	2"x8"x8'2⅝"
Roof Slats	32	1"x4"x10'
15-lb. Roofing Felt		100 sq. ft.
Metal Drip Edge	4	8' Lengths
Composite or Wood Shingles		100 sq. ft.
Composite Hip and Ridge Shingles		Needed to cover approximately 60'
Aluminum Cap	1	
Railing		
Square-End Rails	6	2"x4"x32¾"
Mitered Rails	8	2"x4"x37 11/16"
Balusters	46	2"x2"x27"
Nails & Fasteners		
Metal Post Anchors	8	
Nails		
16d Common		
10d Common		
8d Common		
6d Common		
8d Galvanized Finishing		
Roofing		
Carriage Bolts	8	⅜"x8"
Lag Screws	8	⅜"x3"
3" Galvanized Decking Screws		
2½" Galvanized Decking Screws		
Stair Angles	4	
Framing Angles	2	For stringers
Premixed Cement	As required to set post & step footings below frost line	

T his eight-sided gazebo gets a special touch of elegance from its high, gracefully curved roof. The roof is created with curved rafters sheathed with slats. Of course you can simplify construction by using straight rafters instead.

Like the other gazebos in this book, this one is supported by 2x8 beams bolted to 4x4 posts. The beams support 2x6 rafters, which are covered with 5/4-inch decking boards. The deck is 8 feet across. The distance from the deck to the

Overall View

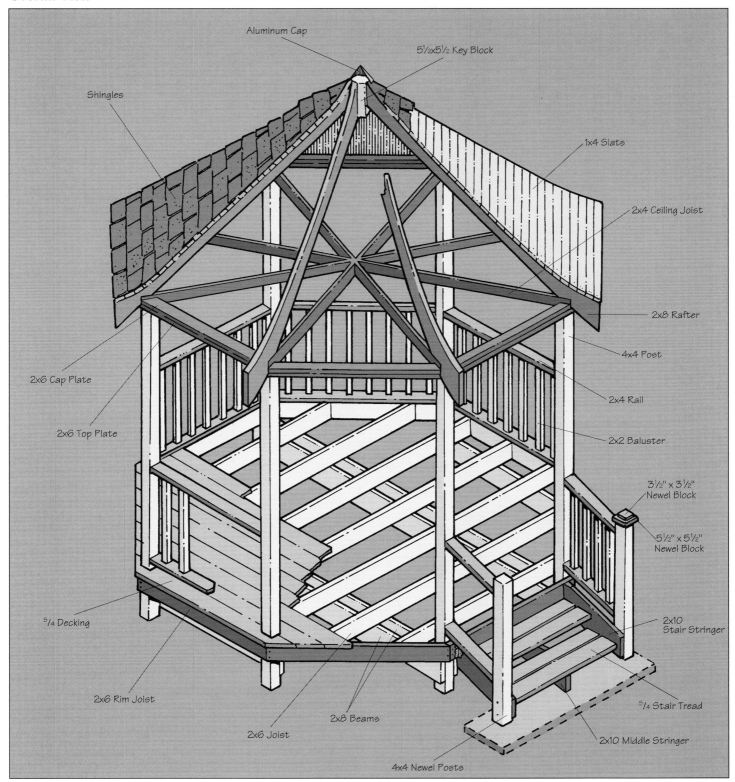

Aluminum Cap

5½x5½ Key Block

Shingles

1x4 Slats

2x4 Ceiling Joist

2x8 Rafter

4x4 Post

2x6 Cap Plate

2x4 Rail

2x6 Top Plate

2x2 Baluster

3½" x 3½" Newel Block

5½" x 5½" Newel Block

2x10 Stair Stringer

5/4 Decking

5/4 Stair Tread

2x6 Rim Joist

2x10 Middle Stringer

2x8 Beams

2x6 Joist

4x4 Newel Posts

top plate is 6 feet 6 inches. The materials list and drawings for this project provide specific lengths for the framing lumber. These lengths would be accurate if all framing lumber were exact in width and thickness measurements and if you managed to locate all posts and make all cuts with pinpoint accuracy. But the real world isn't like that. So measure as you go, adjust as necessary, and use the stated dimensions as a guide only.

Before you begin, study the "Overall View" and the "Framing Plan."

Framing Plan

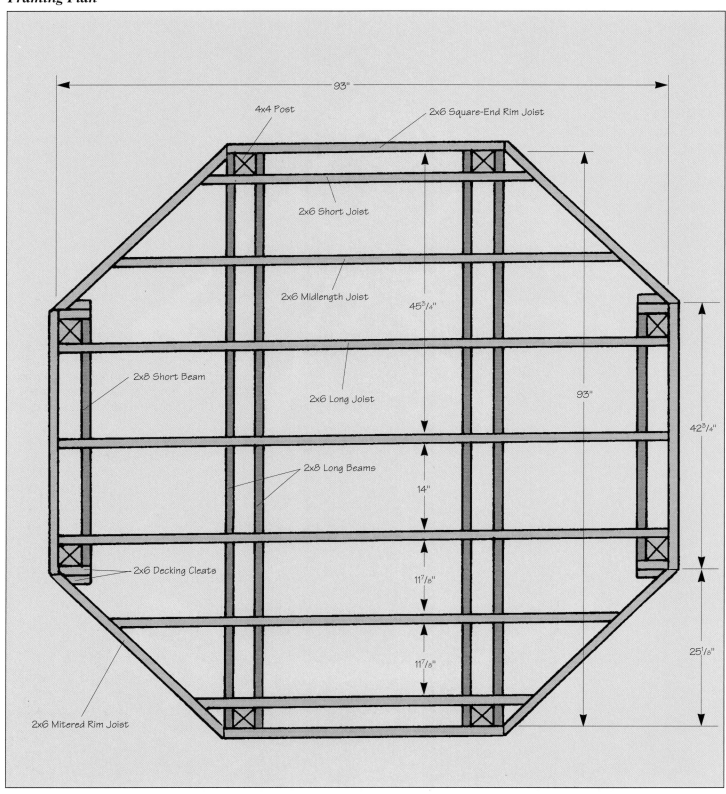

PLAN AND BUILD THE DECK

As with any project, careful planning and precise layout are essential, so take your time. This eight-sided building will require some fairly complex cutting and joinery; time invested now will eliminate the need to do any time-consuming alterations later.

Don't let the complexity of the octagonal shape discourage you. The layout and foundation work required for this project are basically the same as for the simpler projects.

You can incorporate any of the custom options into this project. Just be sure that you understand how these changes could affect the structure. Be prepared to make any necessary alterations to the following directions to accommodate your design.

1. Lay Out Posts

Begin by constructing batter boards with strings to lay out a 93-inch square. See "Groundwork" on page 49 for instruction on how to set up batter boards. Use a felt-tipped pen to make a mark $26^5/8$ inches from each corner. These marks locate the outside corners of the eight posts. From these points, locate the center of each post. This will be the center of your post holes.

2. Set Posts

The eight posts that support the roof are 10 feet long. However, this is not the final post length. You'll cut the posts to final height after you install the deck.

Set the posts on concrete footings that rest on undisturbed soil beneath the frost line. The posts must be in their proper locations and exactly plumb for the floor and roof components to fit properly. Place the eight concrete footing and metal post anchors according to the instructions in "Groundwork" on page 49.

3. Place Step Footing

Build a support for the bottom of the stair stringers and railing posts by placing a 4-inch-thick concrete slab at the base of the chosen step location. Make this slab 18x40 inches, with the front edge of the slab 26 inches from the outside rim joist. Make the surface of the slab flush with the ground.

1. Lay Out Posts

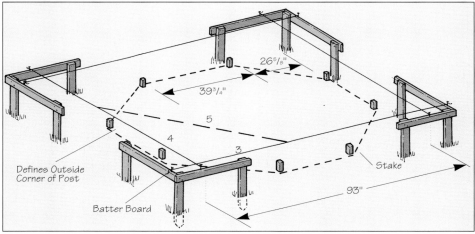

2. Set Posts

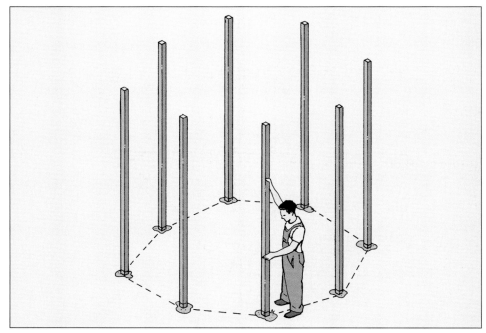

3. Place Step Footing

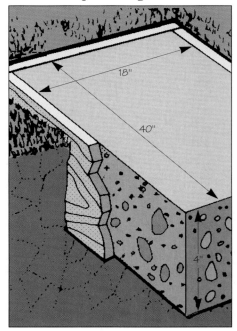

4. Establish Deck Height

The finished deck height will be 16 inches above grade. This allows for a simple two-riser step design. Mark this 16-inch height on one of the posts and transfer this dimension to all other posts using a line level or water level. Once the deck height is marked, measure down 1 inch to allow for the thickness of the deck boards. This marks the top of the joists. Now measure down an additional 5$\frac{1}{2}$ inches (the width of the joists) to locate the top of the beams. Mark this height.

5. Install Beams

As shown in the "Framing Plan," the joists are supported by four long beams and two short beams. Note that the short beams extend 3 inches past the posts on each end. Cut these beams to length.

Through-bolt the long beams to the posts with two $\frac{3}{8}$x8-inch carriage bolts at each post location. Attach the two short beams to the inside of the posts with two $\frac{3}{8}$x3-inch lag screws into each post.

6. Install Joists

Measure and cut the square-end rim joists and attach them to the posts with 16d nails. Doubled decking cleats attached to the posts provide nailing for decking and for the mitered rim joists. Measure and cut the decking cleats with a 45-degree miter on the end of the outer cleats as shown in the drawing. Place the cleats on the short beams and nail them to the posts and the short beam. Measure and cut the mitered rim joists and attach them to the ends of the square-end rim joists with two 8d nails at each connection.

Measure and cut the three long joists. Place them across the long and short beams. Attach the two outer long joists to the inside of the posts and to the square rim joists with 16d nails. Center the middle long joist between the first two. Nail this joist to the rim joists. Toe-nail the long joists to the beams with one 8d nail on each side of each connection.

Measure and cut the two short joists with 45-degree miters at each end. Nail the short joists to the posts and to the mitered rim joists. Measure and cut the midlength joists to fit between the mitered rim joists, centered between the short joists and long joists. Nail the mitered ends of the midlength joists to the rim joists and toe-nail them to the long beams.

7. Lay Out End Stringers

The eight-sided gazebo uses a "housed stringer" design that is identical to the stairs shown in the other gazebos in this book. However, the elegance of the eight-sided gazebo has been enhanced by the addition of stair rails. These rails are optional and you could, in fact, add them to any gazebo in this book.

The stair has a rise of 5$\frac{3}{8}$ inches and a run of 11$\frac{3}{8}$ inches. To make

4. Establish Deck Height

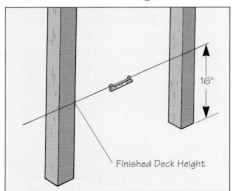

Finished Deck Height

16"

5. Install Beams

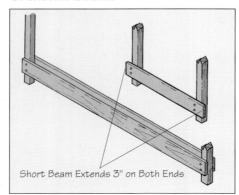

Short Beam Extends 3" on Both Ends

6. Install Joists

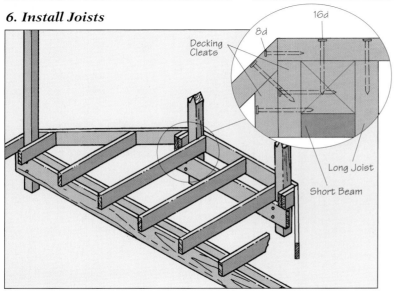

Decking Cleats

8d

16d

Long Joist

Short Beam

7. Lay Out End Stringers

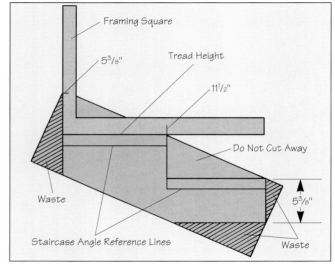

Framing Square

5$\frac{3}{8}$"

Tread Height

11$\frac{1}{2}$"

Do Not Cut Away

5$\frac{3}{8}$"

Waste

Staircase Angle Reference Lines

Waste

the end stringers, start with two pieces of 2x10, each about 30 inches long. Place a framing square on a stringer as illustrated so that the 5³/8-inch mark on the outside of the square's tongue and the 11¹/2-inch mark on the outside of the square's blade both align with the top edge of the stringer.

Mark out the rise and the run. Extend the rise line to the bottom of the stringer. You'll cut along this line to make the upper end of the stringer. Now move the square down to lay out the second step, as shown in the drawing. Use the square to lay out the cuts for the front and bottom of the stringers. Measure down 1 inch from the top of the treads and draw layout lines for the stair angles. Lay out the other end stringer.

8. Lay Out Middle Stringer

You will have to include a middle stringer to support the 32³/4-inch-long tread. The middle stringer is designed so that its risers will be recessed 1 inch behind the front of the treads. As you did for the end stringers, use the framing square to lay out the rise and run cuts and

the bottom cut. Note that to mark out the top step, the tongue of the square is at 6³/8 inches while the blade is at 13¹/2 inches. For the second step the tongue is at 6⁷/8 inches while the blade is at 14¹/2 inches. To lay out the bottom rise, start from the 11¹/2-inch mark on the blade and draw a 4³/8-inch-long perpen-dicular line as shown in the illustration for this step. You can do most of the cutting for the middle stringer with a circular saw. Finish with a handsaw.

9. Assemble Stairs

The hardware that connects the treads to the stringers is called a stair angle. Nail the stair angles to the stringers with the nails recommended or provided by the manufacturer. Working with the stringers upside down, nail the stair angles to the bottom of the treads. Each tread is made of two pieces of 5/4x6-inch decking. Cut the treads to 32³/4 inches long. Attach the front tread pieces flush to the front of the stringers. Leave ¹/2 inch space between the front and back treads. This improves drainage from the steps.

Nail the middle stringer to the front square-end rim joist, centering it between middle front posts. Use two 16d nails driven through the inside face of the beam. Put the stair assembly in place over the middle stringer. Attach it to the front rim joist with framing anchors. Fasten the treads to the middle stringer using two 8d nails at each connection. When the bottom of the stringer sits flat on the concrete slab, the top point of the stringer should extend about 1 inch above the header joist. This is because the calculation for the rise and run of the stair included the 1-inch-thick decking. However, the decking will overhang the header slightly. To allow for this, use a handsaw to cut the top of the stringer flush with the header after you install the stringers.

Cut the two newel posts 41¹/4 inches long. Attach them to the bottom of the stringers with two 16d nails at each side connection. Nail through the stringers into the posts. Make sure the posts are plumb before you nail.

8. Lay Out Middle Stringer

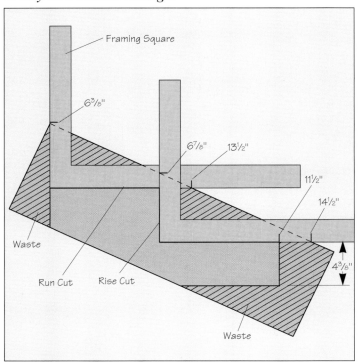

Framing Square

6³/8"

6⁷/8"   13¹/2"

11¹/2"

14¹/2"

4³/8"

Waste

Run Cut   Rise Cut

Waste

9. Assemble Stairs

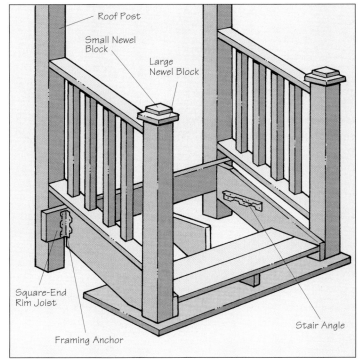

Roof Post

Small Newel Block

Large Newel Block

Square-End Rim Joist

Framing Anchor

Stair Angle

10. Assemble Stair Rails

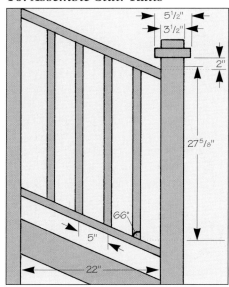

11. Install Decking

10. Assemble Stair Rails

The stair rails will be attached to the two front roof posts. Mark these posts 34¼ inches from the top of the rim joist. This will be the top of the top rails. Make another mark 5¾ inches from the top of the rim joist. This will be the top of the bottom rails. Now mark where the tops of the rails will meet the rail posts. These marks will be at 10¾ inches from the ground and 2 inches from the top of the post. Theoretically, the rails should be 24¾ inches long with parallel 66-degree cuts on each end. But it's best to scribe

these cuts to fit. Begin by cutting the four stair rails to about 30 inches long. Now align the rails to the marks and scribe the angle cuts at each end. Make these cuts. Screw the rails to the posts with two 3-inch galvanized deck screws at each connection. Screw the small newel block on top of the large newel block with two 3-inch decking screws. Toe-nail the blocks to the newel post top with 8d galvanized finishing nails. Cut the eight 2x2-inch balusters to 27⅝ inches long with 66-degree angles on each end. Attach the balusters with 3-inch galvanized decking screws through the bottom rails, spacing the balusters 5 inches apart on center, as shown. Toe-screw the balusters into the top rails.

11. Install Decking

Install the 1¼x6-inch decking boards perpendicular to the joists using two 8d nails at each joist location. Position the first deck board so that its side overhangs a rim joist by ½ inch. Leave it a couple of inches long on each end; you'll trim the deck boards to length after they are all in place. Use the thickness of a 10d nail as a gauge to leave space between the deck boards. When you get within a few boards of the opposite side, check the distance left. You may be able to adjust your spacing slightly to avoid ripping the last board to width. Even if you do have to rip the last board you can make sure it remains wide enough so you can screw or nail it down without splitting.

Snap a line around the perimeter of the deck, leaving the ½-inch overhang. If you have a steady eye and hand you can trim the boards using a circular saw without a guide. Otherwise, you can tack a board to the deck to guide the saw. You'll need to cut some of the boards with a handsaw because the posts will get in the way of the power saw.

FRAME THE ROOF

This gazebo uses eight identical curved rafters. It differs from other gazebos in the book in that the roof and posts are tied with ceiling joists. The rafter bird's mouths land on top of the end of the joist.

To lay out the classically graceful rafters you'll use a simple batten bending technique borrowed from boat builders. The curves are easily cut with a saber saw.

1. Cut Posts

Measure up one post 78 inches from the deck floor. Use a line level to transfer this height to the other posts. Mark and cut the posts to this height.

1. Cut Posts

2. Install Top Plates

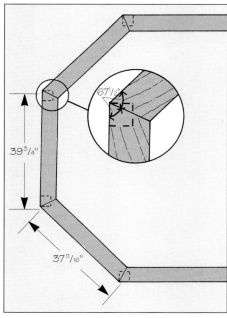

2. Install Top Plates

In this gazebo, the top plates and the cap plates are made of 2x6 lumber. As shown in the drawings, the top plates must meet flush to the outside corner of each post. For this to happen, the plates must be cut with 67$\frac{1}{2}$-degree miters at each end (cutting off 22$\frac{1}{2}$ degrees). There will be two alternating plate lengths as shown in the drawing. Measure between the outside corners at the tops of your posts; your distances could be slightly different than the dimensions shown in the drawing and materials list. Cut the top plates with opposing 67$\frac{1}{2}$-degree angles on each end to meet over the posts. Nail the top plates to the top of the posts with 16d nails.

3. Install Ceiling Joists

There are two long ceiling joists that span the width of the gazebo. Measure from outside corners of opposing posts to get the length of these two joists. Then make a 1$\frac{1}{2}$-inch-wide by 1$\frac{3}{4}$-inch-deep notch in the center of each one so that they form a lap joint as shown. Toe-nail these joists to the posts with 8d nails. Notice in the detail that the joists overhang the faces of the posts slightly. Now measure and cut the short joists with 45-degree bevels on both sides of the ends that meet the long joists. Toe-nail these joists into the long joists and the top plates with 8d nails.

Measure between the ceiling joists to get the length of the cap plates. Cut opposing 67$\frac{1}{2}$-degree miters on both ends of each cap plate. Fasten the cap plates to the top plates with 10d nails. Toe-nail the cap plates to the ceiling joists with 8d nails.

4. Make the Key Block

At the peak of the roof, the rafters meet an eight-sided key block made from a 12-inch-long piece of 6x6.

3. Install Ceiling Joists

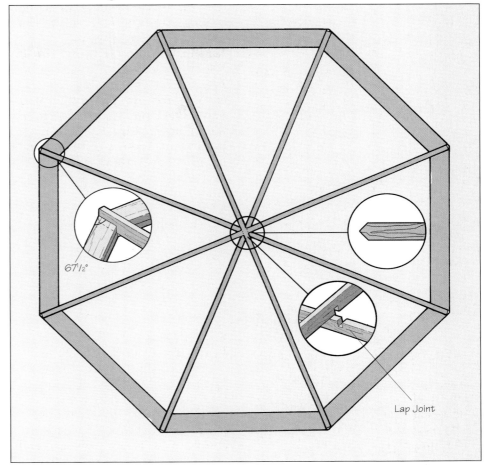

67$\frac{1}{2}$°

Lap Joint

4. Make the Key Block

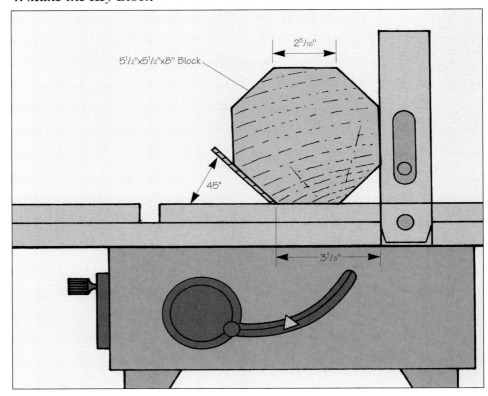

5$\frac{1}{2}$"x5$\frac{1}{2}$"x8" Block

2$\frac{5}{16}$"

45°

3$\frac{7}{2}$"

Make the block on the table saw.
Set the rip fence 3⁷/₈ inches from
the blade. Set the blade about
3 inches high and tilt it 45 degrees.
Remove the four corners.

5. *Make Pattern Rafter*

The eight curved rafters have a rise
of 15 inches per 12 inches of run.
If the perimeter of your gazebo
came out exactly as planned, you
can use the rafter dimensions
shown in the drawing. If not, see
"Roof Framing" on page 58 for
information on determining rafter
length. In any case, begin by
making a pattern rafter from a
2×8×10-foot-long board. Lay out
and cut the bird's mouth and
plumb cuts before laying out the
curve at the top of the rafter.
To lay out the tail plumb cut, align
the 15-inch mark on the framing
square blade and the 12-inch mark
on the framing square tongue to
the top of the rafter as shown.
Scribe the tail plumb cut along the
blade. Slide the square 12 inches
up the rafter to lay out the bird's
mouth plumb cut. The bird's
mouth seat cut is a 2³/₄-inch line
square to the plumb cut. To lay
out the peak cut, place the framing
square on the rafter as shown,
with the 15-inch mark on the inside of
the blade and the 12-inch mark
on the inside of the framing square
tongue aligned to the bottom of
the rafter. Scribe the peak cut
on the inside of the blade. Make
the cuts.

6. *Cut Rafter Curves*

The graceful curves along the top
of the rafters are quite easy to
make. The secret is to lay them
out using a ¹/₄-inch-thick strip of
clear softwood as a bending batten.
A strip ripped off a piece of 2-by
lumber will work fine, as long as
there are no knots.

Drive seven 4d finishing nails
halfway into the pattern rafter at
the points shown in the drawing.
The center nail is centered along
the top and width of the rafter.

5. Make Pattern Rafter

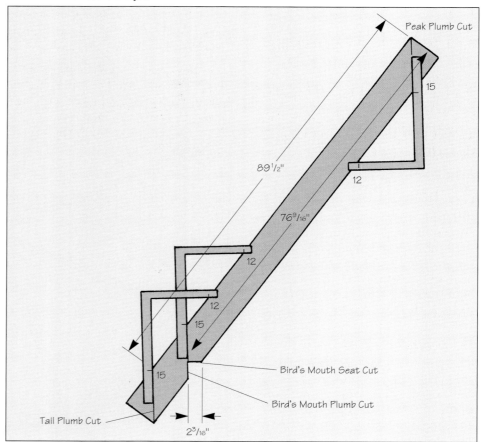

6. Cut Rafter Curves

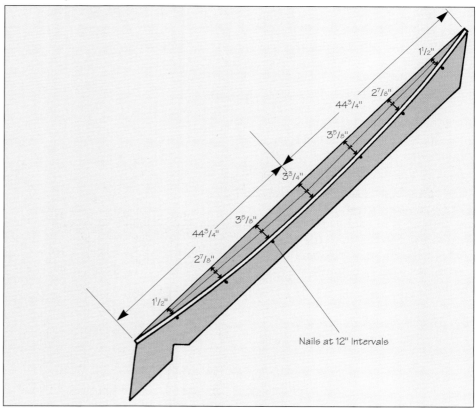

All the other nails are spaced at 12-inch intervals. All distances are measured square to the top of the rafter. Bend the batten around the center nail as shown in the drawing. Scribe a line along the length of the batten on the side closest to the top of the rafter. Remove the batten and nails. Cut the curve with a saber saw. Use the pattern rafter to cut the remaining rafters.

7. *Install Rafters*

Toe-nail two rafters to opposing sides of the key block. With a helper, position the assembly on the ceiling joists.

Toe-nail the rafters through their bird's mouths into the top of the ceiling joists with 8d nails. Put the other rafters in position one at a time, toe-nailing them to the key block and joists.

8. *Install Railings*

Like the rim joists, three of the rail assemblies meet the posts squarely and four meet the posts with 45-degree miters. The deck railings are assembled and installed in the same way as the stair railings except for two slight differences: (1) the balusters are cut square at the end and (2) the deck balusters are spaced $5\,^{11}/_{16}$ inches on center for the square-end rails and $5\,^{3}/_{8}$ inches on center for the mitered rails.

9. *Complete the Roof*

Because plywood can't follow the curves of the rafters, the roof is sheathed with 1x4 slats nailed to the rafters with 6d nails. Size the slats for one section of the roof at a time and fit them carefully in place. Cover the slats with 15-pound roofing felt and shingle the roof with composite or wood shingles. Detailed roofing options are given in "Roofing" on page 66.

7. *Install Rafters*

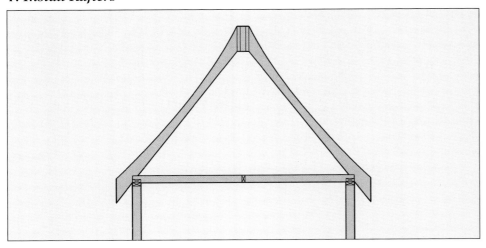

8. Install Railings

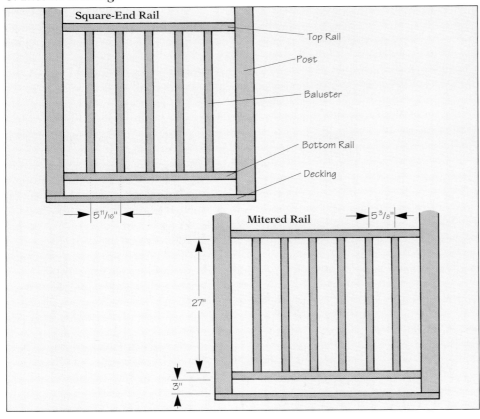

9. *Complete the Roof*

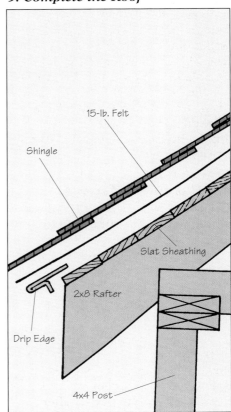

Pavilion
WITH GABLE ROOF

CUTTING & MATERIALS LIST

Name	Quantity	Size
Pavilion Framing		
Posts	8	4"x4"x8'
Top Plates	2	2"x4"x12'
Cap Plates	2	2"x4"x12'
Roof Framing		
Top Chord	8	2"x4"x94"
Bottom Chord	4	2"x4"x12"
Long Brace	8	2"x4"x41"
Short Brace	8	2"x4"x18³⁄₁₆"
Purlin Blocks	24	2"x4"x46"
Plywood Siding	2	¹⁄₂"x4'x8'
Fly Rafters	4	2"x4"x94¹¹⁄₁₆"
Lookout Blocks	16	2"x4"x8"
Plywood Sheathing	7	³⁄₄"x4'x8'
Fascia	2	1"x4"x13'5"
15-lb. Roofing Felt		200 sq. ft.
Metal Drip Edge	3	8' lengths
Composite Shingles		200 sq. ft.

Name	Quantity	Size
Nails & Fasteners		
Nails		
16d Common		
12d Common		
10d Common		
8d Common		
6d Common		
Roofing		
Post Anchors	8	
Purlin Clips	80	
Storm or Hurricane Clips	8	
Truss Clip Packs	4	Sized for 2x4 truss system
Premixed Concrete		As required to set post footings below frost line
Ready-Mix Concrete		As required for 4"-thick slab

This pavilion features a gable roof supported by four simple trusses. The roof is supported by eight posts, which are anchored to a concrete deck. As an alternative to the concrete deck, you can install the posts directly in the ground and use another deck scheme such as bricks set in sand.

The roof of this pavilion has a 6-in-12-inch slope for a moderately steep roof that will shed rain and melting snow. The roof is made with plywood sheathing covered with composite shingles. This basic gable-style roof would also be a great opportunity to try your hand at a cedar shingle or shake roof, or you might just decide to opt for a more open lattice-style roof.

Overall View

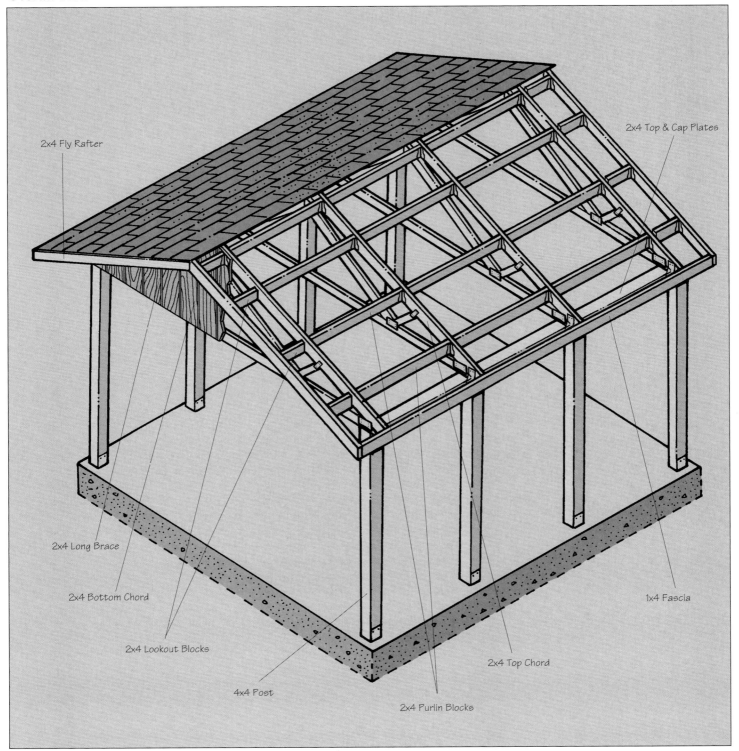

2x4 Fly Rafter

2x4 Top & Cap Plates

2x4 Long Brace

2x4 Bottom Chord

2x4 Lookout Blocks

4x4 Post

2x4 Purlin Blocks

2x4 Top Chord

1x4 Fascia

If you would like to increase the amount of privacy, consider installing lattice on one or more of the walls and planting flowers or vines.

The four trusses are assembled on the ground and then lifted into position. If you like, you can save some work by ordering trusses from a lumberyard.

The trusses are fastened together with four rows of blocking on each pitch. The blocking also provides nailing at the edges and center of the plywood roof sheathing panels.

Study the project drawings for the pavilion until you understand all dimensions and the relationship of all major components.

Framing Plan

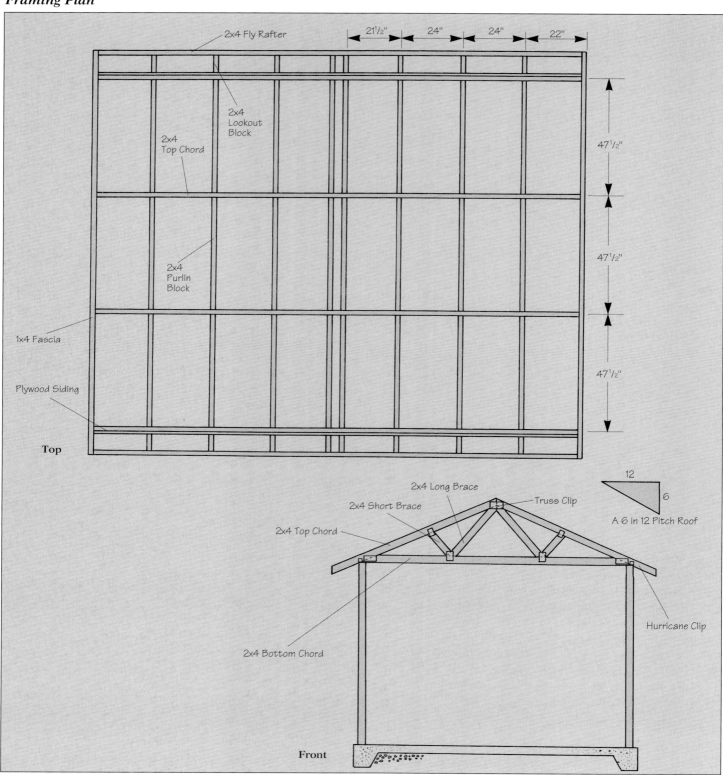

1. Cut Posts

If you have decided to build the pavilion on a slab, then you can cut the posts to length before they are installed. Measure and cut each post at 93 inches. You will have to cut from both sides to make it through the 3$^{1}/_{2}$-inch-thick posts. If you opt not to use a slab, then you will have to cut the posts in place, after installation.

2. Lay Out & Install Posts

As shown in the drawing there are two rows of four posts. The rows are spaced 11 feet 8$^{1}/_{2}$ inches on center. The posts in each row are spaced 46$^{13}/_{16}$ inches on center. If you use a concrete slab foundation, the eight post anchors must be set in the wet concrete when the slab is placed and finished. The best way to do this is to construct batter boards at each corner (see "Groundwork" on page 49). Mark out the exact locations of critical construction points, such as the post anchor locations and slab borders on string lines strung between the batter boards. Use a plumb bob to transfer the points to the surface of the slab so the anchors can be placed in wet concrete with a minimum of measuring and shifting.

If the posts will be set in the ground or anchored to individual footings, stake out locations using the 3-4-5 triangular method (see "Laying Out the Site" on page 50). Posts placed in the ground must be set in concrete 6 inches below the frost line or a minimum of 2 feet deep. Posts should be long enough to stand 93 inches above grade. If you use individual footings for each post, they too must extend a minimum of 2 feet deep or below the frost line.

3. Install Top & Cap Plates

Nail the top plates to the posts with 16d nails. Then nail the cap plate to the top plate with 10d nails.

1. Cut Posts

2. Layout & Install Posts

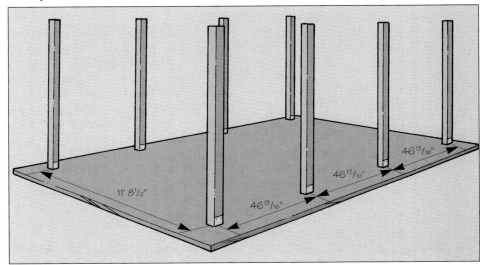

11' 8$^{1}/_{2}$"   46$^{13}/_{16}$"   46$^{13}/_{16}$"   46$^{13}/_{16}$"

3. Install Top & Cap Plates

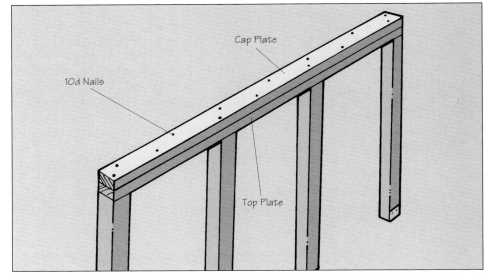

Cap Plate

10d Nails

Top Plate

4. Build Trusses

Build the four trusses on the ground and lift them into place one at a time.

Lay out and cut the truss members to the dimensions and angles shown in the drawing. Start by cutting all the parts for one truss. Lay the pieces out on the slab to make sure they fit properly. When they do, use these pieces as patterns to cut the parts for the remaining trusses.

Use a framing square as shown to lay out the plumb cuts on both ends of the top chords. To do this, align the 6-inch mark on the inside of the rafter square tongue and the 12-inch mark on the square's blade with the top of the chord. The drawing shows the measurements you'll need to cut the angles on the bottom chords and braces.

Assemble the pieces using properly sized truss clips. Position a truss clip over the joint and hammer the barbed tips into the wood. Nail through the clips as specified by the manufacturer. Clips must be installed on both sides of the joint.

5. Raise Trusses

Enlist a helper or two for raising and securing the trusses. Have a ladder and worker on each side. Position the truss between the headers at the post positions. The truss can hang peak down until you are ready to swing it up into position.

6. Fasten Trusses

Raise the end trusses so that they are plumb and flush to the outside of the end posts. It may be necessary to brace the trusses in place before you can secure them to the cap plates and posts with hurricane or storm clips. Position the two middle trusses directly above the center of the middle posts.

7. Install Purlin Blocks

Measure and cut the 2x4 purlin blocks that fit between the trusses. Lengths and positions of these blocks are shown in the "Framing Plan." Install the blocks using purlin clips or toe-nail the blocking using 12d nails.

4. Build Trusses

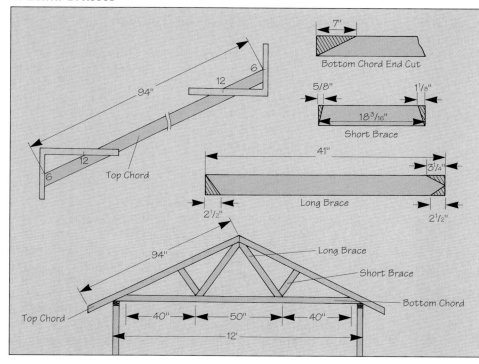

5. Raise Trusses

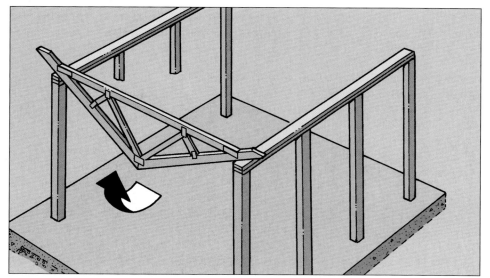

6. Fasten Trusses

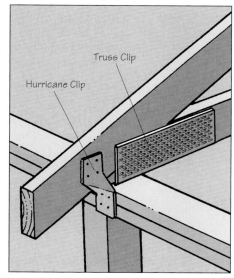

7. Install Purlin Blocks

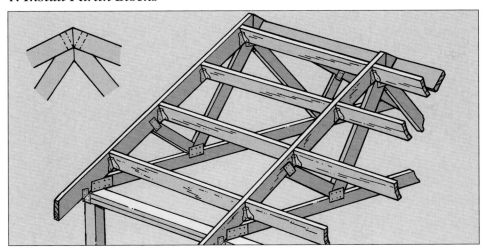

8. Install Gable Panels

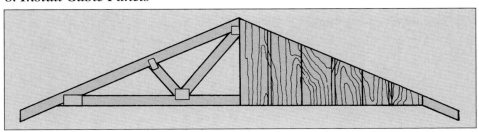

9. Install Lookouts

10. Install Fascia

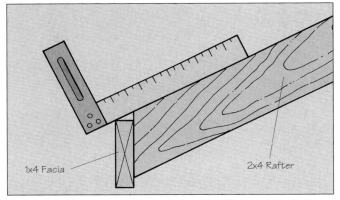

1x4 Facia   2x4 Rafter

8. Install Gable Panels

Size and cut the triangular gable panels from plywood siding such as Textured 1-11. Fasten the panels to the end trusses with 6d nails.

9. Install Lookouts

The lookouts are the pitched overhangs on the gable ends. Each lookout consists of two parts: blocks and fly rafters. Make the fly rafters the same way as the truss top chords, except they will be $^{11}/_{16}$ inch longer to cover the end of the fascia.

Cut the lookout blocks to length, and use 12d nails to fasten the blocks to the fly rafters. Space the blocks so they will line up with the blocking between the trusses. Fasten the blocks through the siding panels to the end trusses with purlin clips or toe-nail them in place.

10. Install Fascia

Use 12d nails to fasten the fascia boards to the ends of the rafters. Use a square to position the fascia so that the sheathing can cover it.

11. Install Roof Covering

Place the plywood roof sheathing so that the lengths of the panels run parallel to the peak. Trim the sheets so all joints butt over a truss. Install the sheathing using 8d nails spaced 12 inches on center.

Cover the roof with 15-pound felt. Install the metal drip edges and composite shingles.

11. Install Roof Covering

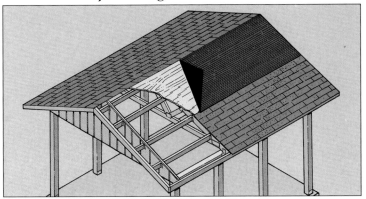

Pavilion

FREESTANDING

CUTTING & MATERIALS LIST

Name	Quantity	Size
Pavilion Framing		
Posts	8	4"x6"x8' (or 10' in ground)
Post Facing	16	2"x4"x8' (or 10' in ground)
Beam Facing	4	2"x4"x15'8"
Beams	4	2"x8"x16'
End Joist Facing	2	1"x4"x14'
Joists	6	2"x6"x14'
Lattice Frame Sides	10	2"x3"x14'
Lattice Frame Crosspieces	24	2"x3"x45"
	16	2"x3"x16½"
Roof Lattice		
Lattice Panels	4	2'x8'
	6	4'x8'
Lattice Panel Trim Cap	10	1"x2"x14'
Frieze Members		
Long Horizontal	4	2"x2"x9'6½"
Short Horizontal	12	2"x2"x43"
Rungs	46	2"x2"x9"

Name	Quantity	Size
Nails & Fasteners		
Post Anchors	8	4"x6"
2¼" Galvanized Decking Screws		
Nails		
16d Common		
10d Common		
10d Button Head		
8d Common		
6d Common		
Adjustable Post Bases	8	4"x6"
2½" Galvanized Decking Screws		
Threaded rod with washers and nuts	16	³/₈"x13"
Premixed Concrete	As required to set post footings below frost line	
Ready-Mix Concrete	As required for 4"-thick slab	

This pavilion is constructed using the standard post, beam, and joist design. The overall roof area is 14x16 feet. This pavilion has a concrete deck floor with the posts attached to adjustable post bases set in the concrete.

If you would like to use another type of floor treatment, such as brick set in sand or simply grass, you can set the posts into the ground or mount them to individual concrete footings. The brick-in-sand base can then be laid around the posts. See "Groundwork" on page 49 and "Customizing Options" on page 88 for details on setting posts and alternate floor treatments.

The roof is constructed of lattice nailed to a frame of 2x3 lumber set between the roof joists. A simple horizontal ladder frieze is added at the roofline. Basic post, beam, and joist members are enhanced using 2-by and 1-by face pieces centered on the members.

The pavilion is supported by eight 4x6 posts. There are two rows of posts with four posts in each row. The rows are 10 feet apart on center. The posts are spaced 49 1/2 inches on center. This spacing allows standard 4-foot-wide sheets of preformed lattice to fit between 2x6 roof joists. Most building suppliers sell 2x8- and 4x8-foot lattice sections. The 2x6 joists are centered over the posts and the 4-foot-wide sheets rest on 2x3 framing attached to the inside of the joists.

Overall View

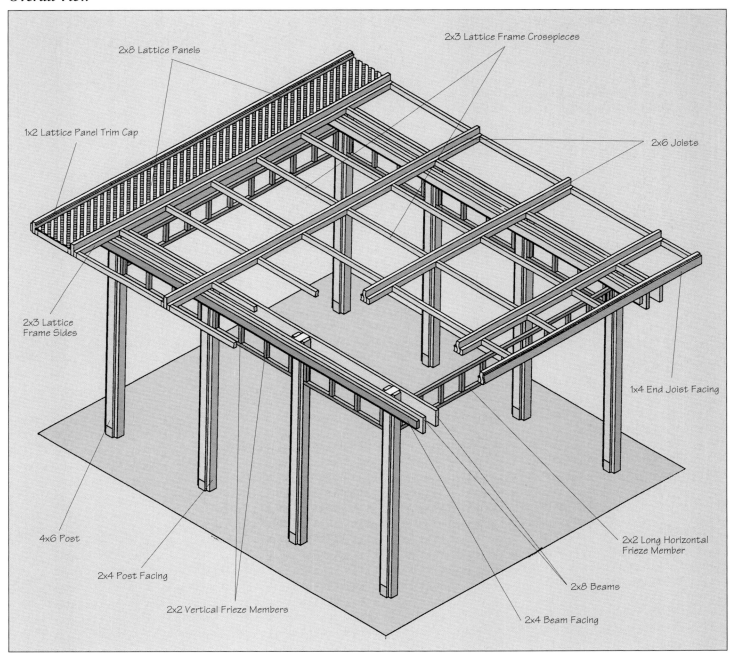

Framing Plan

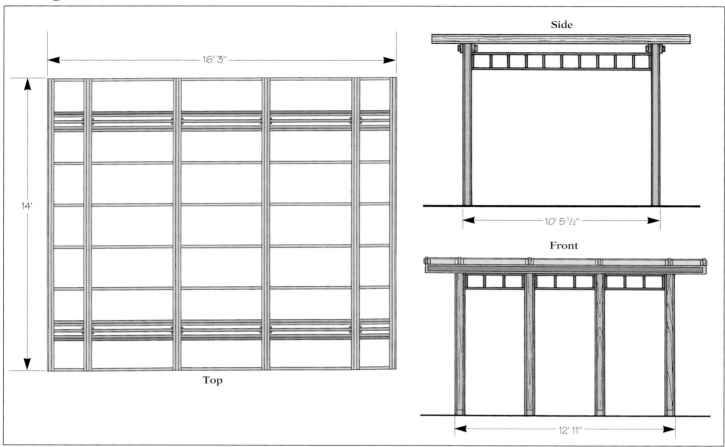

16' 3"

14'

Top

Side

10' 5 1/2"

Front

12' 11"

1. Assemble Posts

Use pressure-treated wood if you plan to set the posts in the ground. Nail the 2x4 post facing boards to the 4x6 posts before anchoring or setting the posts. Use 10d button head nails. These nails have a smaller, more attractive head than common nails. If you are careful, you can drive these nails in without denting the board's surface.

2. Install Posts

If you use a concrete slab foundation, the eight post anchors must be positioned before the concrete sets. The best way to do this is to construct batter boards at each corner. Mark out the exact locations of critical construction points, such as the post anchor locations and slab borders on string lines strung between the batter boards. Use a plumb bob to transfer the points to the surface of the slab so the anchors can be placed in wet

concrete with a minimum of measuring and shifting.

Since the posts will rest on the same slab, you can cut them to length before installation and proceed to Step 4.

If the posts will be set in the ground or anchored to individual footings, stake out locations using the 3-4-5 triangular method outlined in "Laying Out the Site" on page 50. Posts placed in the ground must be set in concrete 6 inches below the frost line, or a minimum of 2 feet deep. Posts should be long enough to stand 8 feet above grade. If you use individual footings for each post, they too must extend below the frost line. Details on post setting options are provided in "Groundwork" on page 49.

3. Trim Posts to Size

Once the posts are installed, measure up 8 feet from the ground or slab along one post, and mark with a pencil. Transfer this dimension to

1. Assemble Posts

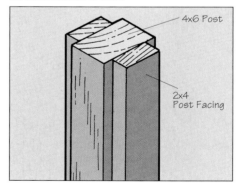

4x6 Post

2x4 Post Facing

2. Install Posts

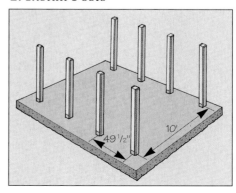

49 1/2"

10'

3. Trim Posts to Size

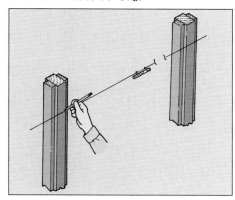

4. Assemble & Install Beams

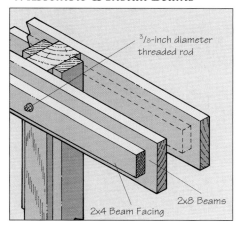

3/8-inch diameter threaded rod

2x8 Beams

2x4 Beam Facing

5. Assemble & Install Joists

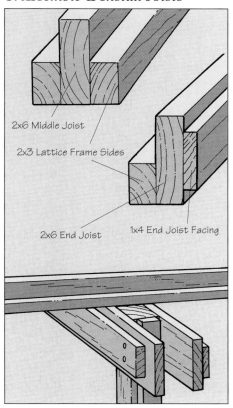

2x6 Middle Joist

2x3 Lattice Frame Sides

2x6 End Joist

1x4 End Joist Facing

all other posts using a line level. Trim the posts to the finished height.

4. *Assemble & Install Beams*

Cut the 2x4 beam facing to length. Center the facing on the beams and fasten it with 10d button head nails.

Lift the beams to the tops of the posts, resting them temporarily on 16d nails partially driven $7^{1}/_{4}$ inches from the top of the posts. Check that the tops of the beams are flush with the post tops. At each post, drill two $^{3}/_{8}$-inch holes through the beams and post, and attach the beams to the post using two 13-inch pieces of $^{3}/_{8}$-inch-diameter threaded rod. Use washers and nuts on both ends of each rod. Remove the 16d nails.

5. *Assemble & Install Joists*

Attach the 1x4 end joist facing to the outside face of the two end joists as shown in the "Overall View." Center the 1x4 on the width of the joist and fasten with 8d nails.

With 10d nails, attach 2x3 lattice frame members to the inside face of the end joists and both faces of the interior joists.The bottom of the 2x3 should be flush with the bottom of the joist.

Position the joist and lattice frame assemblies over the center of the post columns. Remember the distance between the inside edges of adjacent 2x6 joists must be exactly 4 feet to accommodate the lattice panels. Attach the joists to the columns, toe-nailing into the

6. Install Lattice Roof

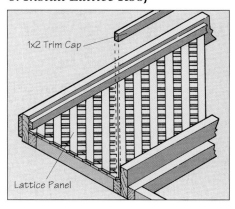

1x2 Trim Cap

Lattice Panel

columns using 16d nails. The ends of the 14-foot-long joists should extend beyond the column center-lines by 24 inches. Install the two end joists by toe-nailing to the beam or by using anchor clips.

6. *Install Lattice Roof*

Complete the 2x3 lattice support frame by installing the frame crosspieces 24 inches on center as shown. Toe-nail the crosspieces in place. Install the crosspieces for one section of the roof at a time. Then install the lattice panel and trim cap to that section before moving on. This will give you more room to position and move the ladder. The beams and joist can bear your weight and the weight of the ladder, but do not climb on or lean against the 2x3 crosspieces or installed lattice.

Position and nail the lattice panels to the 2x3 frame members using 6d nails. All lattice joints must be made over a frame member. Once a section of lattice is nailed to its frame, install the 1x2 lattice panel trim caps on top of the lattice by nailing down into the frame with 8d nails.

7. *Install Frieze*

Measure and assemble the 2x2 frieze sections one at a time. Use $2^{1}/_{2}$-inch galvanized decking screws to attach the 9-inch rungs between the horizontal members of the frieze. Nail the end rungs of each section to the posts with 10d nails.

7. Install Frieze

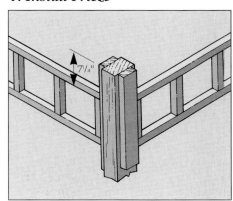

$7^{1}/_{4}$"

Arbor

OPEN-AIR

CUTTING & MATERIALS LIST

Name	Quantity	Size
Posts	4	4"x4"x10'
Beams	4	2"x8"x12'
Roof Joists	9	2"x6"x12'
Roof Slats	24	2"x2"x12'

Name	Quantity	Size
Nails		
16d Common		
10d Common		
8d Common		
Carriage Bolts	8	$^3/_8$"x8"
Premixed Concrete	As required to set post footings below frost line	

You will want to build your arbor using a wood species that is naturally rot resistant, such as cedar or redwood. You also can use pressure-treated lumber which will not harm plants.

Painting or staining the structure will not hinder plant growth, but perennials such as roses and grapes will have to be cut down in a few years when it's time to repaint. Annual vines, however, will give

Overall View

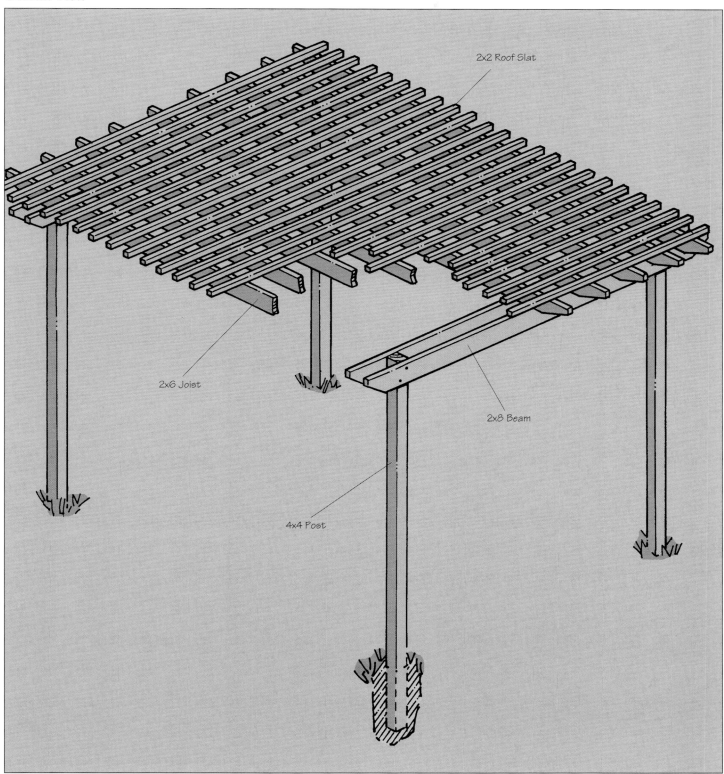

2x2 Roof Slat

2x6 Joist

2x8 Beam

4x4 Post

you the opportunity to repaint in late fall or early spring. This basic arbor has four posts. Each post is centered on the corner of a 9-foot square. With the beam overhangs, the total area is 12×12 feet, with the roof set about 7 feet above grade. To lay out the posts accurately, set up batter boards and strings and use the 3-4-5 method to make sure the layout is square. See "Laying Out the Site" on page 50 for details.

Framing Plan

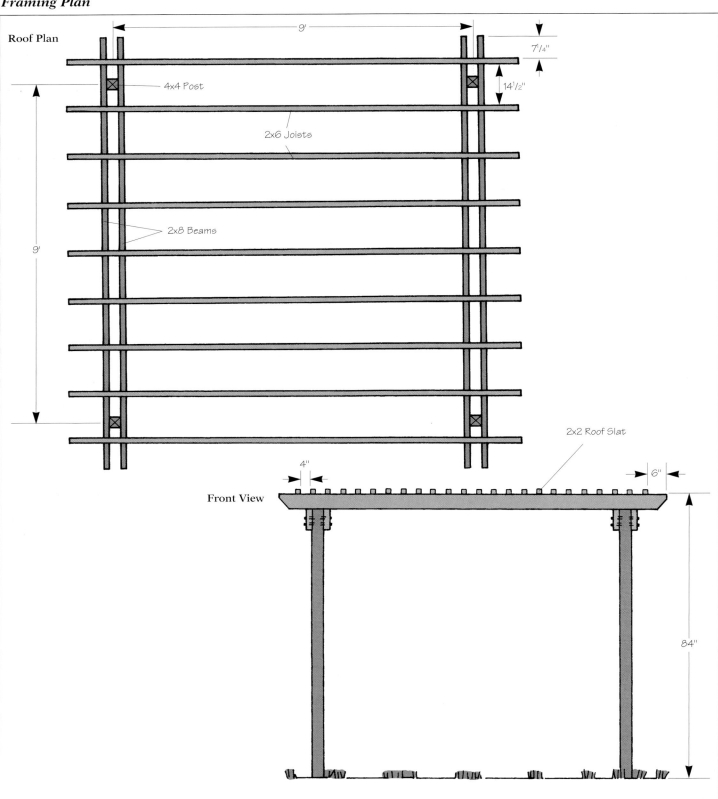

1. Install Posts

The posts are set in concrete 6 inches below the frost line, or a minimum of 2 feet deep. Make sure the posts are long enough to allow you to cut them all off 7 feet above the ground. Before the concrete in the holes hardens, brace the posts on two adjacent sides with stakes and furring strips, checking that the posts are plumb on adjacent sides. Run string past the bottom of the posts to see that they are aligned and set the correct distance apart. Allow the concrete to set up overnight before continuing.

2. Trim Posts to Size

Measure up from the ground on one post 7 feet and mark with a pencil. Transfer this dimension to all other posts using a line level. Trim the posts to the finished height.

3. Install Beams

Cut the four 2x8 beams and the trim ends as shown. Many alternate end cut designs are possible, using straight lines or curved cuts. Lift the beams on to the tops of the posts, resting them temporarily on 16d nails partially driven 7¼ inches from the top of the posts. Check the beams for level. At each post, drill two ³/8-inch-diameter holes through beams and post, and attach the beams to the post using two ³/8x8-inch carriage bolts.

4. Install Joists

Cut and trim the 2x6 joists. Position the joists 16 inches on center on top of the beams. Place the last beam on each side 7¼ inches from the ends of the beams. Make sure there is an equal overhang on both sides of the beams. Toe-nail the joists to the beams with 10d nails.

5. Install Roof Slats

Cut the 2x2 roof slats to 12 feet long. Place the slats across the joists with an equal overhang on both ends of the arbor and with about 6 inches of exposed joist at the cut ends of the joists. Space the slats 4 inches apart. Nail the slats to the joists with 8d nails.

1. Install Posts

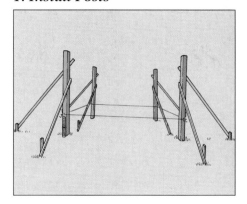

2. Trim Posts to Size

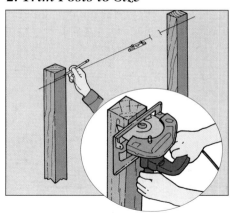

3. Install Beams

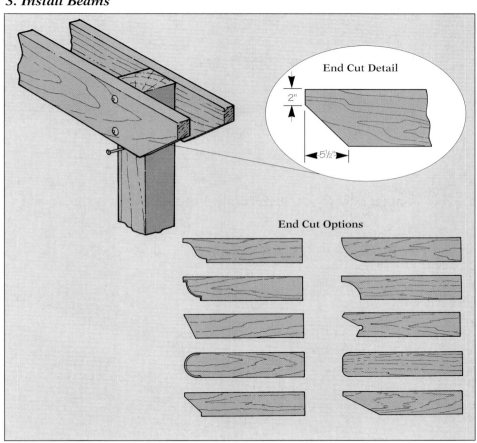

End Cut Detail

2"

5½"

End Cut Options

4. Install Joists

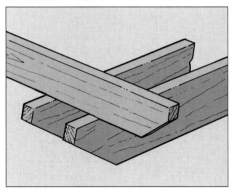

5. Install Roof Slats

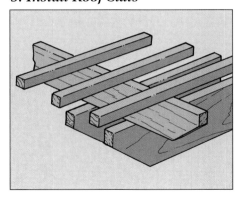

Arbor

WITH DECK

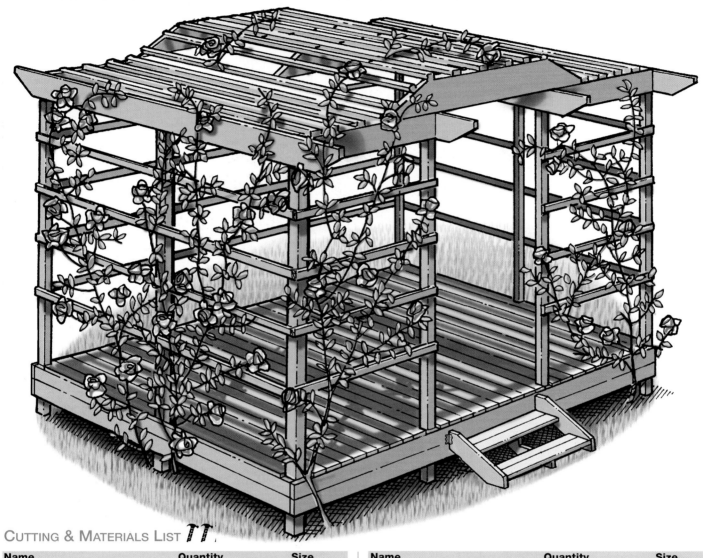

CUTTING & MATERIALS LIST

Name	Quantity	Size
Arbor Deck Framing		
Posts	10	4"x4"x10'
Beams	8	2"x8"x93"
Beam Headers	2	2"x8"x12'
Stringer Joists	2	2"x6"x12'
Joists	3	2"x6"x11'9"
Decking Cleats	6	2"x6"x5"
Decking Cleats	4	2"x6"x6½"
Joist Headers	2	2"x6"x93"
Stair Stringers	3	2"x10"x30"
Stair Treads	4	1¼"x6"x36"
Decking	25	1¼"x6"x10'
Roof Framing		
Beams	4	2"x8"x10'
Crosspieces	6	2"x8"x51"
Top Pieces	3	2"x8"x62"

Name	Quantity	Size
Roof Slats	28	2"x2"x96"
Side Slats	8	1"x4"x93"
Front and Rear Slats	16	1"x4"x51¾"
Nails & Fasteners		
Machine Bolts	20	⅜"x7½"
Nails		
16d Common		
10d Common		
8d Common		
8d Button Head		
Post Anchors	10	
Stair Angles	4	
Framing Angles	2	For stringers
Premixed Concrete		As required to set post & step footings below frost line

This arbor with deck is a wonderful way to create a private retreat in your own backyard. You'll enjoy the convenient, clean, flat surface of a deck while surrounded by the natural shade and privacy provided by growing vines. The deck shown is 8×12 feet, a cozy structure that still provides plenty of room for entertaining. The walls of the arbor use widely spaced 1×4 slats to support vines. If you want a more open look, you can omit the slats on one or more sides of the arbor.

Overall View

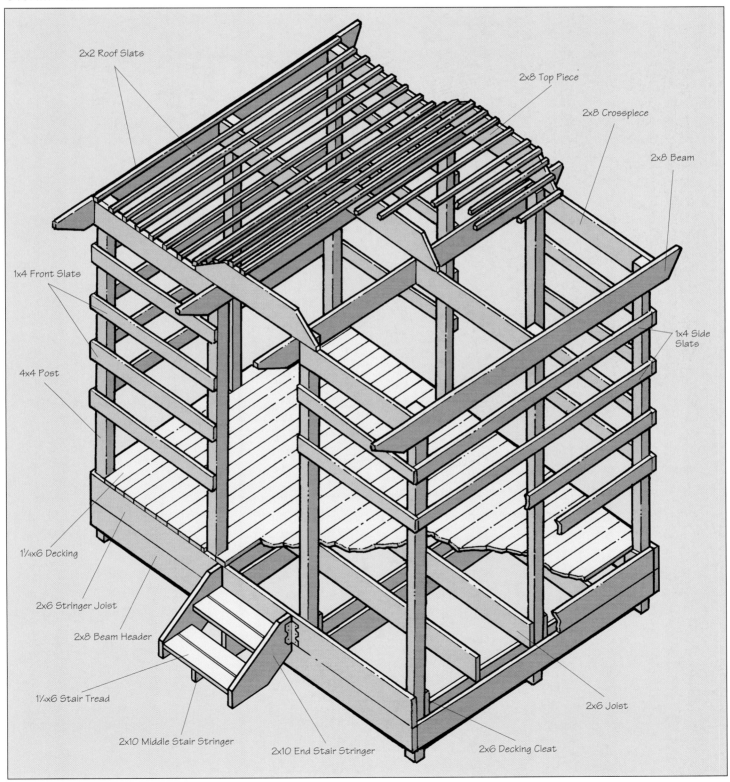

2x2 Roof Slats

2x8 Top Piece

2x8 Crosspiece

2x8 Beam

1x4 Front Slats

1x4 Side Slats

4x4 Post

1¼x6 Decking

2x6 Stringer Joist

2x8 Beam Header

1¼x6 Stair Tread

2x10 Middle Stair Stringer

2x10 End Stair Stringer

2x6 Decking Cleat

2x6 Joist

For your arbor you will want to use wood that is naturally rot resistant, such as cedar or redwood. You also can use pressure-treated lumber, which will not harm plants. An alternative is to use pressure-treated wood for the posts and cedar or redwood for the rest of the structure.

Study the "Overall View" and the "Framing Plan" before you start building your arbor with deck. Measure and cut as you work. This will let you correct any slight measurement errors before they accumulate into big problems.

Framing Plan

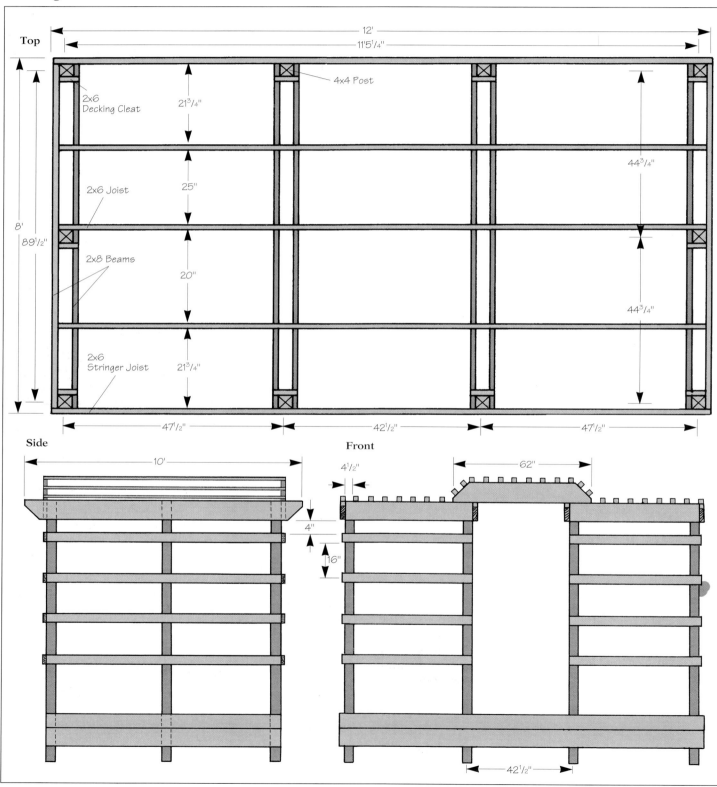

CONSTRUCT THE DECK

The basic structural components of the deck are 4x4 posts that support the deck beams and roof, 2x8 beams that bolt to the posts and support the floor joists, and 2x6 joists, stringer joists, and joist headers that fasten to the beams and support the 1¼-inch-thick decking. Lay out the locations for the 10 posts as shown in the "Framing Plan." It is essential that your post layout be square; use the 3-4-5 method described in "Laying Out the Site" on page 50.

1. Install Posts

The posts are 10 feet long. You will cut the posts to size after you install the deck. The posts must be properly positioned and exactly plumb for the floor and roof components to fit properly. Place the 10 concrete footings and metal post anchors according to the instructions given in "Groundwork" on page 49.

2. Place Step Footing

Build a support for the bottom end of the step stringers by placing a 4-inch-thick concrete slab at the base of the step location. The slab measures 18x43 inches, with the front edge of the slab 26 inches out from the edge of the deck. Make the surface of the slab flush with the ground.

3. Establish Deck Height

The finished deck height above grade is 16 inches. This allows for a simple two-riser step design. It also keeps framing members about 2 inches above the ground. Mark the finished height on one of the posts and transfer this dimension to all other posts using a line or water level. Measure down 1¼ inches from this line to find the height of the top of the joists. Measure down an additional 5½ inches to locate the top of the beams.

4. Install Beams

The beams are formed from two 2x8s through-bolted to the posts.

1. Install Posts

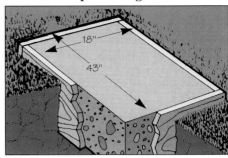

2. Place Step Footing

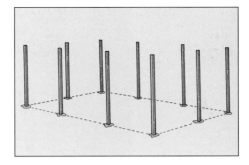

3. Establish Deck Height

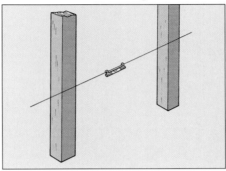

4. Install Beams

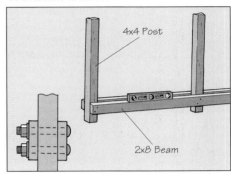

4x4 Post

2x8 Beam

5. Install Joists

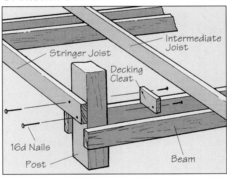

Stringer Joist
Intermediate Joist
Decking Cleat
16d Nails
Post
Beam

6. Install Joist Headers

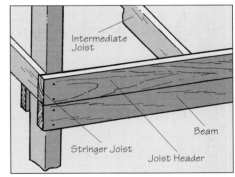

Intermediate Joist
Beam
Stringer Joist
Joist Header

Temporarily tack-nail the beams to each post at the correct height and check for level. Attach the remaining beams in the same manner, leveling them with the first beam. Lay a straight 2x4 diagonally across the beams and check for level.

When all the beams are in position, drill two ⅜-inch-diameter holes through each assembly and install the bolts, washers, and nuts. Nail the two beam headers on with 16d nails.

5. Install Joists

The stringer joists are 3 inches longer than the other joists so they can cover the ends of the headers, making a clean front view. Attach the stringer joists to the posts with two 16d nails at each connection.

Position the remaining joists across the beams, spacing them as shown in the "Framing Plan," and toe-nail in place.

The decking cleats provide support for the decking boards whenever a board ends at a post. Attach the cleats to the posts with 16d nails.

6. Install Joist Headers

Use 16d nails to face-nail the joist header to the exposed ends of the joist at the sides of the deck. Nail the headers to the posts.

MAKE THE STAIRS

The deck uses a two-step "housed stringer" stair design. The 1¼-inch-thick stair treads are fastened between two 2x10 stringers. The connection between treads and stringers is made with a piece of hardware called a stair angle.

1. Cut End Stringers.

The stair has a rise of 5³⁄₈ inches and a run of 11¹⁄₂ inches. Place a framing square on a stringer, as illustrated, so that the 5³⁄₈-inch mark on the outside of the square's tongue and the 11¹⁄₂-inch measurement on the outside of the square's blade both align with the top edge of the stringer.

Mark out the rise and the run. Extend the rise line to the bottom of the stringer. You'll cut along this line to make the upper end of the stringer. Now move the square down to lay out the second step as shown. Use the square to lay out the cuts for the front and bottom of the stringer. Measure down 1¼ inches from the top of the treads and draw layout lines for the stair angles. Lay out the other end stringer. Make the cuts at the front back and bottom of the end stringers.

2. Cut Middle Stringer

The middle stringer is designed so that its risers will be recessed 1 inch behind the front of the treads. As you did for the end stringers, use the framing square to lay out the rise and run cuts and the bottom cut. Note that to mark out the top step, the tongue of the square is at 6³⁄₈ inches while the blade is at 13¹⁄₂ inches. For the second step the tongue is at 6⁷⁄₈ inches while the blade is at 14¹⁄₂ inches. To lay out the bottom rise, start from the 11¹⁄₂-inch mark on the blade and draw a 4³⁄₈-inch-long perpendicular line as shown in the illustration for this step. You can do most of the cutting for the middle stringer with a circular saw. Finish with a handsaw.

3. Assemble Stairs

Nail the stair angles to the end

1. Cut End Stringers

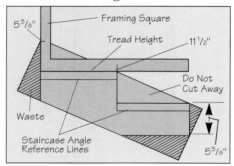

2. Cut Middle Stringer

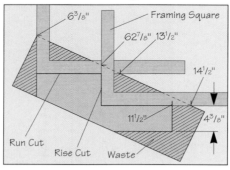

3. Assemble Stairs

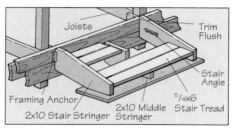

stringers with the nails recommended or provided by the manufacturer.

Each tread is made of two pieces of 1¼x6-inch decking. Cut the treads to 36 inches long. Working with the stringers upside down, nail the stair angles into the bottom of the treads. Attach the front tread pieces flush to the front of the end stringers. Leave ½ inch between the front and back treads to improve drainage.

Toe-nail the middle stringer to the front beam, centering it between front entry posts. Use two 8d nails through each side of the stringer. Put the stair assembly in place over the middle stringer. Attach it to the joist stringers with framing anchors, then fasten the treads to the middle stringer using two 8d nails at each connection.

When the bottom of the stringers sits flat on the concrete slab, the top

point of the end stringers should extend about 1¼ inches higher than the stringer joist. This is because the calculation for the rise and run of the stair included the 1¼-inch-thick decking. However, the decking will overhang the header slightly. To allow for this, use a handsaw to cut the top of the end stringers flush with the joist after the stringers are installed.

COMPLETE THE DECK

Two tasks remain: first you'll install the decking, then you will cut the posts to final height. This way, the roof will be the proper height from the deck even if deck height is slightly different than you planned due to measuring errors or slight variations in lumber dimensions.

1. Install Decking

Install the decking boards perpendicular to the floor joists, starting at one side of the deck. Let the boards overhang the stringer joists. You'll cut them all off even later. For better appearance, let the edge of the first board overhang ½ inch. Several deck boards must be notched to fit around the posts. When cutting these notches, leave about ⅛ inch of

1. Install Decking

2. Measure & Cut Posts

clearance around the post. Both ends of each piece of decking must be supported, either by the joist headers, stringers, joists, or decking cleats.

Nail the decking to each joist with two 8d nails driven at an angle or with deck fastening clips. Space the deck boards with 10d nails.

After every three or four boards, measure to make sure that the boards are running parallel to the joist headers. As you near the opposite end of the deck, be aware that it may be necessary to rip the last board to fit, or alter the spacing of the last few boards so you don't come up short. Plan ahead by laying the last few deck boards in place before nailing them. Remember, you want the last board to overhang the back header by about 1/2 inch.

Snap chalk lines across the ends of the deck boards 1/2 inch from the outside faces of the stringer joists. If you have a steady hand you can use a circular saw to cut freehand along the lines. Otherwise, tack a board to the deck as a guide for the saw. The posts will get in the way of the circular saw, so you'll have to cut a few boards off with a handsaw.

2. *Measure & Cut Posts*

Measure up 84 inches from the deck floor along one of the posts. Use a line level or a water level to transfer this height to all other posts. Mark and cut the roof support posts off at this height.

Construct the Arbor

The arbor roof has 10-foot-long beams that are attached to the posts and run from the front to the back of the arbor. Six crosspieces run between inner and outer beams. Three top pieces run along the middle of the roof, creating an arch from front to back. The entire roof structure

is covered with 2x2 slats. The walls are covered with slats spaced 16 inches on center.

1. *Cut & Install Beams*

Trim the ends of the four 2x8 beams as shown in the drawing. Nail the beams across the sides as shown in the "Overall View," making sure they are flush to the tops of the posts. Use four 16d nails for each connection.

2. *Cut & Install Crosspieces*

Cut six 2x8 crosspieces to fit between the beams. Drive 16d nails through the crosspieces into the posts and through the beams into the ends of the crosspieces. Use three nails at each connection.

3. *Cut & Install Top Pieces*

Cut three 2x8 top pieces to 62 inches long. Give them the same decorative end cuts as the beams. Place the top pieces across the middle beams as shown, aligning them with the crosspieces. Toe-nail the top pieces to the middle beams with 10d nails.

4. *Install Slats*

Measure from the outside faces of the front crosspieces to the outside faces of the rear crosspieces. Cut the 2x2 roof slats to this length. Nail the slats in place with 8d nails, spacing them 4 1/2 inches apart.

Cut eight 1x4 slats to fit across the sides of the arbor as shown in the "Framing Plan." To position the highest slat on each side, measure down 4 inches from the beams. Position the remaining three slats on each side 16 inches on center as shown. Fasten the slats to the posts with two 8d button head nails at each connection. If you are careful, you should be able to drive the nails home without denting the slats.

Now cut 16 1x4 slats for the front and rear of the arbor. Make these slats long enough to cover the edges of the side slats and cover

1. *Cut & Install Beams*

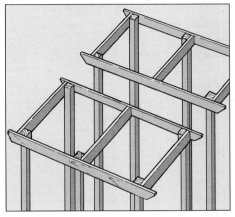

2. *Cut & Install Crosspieces*

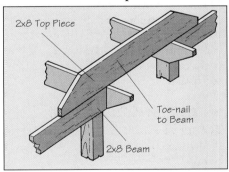

3. *Cut & Install Top Pieces*

2x8 Top Piece
Toe-nail to Beam
2x8 Beam

4. *Install Slats*

the fronts of the entry posts as shown in the "Framing Plan." Nail these slats in place in the same manner as the side slats.

Arbor

WITH PICNIC TABLE

CUTTING & MATERIALS LIST

Name	Quantity	Size
Arbor Framing		
Posts	2	6"x6"x10'
Beams	4	2"x8"x63"
Roof Joists	5	2"x6"x9'
Lattice Slats	18	2"x2"x63"
Table Materials		
Tabletop V-Braces	4	2"x4"x18"
Tabletop	6	2"x6"x72"
Tabletop Support Ribs	3	2"x4"x33"
Bench Materials		
Bench Legs	4	4"x4"x36"
Seat Boards	4	2"x6"x72"
Seat Braces	8	2"x4"x10"

Name	Quantity	Size
Nails & Fasteners		
Nails		
16d Common		
10d Common		
Carriage Bolts	4	$^{3}/_{8}$"x7"
3" Galvanized Decking Screws		
	8	$^{3}/_{8}$"x7"
Premixed Concrete	As required to set posts & legs below frost line	

This arbor and picnic table combination is perfect for gardens where space is at a premium. Like the basic arbor, this arbor with table consists of beams, joists, and slats supported by posts. In this case, only two posts are used, and they support a table as well as the arbor. The posts are set in the ground, anchored in concrete. You can build the arbor and table alone and use it with separate benches or chairs. Or you can build permanent benches supported by their own posts as described here.

For your arbor, you will want to use wood that is naturally rot resistant, such as cedar or redwood, or use pressure-treated lumber, which will not harm plants. One option is to use pressure-treated posts and cedar or redwood for the rest of the project.

A word of advice: Don't plant flowering vines on this arbor. The flowers will attract bees and make the table a dangerous place to eat.

Overall View

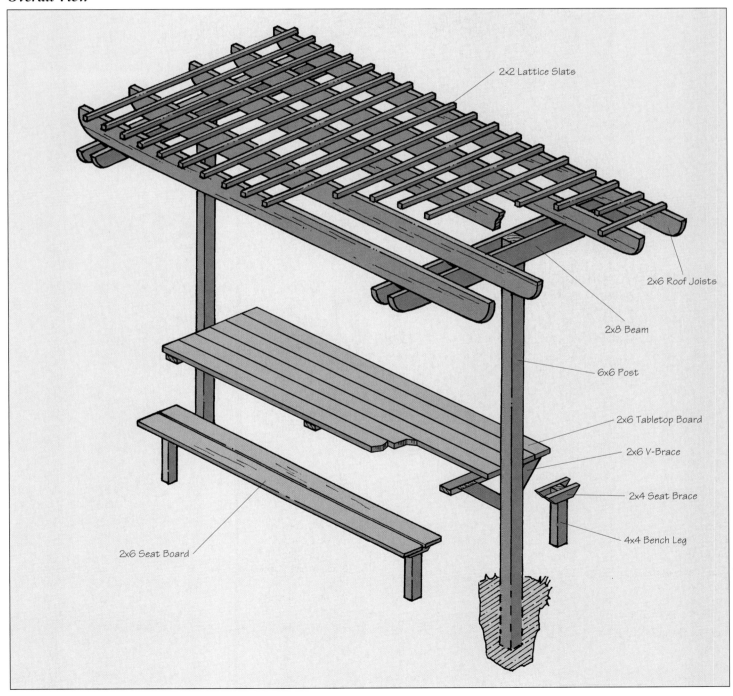

2x2 Lattice Slats

2x6 Roof Joists

2x8 Beam

6x6 Post

2x6 Tabletop Board

2x6 V-Brace

2x4 Seat Brace

4x4 Bench Leg

2x6 Seat Board

Framing Plan

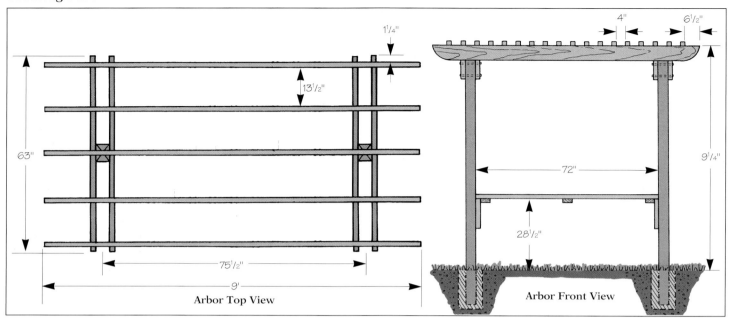

13½"

1¼"

63"

75½"

9'

Arbor Top View

4"

6½"

9¼"

72"

28½"

Arbor Front View

1. Locate & Install Posts

Measure two post holes 75½ inches on center. Dig holes at least 2 feet deep, making sure that the posts extend at least 6 inches below the frost line. Set the post in the holes and fill the holes with concrete. Brace the posts with stakes and furring strips on two adjacent sides, and check for plumb with a carpenter's level. Run a string across the bottoms of the posts to make sure they are in line with each other. Let the concrete set overnight before continuing.

After the concrete has set, measure up from the ground on one post 91¼ inches and mark with a pencil. Using a line level, run a tight string to the other post and mark it. Trim the posts to finished height.

2. Install Beams

Cut the four beams to 63 inches long. Choose a curve design and draw it on the end of one beam. Cut the curve with a saber saw, sand it smooth, and use it as a template for the other beam ends. See page 147 for end cut options.

Lift the beams to the tops of the posts, resting them temporarily on 16d nails partially driven 7¼ inches from the top. Check that the beams and posts are flush on top. At each

1. Locate & Install Posts

post, drill two ⅜-inch-diameter holes through the beams and post, and attach the beams to the post using two ⅜x9-inch carriage bolts.

3. Install Roof Joists

Cut the roof joists 9 feet long. As with the beam ends, draw a curve on the end of one joist, then cut and sand it to use as a template for the other end cuts. Space them across the beams, and toe-nail into place with 10d nails. Metal ties also can be used to install the joists.

4. Cut & Nail Lattice Slats

Cut 2x2 slats to 63 inches long. Position the first slat 6½ inches from one end of the joists. Space the remaining slats 4 inches apart on the joists and fasten all slats with 10d nails.

2. Install Beams

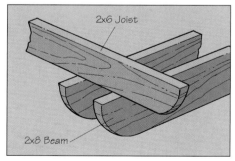

⅜"x9" Carriage Bolt

16d Nail

3. Install Roof Joists

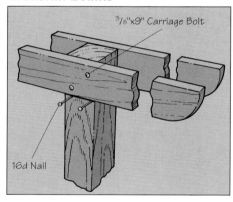

2x6 Joist

2x8 Beam

4. Cut & Nail Lattice Slats

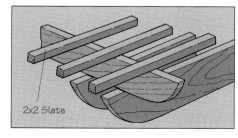

2x2 Slats

5. *Assemble V-Braces*

Cut tabletop V-braces to the dimensions shown in the drawing. Cut 45-degree miters on each end. Mark a line on the inside of one post 28½ inches off the ground. From that mark, run a line level and mark the other post. Draw a pencil line down the middle of the inside faces of the posts beneath the 28½-inch mark. Align the top of the V-brace at the 28½-inch mark, and center the brace to the middle line. Tack each piece in place with one 16d nail. When all four brace pieces are in place, check each assembly with a level, then add another nail to each piece to secure the braces in place.

6. *Make Tabletop*

Measure and cut six 2x6 pieces to fit between the posts. Next, cut three 2x4 tabletop support ribs. Square up the 2x6 tabletop pieces with a framing square, and use 3-inch galvanized decking screws to fasten one support rib across the center of the pieces. Put the tabletop in position on the V-braces. Mark the thickness of the braces on the bottom of the tabletop. Remove the tabletop and screw the two end ribs in place along the lines you scribed from the braces. Put the tabletop back on the braces. Secure the tabletop by screwing through the braces into the end ribs with 3-inch screws.

7. *Install Bench Legs*

Center the bench legs on points that are 8 inches from the sides of the table, 60 inches apart, and equidistant from the ends of the table. Dig bench leg holes that are at least 18 inches deep. Place the bench legs in the holes and fill the holes with concrete. Run a string across the bottoms of the posts to make sure they are in line with each other. Check that the posts are plumb. Brace the posts with furring strips, if neccessary. Allow the concrete to set overnight. Then trim one post to 14½ inches from the ground. Use a string and line level to mark the same height and trim the other posts.

8. *Make Bench Seats*

Cut four 2x6 seat boards to 72 inches. Then cut eight 2x4 seat braces to 10 inches. Miter the ends of the braces 45 degrees as shown. Tack each brace piece to the post with one 10d nail. Check that the braces are level. Drill ³/₈-inch-diameter holes through the braces and 4x4 bench posts. Fasten the braces to the posts with ³/₈x7-inch carriage bolts. Center a pair of seat boards on each pair of braces, leaving ½ inch of space between the boards. Fasten the boards to the braces with 3-inch galvanized decking screws. Be sure to drive the screws below the surface. Round off the edges of the tabletop and seat boards with a few passes of a block plane to prevent splinters.

5. Assemble V-Braces

6. Make Tabletop

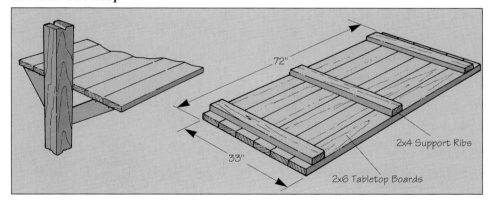

2x4 Support Ribs
2x6 Tabletop Boards
72"
33"

7. Install Bench Legs

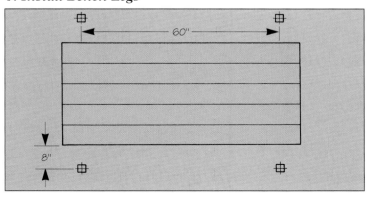

60"
8"

8. Make Bench Seats

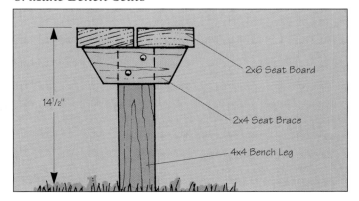

2x6 Seat Board
2x4 Seat Brace
4x4 Bench Leg
14½"

Glossary

Actual Dimensions The exact measurements of a piece of lumber after it has been cut, surfaced, and left to dry. Example: A 2×4's actual dimensions are 1½×3½.

Arbor An openwork structure that usually consists of slats or lattice that support climbing vines.

Baluster A vertical railing member that supports the upper and lower rails.

Beam A framing member used to support joists.

Bird's Mouth A notch in a common rafter that fits over the cap plate. It consists of a level cut, called the seat cut, and a short plumb cut.

Bull Float A flat metal tool equipped with a long handle used to bring sand and cement to the surface of poured concrete, while knocking down the small ridges left by screeding.

Cap Plate Horizontal framing member that goes on top of the top plate, tying walls together.

Ceiling Joist Roof framing member that spans the width of a building.

Chalkline String or cord that is covered with colored chalk. It is snapped against a surface to make a mark for cutting or aligning.

Chromated Copper Arsenic (CCA) A chemical used to pressure-treat wood to make it resist decay.

Clinching Bending over the exposed tip of a nail, after it has been driven through a board.

Color Value The lightness or darkness of a color.

Color Wheel A chart that identifies associations between colors.

Common Rafter A rafter that meets the cap plate with a bird's mouth cut and the ridge or key block with a plumb cut.

Complementary Colors Any two colors opposite each other on the color wheel.

Composite Shingles Commonly made of asphalt and fiberglass. They are often made into a three tab strip, which is one of the most popular roofing materials available.

Crook A deviation in a piece of lumber from a flat plane on the narrow face, end to end. A crook makes wood unsuitable for framing.

Curing The slow chemical action that hardens concrete.

Decay The destruction of wood by fungi or insects.

Deck Height The height above grade of the top of the decking.

Decking Boards or plywood nailed to joists to form the deck surface.

Decking Cleats Small pieces that provide support for the decking boards whenever a board ends at a post.

Dipping A treatment where wood is immersed in a bath of sealant for several minutes, and then allowed to air-dry.

Fascia The horizontal lumber placed at the roofline that covers the ends of the rafters.

Footing The concrete base that supports posts or steps.

Form Lumber set around the edge to define the shape of the concrete slab.

Framing Square A piece of steel or aluminum that forms an "L" shape. Used to figure rise and run of stringers and roofs, to check for square, and to strike square cutting lines.

Frieze An ornamental horizontal band that is positioned near the roofline.

Frost Heave Shifting or upheaval of the ground due to alternate freezing and thawing of water in the soil.

Frost Line The maximum depth to which soil freezes in winter. Your local building department can provide information on the frost line depth in your area.

Gable Roof A roof with two slopes forming triangles on the ends.

Galvanizing Coating a metal with a thin protective layer (e.g., zinc) to prevent rust. Connectors and fasteners should be galvanized for outdoor use.

Gazebo A freestanding structure intended to offer a panoramic view of the surrounding scenery.

Grade The ground level. On-grade means at or on the natural ground level.

Hand Edger A hand tool used to round the edges of a concrete slab.

Hardwood Wood that comes from deciduous trees (those that loose their leaves in fall).

Hip Jack Rafters Short rafters that run between the cap plate and a hip rafter.

Hip Rafter A rafter that runs diagonally from the ridge to the corners of a building.

Hurricane Ties Connectors used to secure rafters and trusses to the top plates.

Joist One in a series of parallel framing members that supports a floor or ceiling load. Joists are supported by beams or bearing walls.

Joist Hanger Metal connectors used to join a joist and a beam so that the tops of both are in the same plane.

Key Block A piece of wood at the peak of a gazebo roof designed to meet the rafters.

Kickback The action that happens when a saw suddenly jumps backward out of the cut.

Knots The high-density roots of limbs that are very strong, but are not connected to the surrounding wood.

Lag screw/Lag bolt A large hex-head screw or bolt used to fasten framing members face-to-face; typically used for joining horizontal framing member to posts.

Lattice A cross-pattern structure that is made of wood, metal, or plastic.

Lignin The binding agent that holds the cells in wood together.

Lumber Grade A label that reflects the lumber's natural growth characteristics (such as knots), defects that result from milling errors, and manufacturing techniques.

Miter Joint A joint in which the ends of two boards are cut at equal angles (typically 45 degrees) to form a corner.

Nail Set A pointed tool with one round or square end, used to drive nails below surface level.

Nominal Dimensions The identifying dimensions of a piece of lumber (e.g., 2x4) which are larger than the actual dimensions (1½x3½).

On-center A point of reference for measuring. For example, "16 inches on center" means 16 inches from the center of one post to the center of the next post.

Pastel Colors Colors mixed with white.

Pavilion A rectangular structure with a slat, lattice, or gable roof.

Penny (abbr. "d") Unit of nail measurement; e.g., a 10d nail is 3 inches long.

Permanent Structure Any structure that is anchored to the ground or a house.

Pitch Pocket An accumulation of natural resins in wood.

Plumb Vertically straight, in relation to a horizontally level surface.

Post Vertical framing member (e.g., a 4x4 or 4x6) set on the foundation to support the structure.

Post Anchors Connectors that secure the base of a load-bearing post to a concrete slab or deck.

Posthole Digger A clamshell-type tool used to dig holes for posts.

Premade Lumber Pieces that are factory cut and/or assembled.

Premixed Concrete Bagged, dry concrete that is used for small jobs such as securing individual posts. It is mixed with sand and aggregate.

Pressure-Treated Lumber Wood that has had preservatives forced into it under pressure to make it repel rot and insects.

Primary Colors Three colors (pure red, pure blue, and pure yellow) that cannot be mixed from other colors.

Primer An essential undercoat layer of paint. It provides a good surface onto which to apply layers of paint.

Purlin Clips Connectors used to install purlins (crosspieces) between joists or rafters.

Rafter Tail The part of the rafter that overhangs the wall.

Rafter Ties Connectors used to provide wind and seismic ties for trusses and rafters.

Rail A horizontal member that is placed between posts and used for support or as a barrier.

Ready-mix concrete Wet concrete that is transported from a concrete supplier in a cement truck with a revolving drum. The concrete is ready to pour.

Redwood A straight-grain weather-resistant wood used for outdoor building.

Ridge The uppermost horizontal line of the roof.

Rim Joist Joist at the perimeter of a structure.

Rise The vertical distance between the cap plate and the peak of a roof.

Roofer's Hatchet A specialized tool combining a nonskid hammer head with a hatchet. It also has an adjustable pin for gauging shingle exposure, and a wrist strap to prevent it from falling off the roof.

Run The measure of the horizontal distance over which a rafter rises.

Screeding Using a straight 2x4, moved from one end of a concrete pour to the other, to strike off excess concrete.

Secondary Colors Three colors (orange, green, and violet) that are mixed from equal amounts of two primary colors.

Skewing Nails driven into wood at opposing angles to hook the boards together.

Slope Number of inches a roof rises per 12 inches of run. Example: A shallow roof would be 4 in 12, while a steeper roof would be 9 in 12.

Softwood Wood that comes from coniferous trees (e.g., evergreens).

Spaced Slats 1x4s or 1x6s nailed directly to the rafters.

Spading Inserting a shovel vertically into the concrete to remove air pockets that may have occurred in corners or along the sides of the forms.

Span The horizontal distance covered by a roof.

Split A crack that passes completely through a piece of lumber.

Square Roofing material is sold by the square; one square is equal to 100 square feet. To determine the number of squares on a roof, measure the area and then divide by 100 (add 10 percent to allow for waste).

Stair Angles Clips that support stair treads, eliminating the need for notching the stringers.

Stringer Diagonal boards that support stair treads.

Tacknail To nail one structural member to another temporarily with a minimum of nails.

Tamping Using a rake in concrete work to jab aggregate down and to work out any air bubbles.

Toe-nail Joining two boards together by nailing at an angle through the end, or toe, of one board into the face of another.

Tongue-and-Groove Flooring Floor boards that are milled with a tongue on one edge and a groove on the other edge. The tongue of one board fits into the groove of the next to make a tight, strong floor.

Top Plate Horizontal framing member that forms the top of a wall. In a gazebo, top plates are attached to the top of posts.

Tread The horizontal boards on stairs, supported by the stringer.

UV Absorbers and blockers Particles that absorb, or in the case of blockers, reflect, UV light to minimize its effect on the wood.

UV Inhibitors Compounds that are designed to disrupt the normal chemical action caused by UV light.

V-braces Two pieces of 2x4 that are cut at 45-degree miters to form a V shape. They attach to the posts and help support the picnic table top.

Wane The presence of bark, or lack of wood at an edge.

Waste Cut The part of the cut that can be used for scrap or thrown away.

Index